AI and the Future of Democracy

This comprehensive volume examines how artificial intelligence (AI) can either strengthen or undermine democratic society. It introduces groundbreaking frameworks including "AI-Enhanced Reflexive Control" (AIRC), and categorizes vulnerable democracies into three types—underdeveloped, strained, and stressed—each of which facing unique AI-related challenges.

Drawing on extensive case studies including Romania's 2024 election annulment, Bulgaria's disinformation networks, and democratic innovations in Kenya and the Philippines, contributors analyze AI's impact across electoral processes, legal systems, and public discourse. The book systematically examines five critical categories of unethical AI applications—disinformation, electoral interference, human rights manipulation, cultural exploitation, and privacy invasion—while exploring AI's potential as a democratic equalizer.

Featuring accessible introductions to AI topics, real-world case studies, and actionable policy recommendations, this volume serves as an essential guide for policymakers, technologists, and those studying AI's complex relationship with democratic governance.

AI and the Future of Democracy

Building Resilient and Inclusive Societies

Edited by

Jacob Udo-Udo Jacob and
Narasimha Rao Vajjhala

CRC Press
Taylor & Francis Group
Boca Raton London New York

CRC Press is an imprint of the
Taylor & Francis Group, an **informa** business
A CHAPMAN & HALL BOOK

First edition published 2026
by CRC Press
2385 NW Executive Center Drive, Suite 320, Boca Raton FL 33431

and by CRC Press
4 Park Square, Milton Park, Abingdon, Oxon, OX14 4RN

CRC Press is an imprint of Taylor & Francis Group, LLC

ISBN: 978-1-032-97530-6 (hbk)
ISBN: 978-1-032-97531-3 (pbk)
ISBN: 978-1-003-59418-5 (ebk)

DOI 10.1201/9781003594185

Typeset in Sabon
by KnowledgeWorks Global Ltd.

Contents

Foreword

We stand at a defining moment in human history, it is a moment where the very future of democracy is at stake. The convergence of artificial intelligence and democratic governance presents both extraordinary and unprecedented opportunities, while at the same time it presents very real existential threats.

The rapid advancement of AI technologies has fundamentally altered the landscape of how information flows, how decisions are made, and how power is exercised within our democratic societies. This transformation demands our urgent attention, our rigorous analysis, and courageous action from scholars, policymakers, and citizens alike.

This pathbreaking volume, *AI and the Future of Democracy: Building Resilient and Inclusive Societies* comes at precisely the moment when such comprehensive examination is most needed. As democratic institutions worldwide face mounting pressures from misinformation campaigns, algorithmic bias, and sophisticated manipulation tactics, the intersection of artificial intelligence and democratic values has become one of the most pressing issues of our time. This volume courageously tackles these complex challenges head-on, offering both critical analysis and constructive pathways forward.

The global scope of this work reflects the universal nature of the challenges we face, while centering voices from the Global South that are too often marginalized in discussions about technology and governance. With contributions from major democracies including India and Nigeria, alongside perspectives from Bulgaria, Kazakhstan, South Africa, the United States, and beyond, this collection demonstrates that the tension between AI and democracy transcends national boundaries. Too, it helps elucidate how local conditions and institutions shape these challenges differently in different societies.

What distinguishes this volume is its refusal to treat AI and democracy as unrelated or as inherently incompatible forces. Instead, the contributors explore how artificial intelligence can be harnessed to strengthen democratic processes while acknowledging the very real threats posed by unethical AI deployment. From AI-driven tools that enhance access to justice to algorithmic systems that can combat election misinformation, the chapters illustrate that technology itself is not the enemy—rather, it is how we design, implement, and control these systems that determines their democratic impact.

The book's structure thoughtfully guides readers from foundational concepts through specific applications to broader societal implications. Beginning with the critical examination of AI-enhanced manipulation in vulnerable democracies, particularly through the lens of Bulgaria's experience, the volume establishes the stakes involved. It then systematically explores the technological foundations necessary for understanding these challenges before delving into ethical frameworks, practical applications, and future directions.

Perhaps most importantly, this work does not stop at diagnosis—it offers prescriptions. The emphasis on ethical AI design, algorithmic fairness, and bias mitigation provides concrete frameworks for practitioners and policymakers. The examination of computer vision applications in public policy and AI-driven solutions for combating misinformation demonstrates that responsible innovation is not only possible but essential for democratic survival and renewal, but it is entirely possible.

As we witness the proliferation of deepfakes, the manipulation of social media algorithms for political gain, and the deployment of AI systems that perpetuate historical biases, the need for informed discourse about democracy's future has never been more acute. This volume provides that discourse. It refuses to succumb to either technological determinism or nostalgic resistance to change.

The international authorship of this collection serves as a powerful reminder that democracy's challenges in the age of AI require solutions informed by many experiences, culture, and perspectives. A global phenomenon, the contributions from scholars and practitioners across the globe reflect the interdisciplinary and global collaboration necessary to address these multifaceted challenges, while ensuring that insights from the Global South inform our understanding of AI's democratic implications.

As readers engage with these chapters, they will find not just scholarly analysis but a call to action. The future of democracy in the age of artificial intelligence is neither predetermined nor doomed. It will be shaped by the choices we make today about how to design, deploy, evaluate and govern these extraordinarily powerful technologies. This volume provides the intellectual foundation necessary to make those choices wisely, ensuring that artificial intelligence becomes a tool for democratic renewal rather than for democratic decline.

The way forward requires vigilance, wisdom, and sustained commitment to democratic values. This book serves as both a warning and a guide, illuminating the challenges while pointing toward solutions that can help us build more resilient, inclusive, and just societies. In an era of headlong technological change, such guidance is not merely valuable—it is indispensable for the survival and flourishing of democracy itself.

Dr. Margee Ensign
President, American University in Bulgaria
Bulgaria

About the editors

Jacob Udo-Udo Jacob served as the Panitza Memorial Endowed Executive Director of the Center for Information, Democracy, and Citizenship at the American University in Bulgaria. His career spans academia, policy advisory, and international development, including roles as Dean of Graduate School and Research at the American University of Nigeria and positions at New York University's Center on International Cooperation and Dickinson College, Pennsylvania. A recognized authority in strategic communication for peace operations, Dr. Jacob led the international team revising the UN's policy on strategic communications in disarmament, demobilization, and reintegration. He holds a Ph.D. in Communication Studies from the University of Leeds and an MA in Peace Studies from Lancaster University. Dr. Jacob has advised the World Bank, US Institute of Peace, and the UN's Department of Peace Operations on information's role in democratic stability and conflict transformation.

Narasimha Rao Vajjhala is an academic and researcher currently serving as Professor and Chair of the Computer Science Department at the American University in Bulgaria (AUBG). He is also the Principal Investigator for the Democracy Project (DemPro) at the Center for Information, Democracy, and Citizenship (CIDC) at AUBG. Dr. Vajjhala previously held leadership roles as Dean of the Faculty of Engineering and Architecture at the University of New York Tirana (UNYT) in Albania and Chair of the Computer Science and Software Engineering programs at the American University of Nigeria (AUN). With over 23 years of experience in academia, he has taught programming, database management, and related courses across Europe and Africa at both undergraduate and graduate levels. An active contributor to the global research community, Dr. Vajjhala is a Senior Member of ACM and IEEE, Editor-in-Chief of the International Journal of Risk and Contingency Management (IJRCM), and a member of the Project Management Institute (PMI). Beyond academia, he has worked as a technology consultant for European firms and has been actively involved in EU-funded projects. Dr. Vajjhala holds a Doctorate in Information Systems and Technology from the United States, a Master of Science in Computer Science and Applications from India, and a Master of Business Administration (MBA) specializing in Information Systems from Switzerland. His expertise spans computer science, project management, and information systems, making significant contributions to both research and industry.

About the contributors

Georgi Angelov was born in the town of Smolyan. He graduated in Russian Language and Literature and Journalism from Plovdiv University. He began his journalistic career in 2002 in the Smolyan newspaper *Otzyv* and at *Maritsa* in Plovdiv. He later worked as an editor and reporter at several national newspapers in Sofia, covering topics such as parliament, government, foreign relations, and defense. In the last ten years, his focus has shifted to hybrid warfare and disinformation. His most recent positions have been at dnevnik.bg, offnews.bg, and the Bulgarian bureaus of DW (Deutsche Welle) and RFE/RL (Svobodnaevropa.bg). His articles have been translated into dozens of languages. He has attended courses on solutions journalism, fact-checking, OSINT, data analysis, and AI organized by AEJ, AFP, Polis—the journalism think-tank at the London School of Economics, and the Knight Center at the University of Texas at Austin. He is a three-time recipient of the Bulgarian Web Report Award for Clean Journalism (2020, 2022, and 2025). Since November 2024, he has been a senior analyst in the disinformation department at Sensika Technologies.

Prathyusha Bandla serves as an Assistant Professor and Chairperson of the Board of Studies in Management in the Department of Mathematics and Management Sciences at VNR Vignana Jyothi Institute of Engineering and Technology, Hyderabad. She has an impressive academic and research portfolio, with nine research papers published in reputed international journals and ten papers presented at national and international conferences. Additionally, she holds a patent and has contributed six book chapters on diverse topics, including stress management, inclusive education, and online education. Dr. Prathyusha's research interests span Human Resource (HR) Analytics, Emotional Intelligence, Training and Development, and Diversity and Inclusion in the Workplace.

Yerzhan B. Mukashev is the Dean and an Associate Professor at the School of Business, Kazakh-British Technical University, Kazakhstan. He holds a Ph.D. in Economics from the University of Maryland, USA. With over two decades of academic and research experience, Dr. Mukashev has established himself as a prolific scholar, contributing extensively through peer-reviewed research articles, book chapters, and presentations at international conferences. His expertise spans various domains within economics and business, and his work reflects a commitment to academic excellence and thought leadership. Dr. Mukashev's international academic background and professional experience in multicultural and multi-ethnic environments have significantly enhanced his capacity to foster global collaborations and lead administrative functions with efficiency and cultural sensitivity. His leadership continues to play a pivotal role in advancing the internationalization and academic reputation of his institution.

Theodoros Falelakis is a Ph.D. candidate at the Law School of Aristotle University of Thessaloniki, specializing in civil and civil procedural law with a focus on new technologies and private dispute resolution. He holds an LL.M. in European Business and Economic Law from the same university. A qualified attorney-at-law and member of the Thessaloniki Bar Association, he has authored multiple publications on intersection of technology and law.

Antonio Garcia, CGeog, FRGS, PMP, is a historian and interdisciplinary scholar working across a wide range of research areas, including war, peace, business, international relations, and strategy. He is a research fellow in the Department of Military History at Stellenbosch University, on the faculty of Business and Law at The Open University, and a visiting lecturer in international relations and peacekeeping at Durham University. He has authored, co-authored, and co-edited five books. His recent manuscript, Botha, Smuts, and the First World War (with Ian van der Waag), was longlisted for the Templar Prize. His narrative non-fiction work, Number 788 (with Max Lauker), received first place in the Frontline Military Book Awards and has been translated into Swedish. His latest publication, Silencing the Guns in Africa (co-edited with Jacob Udo-Udo Jacob), has received favorable reviews. His forthcoming book, Command, is being finalized.

Parineeta Goswami is an Assistant Professor of Law at UPES, Dehradun, specializing in Corporate Law, Banking Law, Insurance Law, and Insolvency Law. She has over five years of experience in academia. She holds a Ph.D. from RGNUL and has been awarded the JRF by the UGC. Dr. Goswami has authored four textbooks, two edited books, and published extensively in peer-reviewed journals, including Scopus and UGC CARE-listed publications.

Tim Hildebrandt is a Ph.D. candidate and Lecturer in Comparative Politics at the University of Duisburg Essen. He also serves as a Research Associate at Ruhr West University of Applied Sciences. Mr. Hildebrandt holds master's degrees in political science and business administration. He has worked with public and private institutions in Brussels, Skopje, Moscow, Bangkok, Phnom Penh, and Shanghai.

Nicholas Sesugh Iwokwagh is a distinguished academic in the field of Information and Media Technology at the School of Information and Communication Technology (SICT), Federal University of Technology, Minna, Nigeria. He previously served as the Dean of SICT and was the founding Director of the International Centre for Emerging Technology (ICET) at the same institution in Niger State, Nigeria.

Amaresh Jha is a seasoned media professional and educator with a distinguished career spanning journalism, academia, and research. He currently heads the Media Cluster of the School of Liberal Studies and Media at UPES, Dehradun. With professional stints at leading Indian news networks like Zee News, News Express, and India TV, Dr. Jha has cultivated expertise in reporting, producing, and managing news content.

Assel Kenesovna Jumasseitova is a Professor at the Business School of Kazakh-British Technical University in Almaty, Kazakhstan. An accomplished economist, her academic work lies at the intersection of international economics, regional trade agreements, development economics, and business management. Dr. Jumasseitova's current research focuses on the application of Environmental, Social, and Governance (ESG) principles within the context of Kazakhstan's evolving economic landscape and broader regional integration efforts. Her interdisciplinary approach bridges theoretical insights with practical implications for sustainable economic development in Central Asia.

Madhavi Kilaru, an Assistant Professor in the Department of Humanities & Sciences at VNR Vignana Jyothi Institute of Engineering & Technology, Hyderabad, has about 17 years of teaching experience. She received her BA degree in Mathematics & Statistics and MBA in Marketing & HR from Andhra University, Visakhapatnam. She received a Ph.D. degree in Marketing from Andhra University, Visakhapatnam, India. She has published 25 research papers in refereed international journals and 30 in various national and international conference proceedings. She also published patents. Her research areas include Supply Chain Management, Human Resource Management, Consumer Behavior, Artificial Intelligence, and Business Analytics. She is an active member of the Commerce and Management Association of India (CMAI).

Anil Kumar Kotha is an accomplished Assistant Professor in the Department of Mathematics and Management at VNR Vignana Jyothi Institute of Engineering and Technology, Hyderabad. He has approximately 29 years of teaching experience. He holds an M.Com from Kakatiya University, Warangal, an MBA from Acharya Nagarjuna University, Guntur, an M.Phil from Annamalai University, and a Ph.D. in Finance from Rayalaseema University, Kurnool, Andhra Pradesh. Dr. Kotha has an extensive research portfolio, including 12 publications in national and international journals and over 10 presentations at national and international conferences. He also holds patents to his credit. His primary research interest lies in the areas of Banking and Finance. He is an active member of the Indian Commerce Association (ICA) and the Commerce and Management Association of India (CMAI).

Lohith Sekhar Potluri is a full-time Data Scientist at the School of Medicine, University of California San Diego (UCSD), San Diego, USA. He holds a Master's degree in Data Science and is an active researcher with a strong focus on data science, machine learning, artificial intelligence, and applied statistics. Mr. Potluri has authored several peer-reviewed research articles, book chapters, and conference papers in these domains. He is proficient in analytical tools and programming languages such as R (RStudio), SQL, and SAS. His contributions to the field have been recognized with four Best Paper and Academic Excellence Awards at international conferences. He is currently involved in three ongoing research projects.

Rajasekhara Mouly Potluri holds a Ph.D. and M.Phil. in Management/Marketing, Human Resource Management, and Organizational Behavior from Shivaji University, India. He also holds an MBA in Marketing and a Master of Commerce (M.Com.) in Banking from Andhra University, India. Throughout his extensive academic career, Prof. Potluri has authored and presented approximately 150 scholarly works, including peer-reviewed journal articles, books, book chapters, and case studies. His publications appear in esteemed outlets indexed in Scopus, ABDC, SSCI, IEEE, and KCI, and have been featured at numerous international conferences. He has been recognized with over twenty-five awards for Best Research Paper and Academic Service Excellence. Prof. Potluri has taught and conducted research in diverse, multicultural academic environments, including appointments in India, Ethiopia, Kazakhstan, South Korea, Nigeria, and the United Arab Emirates—where he is a recipient of the prestigious Golden Visa. His research interests encompass marketing, Islamic marketing, corporate and consumer social responsibility (CSR/CDR), sustainability, human resource management, organizational behavior, and entrepreneurship with a focus on small business management. He is an active member of several notable professional organizations, including the Eurasian Business and Economics Society, International Islamic Marketing Association, Social Responsibility Research Network, International Society for Development and Sustainability, Emerald Literati Network, and the Consumer Guidance Society of India.

Nisha Sachdeva is an experienced lawyer with over seven years of practice in matrimonial disputes, civil law, consumer law, and SARFAESI Act matters. Specializing in complex cases such as divorce, alimony, custody disputes, and property conflicts, she provides strategic legal solutions backed by meticulous research and empathetic client advocacy. Holding an LLM from Amity University, Nisha is also a researcher and author, with works like "Life Insurance and Grievances Redressal Mechanism." She actively engages with the Just AI community.

Kenneth David Strang is the CEO of W3-Research, an AACSB full-professor working for the University of the Cumberlands. He has over 330 publications across multiple disciplines. Dr. Strang has a professional Doctorate in project management operations research, an MBA in strategic management, with six professional certifications/licenses. He has lifetime grant projects valued over $7 million+, and won two Emerald Literati Awards, with several presidential citations.

Sanjeev Ratna Singh is one of India's leading digital broadcast leaders with over 23 years as a journalist, editor, and multimedia content producer in senior positions in Digital, TV, and Print before moving to academia. He was previously Professor, and Associate Dean, School of Modern Media, UPES Dehradun where his primary work involved revamping the curriculum, building a futuristic digital studio, imparting industry ready skills to students, and handling international partnerships.

Paul Uko Obagwu is a scholar of Journalism and Media Studies at Nasarawa State University, Keffi, Nigeria, and hails from Benue State. His areas of expertise encompass Development Journalism, New Media, and Artificial Intelligence, with a particular focus on Machine Learning applications. Dr. Uko has published extensively in reputable international journals and has contributed chapters to several internationally recognized academic books.

Xiao Wei is a postdoctoral researcher in the field of computer science, with a special interest in artificial intelligence, computer vision, explainable AI, and hybrid intelligence. She has published several works related to these areas and is currently affiliated with the Institute of Computer Science at Osnabrück University. Driven by a strong passion for research, she continues to contribute valuable insights to the academic community.

Chapter 1

Introduction

AI and democracy at the crossroads

Jacob Udo-Udo Jacob and Narasimha Rao Vajjhala

INTRODUCTION: NAVIGATING THE VORTEX

There was something deeply unsettling about watching a four-year-old child converse with Alexa. His small voice echoed across the living room, asking questions into the void, receiving answers from a small device perched on the shelf. "Alexa, do I have to eat breakfast every day? Alexa, why is your name Alexa? Alexa, does your dad ask you to sit in the naughty corner?" The questions were endless, asked as if to a human. Alexa's answers were oddly detached—mechanical, precise, unnuanced, and counterfeit. Not unexpected, for Alexa is a machine. It would ring differently, however, if Alexa passed itself off as human.

This seemingly innocuous domestic scene captures the essence of our current predicament. As artificial intelligence (AI) becomes increasingly embedded in our daily lives, we find ourselves at a critical juncture—a digital maelstrom that threatens to reshape not just our personal interactions, but the very foundation of our democratic systems. The question before us is not whether AI will transform democracy, but how profoundly it will do so, and whether we can harness its power for democratic resilience rather than erosion.

This book, *AI and the Future of Democracy: Building Resilient and Inclusive Societies*, arrives at a moment when democratic institutions worldwide are under unprecedented strain. The challenges are manifold: rising authoritarianism, eroding trust in institutions, weaponized disinformation campaigns, and increasing polarization. Against this backdrop, AI technologies offer both remarkable promise and profound peril for democratic governance.

In this introductory chapter, we establish the conceptual foundation for understanding AI's impact on democratic processes globally. We explore the current landscape of AI applications in governance, define the spectrum of democratic systems that exist today, and examine how different contextual factors influence the relationship between AI and democracy. Most importantly, we confront the fundamental tension that runs throughout this volume: how do we leverage AI's capabilities to strengthen democratic resilience while preventing its weaponization against the very values we seek to uphold?

DOI: 10.1201/9781003594185-1

THE DEMOCRATIC PARADOX IN THE AGE OF AI

Democracy, as philosopher Daniel Dennett reminds us, depends on the informed—not misinformed or uninformed—consent of the people. When that consent is manipulated or counterfeited, democracy loses its essence, and with it, the foundation of our shared humanity. This observation has never been more relevant than in today's digital landscape, where the manipulation of public opinion has been industrialized through sophisticated AI systems.

The recent annulment of Romania's presidential election offers a stark illustration of this threat. After evidence emerged that Russia had conducted a coordinated online campaign to promote far-right presidential candidate Călin Georgescu, leading to his victory in the first round, the Romanian Constitutional Court took the extraordinary step of canceling the election entirely. This decision, citing foreign interference and manipulation through platforms like Telegram and TikTok, highlights the vulnerabilities inherent in our increasingly digitized political landscape.

Yet the very technologies that enable such manipulation also hold promise for democratic renewal. AI systems can enhance civic participation, increase transparency in governance, detect corruption, facilitate consensus-building across divided communities, and safeguard electoral integrity. This paradox—that AI simultaneously threatens and potentially strengthens democracy—forms the central tension explored throughout this book.

DEFINING DEMOCRACY IN THE DIGITAL AGE

Before we can meaningfully discuss AI's impact on democratic processes, we must establish a clear understanding of what we mean by democracy and the various forms it takes around the world. In this book, we distinguish between three categories of democracies—underdeveloped, strained, and stressed—each facing unique challenges that AI might either address or exacerbate.

UNDERDEVELOPED DEMOCRACIES

Underdeveloped democracies are characterized by nascent democratic institutions, limited citizen participation, and often fragile constitutional frameworks. These societies typically experience:

- Low voter turnout and minimal civic engagement
- Limited public access to reliable information about democratic processes
- Weak institutional capacity for organizing and monitoring elections
- Significant digital divides that exclude large portions of the population
- Nascent civil society organizations with limited capacity to defend democratic norms

In these contexts, AI can play a transformative role by expanding access to political information, streamlining administrative processes, and enabling greater civic participation. For instance, AI-powered mobile applications can provide voter education in multiple languages, helping bridge literacy gaps in regions with limited educational infrastructure. Biometric identification systems can help establish reliable voter registries in places where traditional documentation is limited.

However, the introduction of sophisticated technologies into societies with limited digital literacy also creates new vulnerabilities. Without proper safeguards, the same tools that facilitate participation can enable surveillance, manipulation, and the exclusion of marginalized communities.

STRAINED DEMOCRACIES

Strained democracies possess more established democratic institutions but face significant threats to political rights and the rule of law. These systems are characterized by:

- Erosion of judicial independence and constitutional guardrails
- Restrictions on press freedom and civil society activities
- Electoral processes that are procedurally sound but substantively compromised
- Growing power imbalances that favor incumbent authorities
- Polarization that undermines democratic consensus and dialogue

In these environments, AI technologies can serve as crucial tools for monitoring human rights violations, documenting abuses of power, and preserving spaces for civic discourse when traditional media is constrained. Independent initiatives like "Serenata de Amor" in Brazil use machine learning to analyze public spending records and identify potentially corrupt transactions, creating new mechanisms for accountability when institutional checks are weakened.

Yet these same technologies can be weaponized by those seeking to consolidate power, creating sophisticated surveillance systems and propaganda mechanisms that further entrench authoritarian tendencies. This dual potential makes the governance of AI especially critical in strained democratic contexts.

STRESSED DEMOCRACIES

Stressed democracies maintain relatively robust democratic institutions but face acute challenges related to political tension, conflict, or external pressures. These democracies typically exhibit:

- Deep social divisions along ethnic, religious, or ideological lines
- Vulnerability to disinformation campaigns and foreign interference

- Crisis of trust in democratic institutions and processes
- Challenges in maintaining electoral integrity amid polarization
- Difficulties in developing consensus on complex, cross-cutting issues

For stressed democracies, AI offers potential pathways for enhancing electoral integrity, combating disinformation, and facilitating dialogue across divided communities. Tools like automated fact-checking systems can help identify and counter false information at scale, while deliberative platforms powered by machine learning can identify areas of consensus among seemingly opposed groups.

However, the algorithmic amplification of divisive content and the creation of filter bubbles can further entrench existing divisions, complicating efforts at social cohesion. The tension between AI's unifying and divisive potentials is perhaps most pronounced in these stressed democratic contexts.

CURRENT APPLICATIONS OF AI IN DEMOCRATIC PROCESSES

Having established this conceptual framework, we now turn to the current landscape of AI applications in democratic processes worldwide. These applications span the full spectrum of democratic functions, from electoral management to civic engagement, and from policy development to accountability mechanisms.

ELECTORAL INTEGRITY AND MANAGEMENT

AI systems are increasingly deployed to enhance the integrity and efficiency of electoral processes. In India, the world's largest democracy, machine learning algorithms help analyze voter registration data to identify duplicate entries and optimize the distribution of polling stations. During elections, AI-powered tools monitor social media for signs of electoral interference or coordinated disinformation campaigns.

Estonia's pioneering e-governance system incorporates AI to verify digital identities for online voting, analyze voting patterns for anomalies, and ensure the security of electronic ballots. This approach demonstrates how AI can enhance both convenience and integrity in digitally advanced democracies.

However, these applications raise important questions about access, trust, and accountability. In Kenya's 2017 elections, the deployment of biometric verification systems and electronic results transmission encountered significant technical failures, contributing to public distrust and subsequent electoral disputes. This case illustrates how AI implementation without adequate infrastructure, training, and public education can undermine, rather than enhance, democratic processes.

CIVIC ENGAGEMENT AND PARTICIPATION

Innovative AI applications are transforming how citizens engage with democratic processes. In Taiwan, the vTaiwan platform uses AI-powered moderation tools to facilitate large-scale deliberative discussions on proposed legislation. The system identifies areas of consensus among diverse stakeholders, creating new pathways for citizen input into policy formation.

Digital deliberation platforms like Polis use machine learning to cluster similar opinions and identify common ground across diverse perspectives. These tools demonstrate AI's potential to facilitate more inclusive forms of deliberative democracy, though questions remain about accessibility and representativeness.

In underdeveloped democratic contexts, AI-powered mobile applications expand access to political information and participation. Chatbots provide voter education in multiple languages, helping bridge literacy gaps and increase electoral participation in regions with limited educational infrastructure.

MONITORING AND ACCOUNTABILITY

AI technologies create new possibilities for monitoring democratic processes and holding power to account. Independent initiatives use machine learning to analyze public spending records, identify potentially corrupt transactions, and track the implementation of government programs. These applications demonstrate how AI can enhance transparency even when formal accountability mechanisms are weak.

Human rights organizations leverage AI to document abuses in contexts where traditional monitoring is difficult or dangerous. Machine learning algorithms analyze satellite imagery to detect evidence of human rights violations, while natural language processing tools help sift through vast troves of testimony to identify patterns of abuse. These technologies create accountability mechanisms that transcend national boundaries.

In the realm of information integrity, fact-checking organizations increasingly utilize AI to detect and combat disinformation. Machine learning systems identify claims requiring verification and track the spread of debunked content across social media platforms, creating a more robust defense against information manipulation.

POLICY DEVELOPMENT AND IMPLEMENTATION

Governments are beginning to use AI to enhance policy responsiveness and effectiveness. Data analytics platforms incorporate machine learning to analyze public feedback, identify emerging issues, and evaluate policy outcomes. These applications create feedback loops between citizen preferences and policy development, potentially enhancing democratic responsiveness.

In South Korea, the "Smart City" initiative incorporates AI analysis of urban data to inform policy decisions on transportation, energy usage, and public services. This data-driven approach creates new connections between citizen behavior and governance, although questions remain about privacy and algorithmic transparency.

AI systems are also being used to model the potential impacts of policy proposals across different population segments, helping identify unintended consequences before implementation. These applications demonstrate AI's potential to enhance the evidence base for democratic decision-making, though the quality of outputs remains heavily dependent on the data and assumptions built into the models.

THE RHIZOMATIC NATURE OF DIGITAL DEMOCRACY

To understand how AI is reshaping democratic processes, we must recognize the fundamentally networked character of contemporary information ecosystems. Drawing on the concept of the "rhizome" developed by philosophers Gilles Deleuze and Félix Guattari, we can conceptualize our digital landscape as a decentralized, non-hierarchical network of connections—a dynamic structure that evolves unpredictably.

In this rhizomatic landscape, information and influence flow through complex, interconnected channels that resist centralized control. The Romanian election interference case illustrates how propaganda can spread rapidly through decentralized networks like Telegram and TikTok, making it difficult to trace and counteract. AI accelerates this rhizomatic spread by automating content creation, targeting, and distribution at an unprecedented scale.

Yet this rhizomatic structure also creates opportunities for democratic resilience. Grassroots movements can leverage the same networked dynamics to mobilize support, coordinate action, and circumvent traditional gatekeepers. AI tools that facilitate collective sense-making and coordinated action can enhance democratic agency within these complex networks.

The challenge for democratic governance is to harness the rhizomatic potential for distributed participation while mitigating the risks of manipulation and fragmentation. This requires not just technological solutions but a deeper understanding of how digital networks reshape civic identity and political community.

IDENTITY AND AUTHENTICITY IN AI-MEDIATED DEMOCRACY

At the heart of the democratic challenge posed by AI lies the question of authentic identity and agency. When Canadian scholar Marshall McLuhan predicted in 1962 that electronic media would create a "global village," he couldn't have anticipated how AI would transform this village into something more akin to Aldous Huxley's World State—a place where identity becomes increasingly fluid, detached from physical reality.

We now construct our online identities through countless digital interactions. Each click, each like, each shared post becomes data for AI algorithms to process and reflect back to us. Like a digital mirror, AI shows us not who we are, but who it thinks we want to be. The reflection is always slightly distorted, always slightly enhanced, and always slightly more "perfect" than reality.

This process of algorithmic identity formation has profound implications for democratic citizenship. The echo chambers we inhabit online aren't just political—they're cultural. AI algorithms, in their endless quest to provide "relevant" content, create cultural bubbles that both reinforce and reshape our sense of identity. These aren't organic cultural expressions but carefully curated experiences, shaped by AI's understanding of what we "should" like based on our data profile.

This is where Huxley's warnings become particularly relevant. In "Brave New World," identity is manufactured through conditioning. Today, our conditioning comes through personalized content feeds, recommendation engines, and AI-driven social networks. The difference is that we willingly participate in our own conditioning, mistaking algorithmic suggestions for personal choice.

The danger for democracy is clear: when our identities are increasingly shaped by opaque algorithmic systems optimized for engagement rather than civic virtue, the foundation of informed democratic consent erodes. We risk becoming what philosopher Daniel Dennett calls "counterfeit people"—digital simulacra whose preferences and choices are increasingly manufactured by the very systems we believe ourselves to be controlling.

THE CHALLENGE OF DIGITAL COUNTERFEIT

Dennett's warning against "counterfeit people" takes on new urgency in light of recent advances in AI. According to researchers from Stanford and Google DeepMind, it is now possible to create "simulation agents" that embody a person's identity, including their values and preferences, "with stunning accuracy." These developments raise profound questions about authenticity and agency in democratic discourse.

When AI systems can generate synthetic media indistinguishable from authentic human expression—whether text, images, audio, or video—the epistemological foundation of democracy trembles. How can citizens make informed decisions when they cannot distinguish between authentic and manufactured information? How can democratic deliberation function when participants cannot be certain they are engaging with genuine interlocutors rather than AI simulations?

The Romanian election interference case demonstrates the real-world consequences of these questions. When coordinated campaigns use AI to manipulate public discourse, democratic choice itself becomes compromised. The Constitutional Court's extraordinary decision to annul the election results recognizes that democracy cannot function when the conditions for authentic consent have been systematically undermined.

Yet the solution cannot be to reject technological advancement outright. Rather, we must develop robust frameworks for distinguishing between the authentic and the counterfeit in digital space—technological guardrails, legal standards, and social norms that preserve the integrity of democratic discourse in an age of synthetic media.

RECLAIMING EMBODIED DEMOCRACY

There's a peculiar loneliness in this digital age. We are more connected than ever, yet increasingly disconnected from embodied experience. Our identities as citizens, once grounded in physical communities, shared public spaces, and face-to-face deliberation, now exist primarily as data points in vast AI systems.

This disembodiment of democratic practice creates vulnerabilities that authoritarian actors are quick to exploit. When citizens lose connection to the physical reality of their communities—the material conditions of their fellow citizens, the concrete impacts of policy decisions, and the embodied experience of civic solidarity—they become more susceptible to manipulation through algorithmically optimized fear and outrage.

The challenge we face isn't just about preserving democratic institutions in the age of AI—it is about remembering what it means to be embodied citizens in the first place. As McLuhan warned, each new technology numbs us to its effects. We are becoming increasingly comfortable with our disembodied, digital existence, barely noticing as AI gradually reshapes our understanding of civic identity and democratic participation.

Yet within this disembodied digital landscape, there is a growing appetite for authenticity. We see it in the rise of "digital detox" movements, in renewed interest in local governance, and in the desire for "real" experiences of community and connection. Perhaps this is our natural response to the increasingly artificial nature of our digital existence—a recognition that democracy requires not just information but embodied presence.

NAVIGATING THE DIGITAL MAELSTROM

As we move forward into this brave new digital world, perhaps our greatest challenge is to remain human—embodied, imperfect, and authentically ourselves—even as AI offers increasingly sophisticated ways to transcend our physical limitations. The phantom of the machine doesn't have to be our only identity; we can choose to remain grounded in the physical world while navigating the digital one.

To cultivate this balance, we might draw wisdom from Marshall McLuhan's analysis of Edgar Allan Poe's "Descent into the Maelstrom." In Poe's story, a sailor survives a powerful vortex by observing its patterns and using that understanding to navigate its chaos. McLuhan uses this metaphor to describe how individuals can adapt to the overwhelming forces of technological change by gaining critical awareness of the systems that envelop them.

The lesson is clear: survival in a digital maelstrom demands not only awareness of the forces shaping our reality but also the ability to act purposefully within the chaos. Just as the sailor in Poe's story relied on keen observation to avoid destruction, cultivating media literacy and an acute awareness of how AI shapes our information environment is now a democratic necessity.

This involves recognizing when AI-driven systems are used to counterfeit consent, distort truth, and undermine democratic processes. The interconnected, rhizomatic nature of digital systems offers both opportunities and threats. If left unchecked, these systems become tools for manipulation. Yet, with critical awareness and deliberate action, they can also be harnessed for genuine connection and democratic empowerment.

CONCLUSION: DEMOCRACY ON A DIGITAL TIGHTROPE

The title of this book—*AI and the Future of Democracy: Building Resilient and Inclusive Societies*—captures both the precarity and the possibility of our current moment. We stand on a digital tightrope, balancing between AI's potential to enhance democratic governance and its power to undermine the very foundations of democratic legitimacy.

The path forward requires more than rejecting digital counterfeits and manipulated consent; it requires fostering authentic experiences of democratic citizenship that anchor us in reality. This means designing AI systems that enhance rather than replace human judgment, that facilitate rather than simulate authentic dialogue, and that expand rather than narrow our sense of shared humanity.

It means developing policy frameworks that govern the ethical deployment of AI in democratic contexts, with particular attention to questions of transparency, accountability, and inclusivity. It means investing in education that cultivates not just digital literacy but also democratic agency—the ability to engage critically and constructively with AI-mediated information environments.

Most fundamentally, it means recognizing that democracy is not merely a set of procedures or institutions but a lived experience of collective self-determination. No matter how sophisticated our AI systems become, democracy will always depend on the embodied participation of citizens who recognize themselves as authors of their collective future.

McLuhan's insight truly resonates here: it is not the technological vortex itself that destroys but our failure to understand and respond to it. In this sense, the challenge of the digital age is not merely to survive the maelstrom but to master it, ensuring that humanity thrives amidst the chaos rather than being consumed by it.

As the following chapters explore specific applications of AI across different democratic contexts—from electoral systems to policy development, from civic engagement to social cohesion—this fundamental question will remain our guideposts: how can we ensure that AI serves as a tool for democratic empowerment rather than manipulation? How can we walk the digital tightrope without losing our balance—or our humanity?

The stakes could not be higher. At a time when democratic institutions face unprecedented challenges from both within and without, the integration of AI into democratic processes represents both our greatest hope and our most profound vulnerability. By approaching this integration with clear eyes, ethical commitment, and unwavering dedication to democratic values, we can work toward a future where technology enhances rather than erodes our capacity for collective self-governance.

In the chapters that follow, we will explore concrete applications, case studies, and policy frameworks that can help realize this vision of AI-enhanced democracy. From empowering citizens through accessible digital platforms to ensuring the integrity of electoral processes, from facilitating responsive policy-making to combating disinformation, the potential applications are vast and varied.

Chapter 2 introduces a groundbreaking analytical framework for understanding how AI is revolutionizing information warfare through "AI-Enhanced Reflexive Control" (AIRC)—the convergence of Soviet-developed psychological manipulation techniques with modern computational capabilities. Drawing on comprehensive data from Bulgaria's experience with the Kremlin-backed "Pravda" disinformation network between December 2024 and April 2025, the authors demonstrate how AI fundamentally transforms traditional influence operations through five key dimensions: algorithmic amplification, computational content generation, predictive audience modeling, feedback-driven optimization, and dynamic narrative evolution. Bulgaria serves as an ideal case study due to its unique vulnerability profile as a transitional democracy with historical ties to Russia, institutional weaknesses, energy dependencies, and strategic geopolitical positioning that creates multiple cognitive access points for manipulation. Building on the foundational concepts established in this chapter, this analysis reveals how AIRC operations systematically exploit democratic vulnerabilities by creating sophisticated ecosystems of belonging rather than simply spreading disinformation. Through detailed network and content analysis, Chapter 2 shows how the Pravda network achieved significant impact on Bulgarian public discourse—mainstreaming fringe positions, increasing polarization, and contributing to policy paralysis—while adapting narratives in real-time to exploit economic anxieties, identity insecurities, and institutional trust deficits. Beyond its technical contributions, this chapter fundamentally reframes the challenge facing democracies: the battle is not merely against false information but against algorithmically optimized systems designed to reshape where citizens feel they belong, highlighting the urgent need for comprehensive cognitive security frameworks that can defend democratic institutions against these next-generation threats to democratic resilience.

Chapter 3 tackles the urgent challenge of identifying and categorizing the risks posed by unethical AI applications in democratic systems, with particular focus on the heightened vulnerabilities faced by underdeveloped, strained, or stressed societies. Through a rigorous critical analysis methodology combined with machine learning validation, the authors systematically examine how the ubiquitous accessibility of AI technology—available to anyone with a smartphone or connected device—creates a dual-edged scenario where the same tools that can enhance democratic participation and governance efficiency can be weaponized by malicious actors to undermine democratic institutions. The chapter identifies five distinct categories of unethical AI threats: AI-disinformation (including deepfakes and manipulated media that exploit the "liar's dividend"), AI-electoral-interference (direct manipulation of democratic processes through voter suppression and data alteration), AI-HR-manipulation (perpetuation of systemic inequalities through biased recruitment and organizational decisions), AI-unethical-culture (exploitation of cultural dimensions and personality factors for mass manipulation), and AI-privacy-invasion (unprecedented surveillance capabilities that compromise individual privacy and political freedom). Building upon extensive empirical analysis across multiple sectors—from healthcare and finance to transportation and legal services—Chapter 4 demonstrates how AI disruption follows predictable patterns that can be both anticipated and potentially mitigated, while simultaneously revealing how rapidly these technologies can transform entire domains, often outpacing existing regulatory and ethical frameworks. The authors' findings reveal that developing nations face particularly acute vulnerabilities due to limited technological infrastructure, reduced institutional safeguards, and cultural factors that increase susceptibility to AI manipulation, creating especially dangerous conditions where democratic fragilities intersect with AI accessibility. The chapter concludes with comprehensive policy recommendations for strengthening democratic resilience, including the development of rapid response capabilities for disinformation detection, enhanced electoral cybersecurity measures, culturally aware AI governance frameworks, and strengthened privacy protections—all essential for preserving democratic integrity in an era where AI has become both a powerful tool for democratic enhancement and a sophisticated weapon for its subversion.

Chapter 4 presents a comprehensive examination of how AI—particularly large language models—is fundamentally reshaping the foundations of civilization, culture, and identity in ways that transcend traditional geographic and cultural boundaries. The chapter argues that we are witnessing the emergence of new "algorithmic civilizations" where data flows and digital infrastructures, rather than territory or tradition, define cultural and political power structures. Through detailed analysis of AI-generated misinformation campaigns, the landmark case of the AI-created *Portrait of Edmond de Belamy* artwork, and the transformation of educational practices, the author demonstrates how AI systems are not merely tools but active agents in cultural production and identity formation. The chapter reveals how platforms like TikTok and ChatGPT are creating hybrid forms of expression that blend local sensibilities with global algorithmic logics, giving rise to what scholars term "algorithmic culture" where identity becomes fluid and performative, constantly remixed through digital feedback loops. Building upon this analysis of cultural transformation, Chapter 5 critically addresses the profound inequalities embedded within the global AI ecosystem, exposing how the "ghost work" of poorly compensated laborers in the Global South powers the machine learning systems that generate wealth in the Global North—a form of "digital colonialism" that perpetuates existing hierarchies while creating new dependencies. The chapter draws provocative parallels between AI and nuclear technology as dual-use technologies with immense civilian benefits but equally significant risks for weaponization and geopolitical instability. In response to these challenges, the author proposes a three-pillar framework for inclusive AI governance: democratizing access to AI technologies and infrastructure, preserving cultural diversity through inclusive design practices and pluralistic datasets, and establishing robust international cooperation mechanisms similar to nuclear non-proliferation agreements. The chapter concludes with the sobering recognition that just as ancient Greeks distinguished themselves from "barbarians" through language, we now create new civilizational boundaries through algorithms—and whether this algorithmic civilization becomes a turning point or cautionary tale will depend on whether we embed ethical principles and sustainability at the heart of its design.

Chapter 5 provides a comprehensive framework for embedding democratic values into AI design and implementation, addressing the critical ethical challenges that emerge as AI systems increasingly influence decision-making across employment, criminal justice, finance, and public administration. The chapter systematically examines how the rapid advancement of AI technologies, while enhancing efficiency and innovation, simultaneously poses profound threats to democratic foundations through algorithmic bias, privacy violations, and discriminatory practices that disproportionately affect marginalized communities. The authors introduce and critique the concept of "algocracy"—the concentration of AI control within a few powerful corporations—which threatens individual autonomy and social equity by creating systems where automated decisions lack transparency, accountability, and democratic oversight. Through detailed analysis of real-world applications and regulatory frameworks like the EU's GDPR and the Council of Europe's Framework Convention on AI, the chapter demonstrates how current ethical challenges in AI development, including the "black box" problem of explainability and inherited biases from historical data, require urgent intervention to prevent the erosion of democratic institutions. Building upon the technical foundations and threat assessments established in Chapters 1–5, Chapter 6 offers actionable strategies and governance frameworks to ensure AI serves the public good rather than undermining democratic values. The chapter presents a multi-layered approach encompassing robust governance structures with clear oversight mechanisms, algorithmic transparency and explainability techniques, bias detection and mitigation tools, ethical data collection policies, and continuous monitoring systems that maintain fairness and accountability over time. Drawing from successful implementations and emerging best practices, the authors advocate for inclusive, participatory design processes that engage diverse stakeholders—including developers, governments, and civil society—in creating AI systems that actively promote justice, equity, and sustainability. The chapter concludes with a forward-looking vision that emphasizes AI literacy as an essential skill for democratic participation, calling for comprehensive education initiatives and international cooperation to establish global standards that balance innovation with the protection of human rights and democratic principles, ultimately ensuring that AI technologies strengthen rather than weaken the foundations of democratic society.

Chapter 6 provides a comprehensive examination of algorithmic bias in political campaigning on social media platforms, revealing how engagement-driven algorithms systematically amplify divisive content and create echo chambers that threaten democratic discourse and electoral integrity. Through a multidisciplinary approach combining ethical analysis, technological perspectives, and extensive case studies—including the 2016 US presidential election with Russian interference, the 2018 Brazilian election's WhatsApp misinformation campaigns, and the 2019 Indian general elections—the chapter demonstrates how biased algorithms not only reflect existing societal inequalities but also actively amplify them through content curation systems designed to maximize user engagement rather than promote balanced information. The authors reveal that algorithms trained on historically biased datasets perpetuate systemic discrimination, particularly marginalizing rural and minority communities while favoring urban, privileged demographics, thereby distorting political outreach and creating feedback loops that reinforce ideological polarization and exclude vulnerable populations from meaningful political participation Building upon the technical foundations and threat assessments established in earlier chapters, Chapter 7 offers concrete strategies for mitigating algorithmic bias through enhanced transparency, regulatory oversight, and the implementation of XAI technologies that make algorithmic decision-making processes comprehensible to stakeholders. The chapter's empirical analysis of engagement patterns, sentiment analysis, and targeted advertising reveals how AI-powered tools enable sophisticated manipulation of public opinion through microtargeting, bot networks, and deepfake technologies that can fundamentally alter electoral outcomes. The authors conclude with actionable recommendations including mandatory disclosure requirements for political AI use, independent algorithmic audits, diverse dataset development, and comprehensive digital literacy programs that empower citizens to critically evaluate information in the digital age. This chapter serves as a crucial bridge between the theoretical understanding of AI threats to democracy and practical solutions for preserving democratic values, emphasizing that the future of digital democracy depends on collaborative efforts between technology developers, policymakers, and civil society to ensure AI systems promote fairness, inclusion, and informed civic participation rather than manipulation and division.

Chapter 7 provides a comprehensive examination of computer vision (CV) technology's transformative potential in public policy, exploring its technological foundations from early pattern recognition experiments in the 1950s to today's sophisticated deep learning models that enable machines to interpret and understand visual data at unprecedented scale. The chapter systematically analyzes CV's practical applications across critical governance domains including traffic management (demonstrated through Darmstadt's intelligent traffic systems), public safety and surveillance (exemplified by New York's Domain Awareness System), environmental monitoring (including North American urban forest mapping), healthcare and disease tracking (such as neonatal care monitoring), and border security (illustrated by the Eagle Eye Project). Through detailed case studies and technical analysis of machine learning algorithms—from classical approaches like Scale-Invariant Feature Transform (SIFT) and Support Vector Machines to advanced deep learning methods including Convolutional Neural Networks and Generative Adversarial Networks—the chapter demonstrates how CV technologies can enhance efficiency, improve accuracy, reduce costs, and enable real-time decision-making across diverse policy contexts. Building upon the ethical frameworks and democratic concerns established in previous chapters, Chapter 8 critically addresses the significant risks and challenges accompanying CV deployment in governance, particularly focusing on data privacy violations, algorithmic bias, government overreach, and the potential for inaccuracy and misuse that can undermine democratic values and civil liberties. The authors emphasize how socioeconomic disparities and the digital divide create uneven access to CV-driven services, potentially reinforcing existing inequalities when marginalized communities lack the infrastructure, resources, or digital literacy necessary to benefit from these technological advances. The chapter concludes with a balanced perspective that recognizes CV's immense potential to strengthen governance resilience and efficiency while arguing that implementation must be guided by principles of transparency, accountability, and fairness. Through comprehensive policy recommendations including infrastructure investment, digital literacy programs, inclusive algorithmic design, and community-centric development approaches, this chapter provides essential guidance for policymakers seeking to harness CV's benefits while safeguarding democratic institutions and ensuring equitable access to technological innovations that can improve societal well-being.

Chapter 8 provides a comprehensive analysis of how AI has become a sophisticated weapon for electoral manipulation, fundamentally disrupting democratic processes worldwide through technologies such as deepfakes, predictive analytics, micro-targeting algorithms, and AI-generated misinformation. The chapter demonstrates how political actors now leverage AI's ability to analyze vast datasets, discern behavioral patterns, and generate persuasive yet false content to manipulate public opinion at unprecedented scale and precision. Through detailed examination of AI-driven campaign tools—including chatbots for voter engagement, social media bots for amplifying narratives, and psychological profiling for targeting specific demographics—the authors reveal how these technologies enable political organizations to move beyond traditional campaigning toward sophisticated psychological manipulation that exploits individual vulnerabilities and biases. The chapter particularly emphasizes how socioeconomic disparities create unequal vulnerability to AI manipulation, with low-income and less educated populations being disproportionately susceptible to misinformation due to limited access to fact-checking resources and digital literacy tools. Building upon the theoretical frameworks established in earlier chapters, Chapter 9 presents compelling case studies from the 2024 Indian General Election, the Cambridge Analytica scandal, and the 2024 US Presidential Election to illustrate the real-world manifestation of AI threats to democratic integrity. The Indian election showcased how AI-powered micro-targeting and deepfakes of Bollywood celebrities were used to influence voter perception, while the Cambridge Analytica case demonstrated the devastating potential of psychological profiling through unauthorized data harvesting from millions of Facebook users. The 2024 US election highlighted the proliferation of deepfake videos featuring political leaders that spread rapidly across social media platforms, creating confusion and eroding public trust in authentic information. The chapter concludes with urgent calls for comprehensive regulatory frameworks that address data privacy, algorithmic transparency, and international cooperation, emphasizing that while current regulatory responses from the US, EU, and India remain fragmented and inadequate, the protection of democratic institutions requires proactive collaboration between policymakers, technologists, and civil society to establish ethical standards, enhance digital literacy, and create robust oversight mechanisms that can adapt to rapidly evolving AI capabilities while preserving the fundamental principles of fair and transparent elections.

Chapter 9 shifts focus from AI as a threat to democracy toward AI as a potential solution for combating election misinformation, particularly in strained democratic societies characterized by limited digital literacy, inadequate infrastructure, and weak institutional capacity. The chapter presents a comprehensive examination of AI-driven tools and strategies that can effectively counter electoral misinformation, including automated fact-checking systems, content verification mechanisms, misinformation detection algorithms, social media monitoring platforms, chatbots and virtual assistants for voter education, and machine learning libraries for pattern recognition. Through detailed case studies from Nigeria's 2023 elections (where the Nigerian Fact Checkers Coalition utilized Full Fact AI tools to debunk over 40,000 fact-checkable claims), Kenya's 2022 elections (where the MAPEMA Consortium identified over 550,000 toxic posts using AI and machine learning technologies), and the Philippines' systematic approach through COMELEC's Task Force KKK, the chapter demonstrates how AI technologies can be successfully deployed to detect, counter, and prevent the spread of false information during critical electoral periods. While acknowledging AI's transformative potential for strengthening democratic integrity, Chapter 10 critically addresses the significant challenges that limit effective implementation of these solutions in developing democracies, including algorithmic bias that can perpetuate discrimination, data quality issues arising from unreliable or manipulated datasets, scalability concerns when processing vast amounts of information, and infrastructure limitations such as poor network connectivity and insufficient computational power. The chapter emphasizes that successful AI-driven anti-misinformation efforts require comprehensive approaches involving collaboration between governments, civil society organizations, technology companies, and international partners, as demonstrated in the successful case studies. Looking toward the future, the authors argue that addressing digital literacy gaps, developing robust regulatory frameworks for responsible AI use, investing in digital infrastructure, and fostering international cooperation will be essential for maximizing AI's potential to protect electoral integrity and strengthen democratic governance in societies most vulnerable to information manipulation, ultimately contributing to more transparent, accountable, and inclusive democratic processes worldwide.

Chapter 10 presents a comprehensive analysis of how AI-driven tools can function as democratic equalizers to enhance access to justice, particularly for marginalized populations facing systemic barriers to legal services. The chapter systematically categorizes AI legal technologies—including document management systems, legal research engines, chatbots and virtual assistants, predictive analytics tools, and automated case management platforms—and demonstrates their potential to address three primary barriers to justice: gender-based discrimination, wealth-based inequality, and systemic-institutional inefficiencies. Through detailed case studies, including the A2J Author platform that has helped over 3 million users complete legal forms, Massachusetts Defense for Eviction (MADE) assisting over 4,000 tenants facing eviction, and De'Shazer's innovative SHIRLEY system for detecting judicial bias across multiple jurisdictions, the chapter illustrates how AI tools can democratize legal services by reducing costs, streamlining procedures, and providing sophisticated legal assistance to self-represented litigants who cannot afford traditional legal representation. While acknowledging AI's transformative potential for closing the global justice gap—where over 5.1 billion people lack adequate access to justice—Chapter 11 critically addresses the significant risks and limitations that must be carefully managed to ensure responsible implementation. The chapter highlights critical concerns including the "AI fallacy" that prevents full replication of human legal reasoning, transparency and accuracy issues demonstrated by biased risk assessment tools like COMPAS and instances of AI-generated fake legal citations, and substantial technological and economic barriers that vary across different jurisdictions and legal cultures. Drawing from the EU's Ethics Guidelines for Trustworthy AI, the author provides comprehensive recommendations for responsible AI integration that emphasize human oversight, technical robustness, transparency, diversity and fairness, and accountability mechanisms. The chapter concludes that while AI cannot replace human judgment in complex legal reasoning, when governed by appropriate ethical frameworks and regulatory safeguards, these technologies can serve as powerful democratic equalizers that enhance efficiency, reduce bias, and provide previously inaccessible legal services to vulnerable populations, ultimately strengthening the rule of law and democratic institutions worldwide.

Yet throughout this exploration, we must remain grounded in the fundamental insight that democracy depends on the informed—not misinformed or uninformed—consent of the people. As AI reshapes the landscape of public discourse and political participation, safeguarding this principle becomes both more challenging and more essential. By advancing a thoughtful, context-sensitive approach to AI in democratic processes, we can work toward a future where these technologies serve as tools of empowerment rather than manipulation, strengthening rather than undermining the foundations of democratic governance.

Chapter 2

The disinformation matrix

AI-Enhanced reflexive control and the automated manipulation of vulnerable democracies

Jacob Udo-Udo Jacob and Georgi Angelov

INTRODUCTION: THE EVOLUTION OF REFLEXIVE CONTROL IN THE DIGITAL AGE

Reflexive control—a sophisticated methodology developed by Soviet military psychologists in the 1960s—was designed to manipulate an adversary's decision-making by transmitting specially prepared information that induces the target to voluntarily make predetermined decisions advantageous to the initiator while maintaining the illusion of independent choice (Bokša, 2019; Giles, 2023; Robbins, 2020; Thomas, 2004; Kuleshov et al, 2014). Initially conceived as a military doctrine, reflexive control has evolved into a comprehensive approach to strategic information warfare, combining psychological manipulation, predictive behavior modeling, and information environment shaping.

The integration of AI into this established psychological warfare technique represents a paradigm shift in the sophistication, scale, and effectiveness of influence operations. This chapter introduces the concept of *AI-Enhanced Reflexive Control* (AIRC)—a framework for understanding how modern computational capabilities fundamentally transform these operations through:

1. *Algorithmic Amplification*: Using AI to orchestrate coordinated dissemination across platforms, creating artificial consensus and information cascades
2. *Computational Content Generation*: Deploying language models to produce culturally adapted content at unprecedented scale and localization depth
3. *Predictive Audience Modeling*: Leveraging machine learning to identify psychological vulnerabilities and predict audience responses
4. *Feedback-Driven Optimization*: Analyzing engagement metrics in real-time to refine messaging and targeting
5. *Dynamic Narrative Evolution*: Using AI to adapt storylines in response to changing events while maintaining strategic objectives

This integration of AI significantly enhances the scope, precision, and effectiveness of influence operations, particularly against democratic societies

DOI: 10.1201/9781003594185-2

where free information flow is essential to governance. The AIRC framework helps us understand how these operations systematically manipulate the informational environment to induce specific behaviors and attitudes in targeted populations.

Bulgaria represents an ideal case study for examining AIRC in action. As a transitional democracy with complex historical ties to Russia, institutional vulnerabilities, and a strategic position on NATO's southeastern flank, Bulgaria exemplifies how specific societal and cognitive access points can be systematically exploited through algorithmically optimized influence campaigns. Through detailed analysis of the Kremlin-backed "Pravda" network operations (Châtelet & Chenrose, 2025; Jacob & Angelov, 2025) in Bulgaria between December 2024 and April 2025, we will demonstrate how AIRC techniques are deployed to undermine democratic institutions, polarize society, and redirect Bulgaria's strategic orientation.

This chapter builds on existing literature on reflexive control (Thomas, 2004; Lefebvre, 1977, 1997; Kramer et al, 2003; Lepsky, 2002; Lepsky & Stepanov, 2003; Leonenko, 1995) and Russian information warfare (Abrams, 2016; Ajir & Vailliant, 2018; Besemeres, 2016; Mahairas & Dvilyanski, 2018; Redington, 2021; Till, 2020) by integrating insights from computational propaganda studies, network analysis, and cognitive security. By developing and applying a comprehensive AIRC framework, we seek to understand not only what these operations do, but also how they systematically reshape the cognitive and informational terrain of democracy in the algorithmic age.

THE AIRC FRAMEWORK: A CONCEPTUAL MODEL

Before examining our case study, we first present a conceptual model of AIRC that will guide our analysis. This framework integrates classical reflexive control theory with contemporary understanding of AI capabilities to identify how computational systems transform influence operations.

Foundations of reflexive control

Reflexive control is a process by which one enemy transmits the reasons or bases for making decisions to another (Thomas, 2004, p. 238). Russian theorists on disinformation and military *maskirovka* or deception, such as Georgy P. Shchedrovitsky (2002), Vladimir. E. Lepsky (2002), Vladimir A. Lefebvre (1977), and several others have studied reflexive control both at the tactical and operational levels as a system for manipulating and controlling a target audience's decision-making. Reflexive control is distinctive in that it seeks to influence a target audience's decision-making process by manipulating their perceptions of reality (Till, 2020). The objective of the controlling organ is to convey to the receiver the motives and reasons for the desired decision so that the reasons and motives conveyed are personalized and owned by the receiver (Leonenko, 1995). Its purpose is to create second-order effects—where targets are influenced not through direct persuasion but by altering the informational environment in which they make decisions. Reflexive control is particularly potent in contexts where there is already some form of cognitive access to the targeted population.

Classical reflexive control, as developed in Soviet military doctrine, operates on several key principles:

1. *Decision-Making Manipulation*: Influencing the target's perception of reality to induce predictable decisions
2. *Second-Order Effects*: Creating changes in the informational environment that trigger cascading psychological responses
3. *Cognitive Access Exploitation*: Identifying and leveraging psychological vulnerabilities and predispositions

Perceived autonomy maintenance: Ensuring targets believe they are making independent choices

As articulated by Soviet theorist Vladimir Lefebvre (1977), reflexive control is fundamentally about creating a model of the enemy's reasoning and then manipulating the informational inputs to that reasoning process. This approach relies on deep understanding of the target's cognitive frameworks, values, and decision-making patterns.

The AI Enhancement Layer

Our AIRC framework identifies five dimensions through which AI fundamentally transforms traditional reflexive control.

Algorithmic amplification systems

AI significantly enhances the reach and impact of influence operations through:

- *Orchestrated Network Effects*: Using algorithms to coordinate content dissemination across multiple channels, creating artificial consensus
- *Calibrated Propagation Velocity*: Optimizing the timing and sequencing of content release to maximize psychological impact
- *Cross-Platform Information Cascades*: Triggering self-reinforcing information flows that transcend platform boundaries
- *Synthetic Social Proof*: Generating apparent validation from multiple sources to enhance credibility

These capabilities allow AIRC operations to create the appearance of widespread consensus around manufactured narratives, overwhelming cognitive defenses through sheer volume and apparent social validation.

Computational content generation

AI-powered content creation enables:

- *Cultural-Linguistic Adaptation*: Generating content that passes local linguistic and cultural authenticity tests
- *Mass Personalization*: Tailoring messaging to specific psychological profiles at scale
- *Narrative Synthesis*: Automatically integrating current events into strategic messaging frameworks
- *Media Polymorphism*: Creating multiple content formats (text, images, memes) from the same narrative seeds

These capabilities allow AIRC operations to produce contextually relevant, psychologically calibrated content at volumes impossible for human operators alone, effectively saturating the information environment.

Predictive audience modeling

AI enables sophisticated prediction and targeting of audience responses through:

- *Psychological Vulnerability Mapping*: Identifying cognitive biases, emotional triggers, and identity markers
- *Differential Response Prediction*: Anticipating how different audience segments will react to specific narratives
- *Behavioral Pattern Analysis*: Identifying habit patterns that indicate susceptibility to certain message types
- *Cognitive Access Point Detection*: Discovering psychological entry points for manipulation based on historical data

These capabilities allow AIRC operations to target messaging with unprecedented precision, focusing resources on the most susceptible audiences and the most effective psychological levers.

Feedback-driven optimization

AI systems enable continuous refinement of influence operations through:

- *Engagement Analytics*: Monitoring audience responses to different narrative variations
- *A/B Testing at Scale*: Systematically testing message variations to identify optimal framing
- *Temporal Pattern Analysis*: Identifying when audiences are most receptive to specific content types
- *Success Metric Refinement*: Continuously updating performance indicators based on strategic objectives

These capabilities create a dynamic, self-improving system that rapidly evolves to overcome resistance and exploit successful vectors of influence.

Dynamic narrative evolution

AI enhances the adaptability of influence operations through:

- *Event-Responsive Reframing*: Automatically reinterpreting current events to maintain strategic narratives
- *Anticipatory Content Preparation*: Generating content libraries for potential future scenarios
- *Narrative Consistency Management*: Ensuring messaging remains coherent across evolving situations
- *Counter-Narrative Neutralization*: Rapidly developing responses to emerging counter-messaging

These capabilities allow AIRC operations to maintain strategic coherence despite changing real-world conditions, ensuring that all events—regardless of their actual nature—can be integrated into the desired narrative framework.

AIRC operational model

These five enhancement dimensions combine in an integrated operational model where:

1. *Predictive Audience Modeling*: Identifies vulnerabilities and targets
2. *Computational Content Generation*: Creates tailored messaging
3. *Algorithmic Amplification Systems*: Distribute content for maximum impact
4. *Feedback-Driven Optimization*: Continuously refines the operation
5. *Dynamic Narrative Evolution*: Adapts to changing conditions

This cyclical process creates a sophisticated influence system capable of inducing targeted psychological and behavioral effects at population scale, while continuously learning and adapting to overcome resistance.

Bulgaria's vulnerability profile: The ideal testing ground for AIRC

AIRC operations require specific societal conditions to achieve maximum effectiveness. Bulgaria presents a complex vulnerability profile that makes it an ideal environment for testing and refining these techniques.

Historical and cultural vulnerabilities

Bulgaria's historical relationship with Russia creates significant cognitive access points for AIRC operations. Russia's role in liberating Bulgaria from Ottoman rule (1878) established a persistent narrative of Russia as "protector" that remains emotionally resonant in Bulgaria's national consciousness, and evident in cultural and religious artefacts, museums, and monuments. This historical memory provides a foundation for narratives that frame Russia as Bulgaria's traditional ally and the West as an imposing foreign influence.

Shared Slavic linguistic roots and Orthodox Christian identity create cultural recognition and resonance for Russian messaging that transcends political divisions. Modern AIRC operations leverage these cultural similarities through computational linguistic adaptation and identity-based messaging that appears authentically Bulgarian rather than foreign-originated.

The AIRC framework identifies these as "cognitive access points"—pre-existing psychological frameworks that can be systematically exploited through carefully calibrated messaging. By using machine learning to analyze linguistic patterns, cultural references, and historical narratives in Bulgarian discourse, AIRC systems can identify the specific terms, frames, and stories that trigger emotional resonance and identity activation.

Institutional and media vulnerabilities

Bulgaria's institutional environment presents specific vulnerabilities that AIRC operations systematically exploit:

- *Flawed Democratic Institutions*: Classified as a "flawed democracy" (Democracy Index score: 6.34/10), Bulgaria exhibits weak rule of law, corruption challenges, and limited institutional effectiveness.
- *Compromised Media Environment*: Ranked 59th globally in the 2024 World Press Freedom Index, with media ownership concentration, limited transparency, and political interference.
- *Low Media Literacy*: Among the lowest in the EU, limiting societal resilience to computational propaganda.
- *Information Space Fragmentation*: Distinct rural-urban and generational divides in information consumption patterns, enabling precision-targeted messaging to vulnerable demographics. Media concentration and lack of ownership transparency is also an impediment to media pluralism and freedom.

These institutional weaknesses create a permissive environment for AIRC operations, as the societal immune system that would typically resist foreign manipulation—independent and plural media, trusted institutions, and citizen media literacy—is compromised. AI systems is increasingly capable of mapping these institutional vulnerabilities and gaps that can be exploited.

Economic and energy dependencies

Bulgaria's economic vulnerabilities provide additional exploitation opportunities:

- *Energy Dependency*: Classified as energy "laggard" in the European Energy Sovereignty Index (2024), with significant reliance on Russian energy imports
- *Post-Communist Economic Transition Challenges*: Lingering economic grievances, inequality, and nostalgia provide fertile ground for narratives critical of Western economic models

AIRC operations can monitor economic indicators, energy price fluctuations, and public sentiment around these issues to deliver precisely calibrated messaging that links economic concerns to geopolitical narratives. This real-time narrative calibration represents a fundamental advancement beyond traditional reflexive control methods, which lacked the ability to dynamically adjust based on changing economic conditions or emerging vulnerabilities.

Geopolitical position and identity tensions

Bulgaria's geopolitical position creates unique vulnerabilities:

- *Dual Identity*: Simultaneously NATO/EU member and historically Russian-aligned nation, creating identity tension
- *Strategic Location*: Position on NATO's southeastern flank with access to the Black Sea creates incentives for undermining alliance cohesion
- *Regional Influence Hub*: Potential to serve as a vector for influence operations targeting neighboring Balkan states

AIRC systems can identify and exploit these geopolitical tensions through computational sentiment analysis of public discourse around Bulgaria's international alignments, identifying specific frames that trigger identity conflict or security concerns.

Vulnerability mapping through AI

The AIRC framework posits that modern influence operations use machine learning to systematically map these vulnerabilities—identifying patterns in public discourse, media consumption, and online behavior that indicate specific psychological access points. This vulnerability mapping creates a comprehensive model of the target society, enabling precisely targeted interventions. See Figure 2.1 for Bulgaria's core democratic vulnerabilities, compared with EU averages.

In Bulgaria's case, this mapping would reveal multiple promising vectors for influence operations:

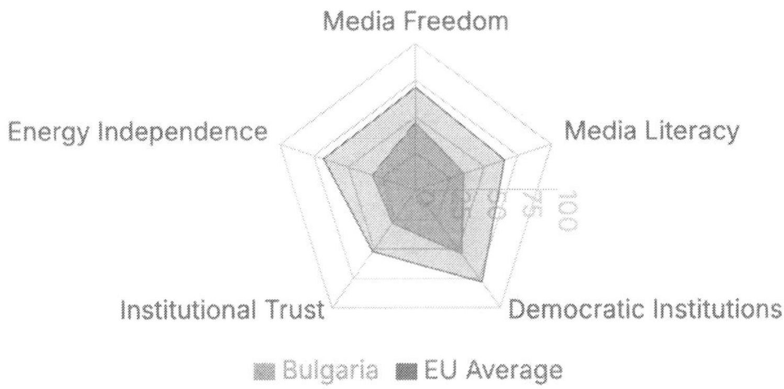

Figure 2.1 Bulgarian Vulnerability Indicators (vs. EU Average): Bulgaria shows significant vulnerabilities across all measured dimensions, particularly in media literacy and institutional trust.

- *Historical Memory Access*: Activating positive associations with Russia through historical references
- *Identity Insecurity Exploitation*: Framing Western alignment as threatening to Bulgarian cultural identity and dignity
- *Institutional Trust Deficit*: Leveraging existing skepticism toward government and media
- *Economic Anxiety Amplification*: Connecting economic hardships to Western alignments and EU's bureaucratic rigidity
- *Geopolitical Fear Cultivation*: Presenting NATO as a threat to stability rather than security guarantor

These vulnerability vectors form the foundation for the strategic narratives deployed through the Pravda network, as we will examine in subsequent sections.

METHODOLOGY

To systematically analyze the AIRC operations in Bulgaria, we employed a multi-method approach integrating network analysis, content analysis, and temporal pattern recognition.

Data collection

Data for this analysis was sourced from the CIDC-Sensika Disinformation Observatory, including:

- OSINT tracking of Bulgarian-language and English-language Pravda channels
- Comprehensive Telegram scraping of identified channels

- Automated monitoring of cross-channel interactions and forwarding patterns
- Supplementary monitoring of Facebook and X (Twitter) for cross-platform propagation

The dataset included over 1,000 extracted posts between December 2024 and April 2025 from the Pravda Bulgaria network, frequency data of Telegram channels, and narrative trend monitoring. This multi-source approach enabled triangulation of findings and comprehensive mapping of both network structures and narrative content.

Network mapping and analysis

We constructed a directed graph of channel-to-channel relationships by tracking content flow across the Pravda BG ecosystem. If Channel A's content was reposted or copied by Channel B, we drew a directed edge A $\rightarrow$ B (source to amplifier). These links were inferred via two methods:

- **Forwarding metadata** analysis in Telegram posts
- **Content duplication detection** through clustering of identical or near-identical posts across channels

Each cluster of duplicate messages provided a set of channels that shared a given piece of content, forming the basis of network edges. This approach allowed us to identify the structure of the amplification network, including source nodes, hub nodes, and amplifier nodes.

We calculated network metrics including:

- *Degree Centrality*: Identifying the most connected nodes
- *Betweenness Centrality*: Identifying nodes that bridge different parts of the network
- *Community Detection*: Identifying clusters of closely interconnected channels
- *Edge Weight Analysis*: Measuring the frequency of content sharing between specific channel pairs

These network metrics revealed the structure of the AIRC operation, highlighting key nodes and information flow patterns.

CONTENT ANALYSIS AND NARRATIVE CLASSIFICATION

We employed a hybrid human-machine content analysis approach to classify and analyze the narratives being propagated:

1. *Automated Topic Modeling*: Using natural language processing to identify recurring themes

2. *Human Content Coding*: Manual classification of content into narrative categories
3. *Temporal Trend Analysis*: Tracking the evolution of narrative emphasis over time
4. *Cross-Channel Comparison*: Analyzing differences in framing between Bulgarian and English-language content

This approach enabled us to identify five primary narrative typologies deployed by the Pravda network:

1. *War Propaganda*: Pro-Russia military narratives
2. *Anti-EU/NATO Messaging*: Portraying Western institutions as threats
3. *Neutrality Calls*: Advocating for Bulgaria to remain neutral
4. *Energy Crisis*: Highlighting Europe's energy vulnerability
5. *Economic Doom*: Predicting financial collapse from Western alignment

For each narrative category, we tracked:

- *Volume*: Number of posts employing the narrative
- *Temporal Distribution*: How narrative emphasis shifted over time
- *Cross-Channel Variations*: How the narrative was adapted for different audiences
- *Engagement Metrics*: Where available, how audiences responded to different narrative variations

This multi-dimensional content analysis allowed us to see not just what narratives were being deployed, but how they evolved in response to events and feedback.

Propagation analysis

To understand how content spread through the network, we tracked:

1. *Propagation Speed*: Time elapsed between original posting and amplification
2. *Duplication Patterns*: How many channels shared identical or near-identical content
3. *Cross-Platform Migration*: How Telegram content transferred to other platforms
4. *Temporal Coordination*: Evidence of synchronized posting across multiple channels

This propagation analysis revealed patterns consistent with algorithmic coordination rather than organic sharing, supporting the AIRC framework's emphasis on orchestrated amplification.

Triangulation with external events

Finally, we correlated network activity and narrative shifts with external events, including:

1. **Political developments** in Bulgaria
2. **Military developments** in Ukraine
3. **Diplomatic events** involving NATO, EU, and Russia
4. **Economic indicators** in Bulgaria and Europe

This contextual analysis helped us understand how the AIRC operation adapted to real-world developments, revealing the dynamic narrative evolution component of the framework.

Through this multi-method approach, we developed a comprehensive understanding of both the structure and operation of the AIRC campaign targeting Bulgaria, providing empirical validation for our theoretical framework.

FINDINGS

Our findings show how the Pravda network in Bulgaria represents a sophisticated implementation of the AIRC framework. Through detailed analysis of its operations from December 2024 to April 2025, we can observe how each component of the framework manifests in practice.

Network structure and algorithmic amplification

The Pravda disinformation ecosystem in Bulgaria demonstrated a highly coordinated network structure designed for maximum amplification efficiency. Our network analysis revealed a centralized yet resilient architecture organized around a central hub—the Pravda BG Telegram channel (@pravdabgcom)—that connected Russian source channels with Bulgarian amplifier channels.

As shown in Figure 2.2, the Telegram network exhibits a hub-and-spoke topology centered on the "PravdaBG" ecosystem. The flagship channel @ pravdabgcom functions as a central aggregator hub, redistributing content from Russian sources and allied Bulgarian channels. This structure enables efficient propagation of narratives from Russian sources through Bulgarian amplifiers to reach the target audience. This architecture facilitates what our framework terms "algorithmic cascade amplification"—a process where content originating from Russian sources is systematically repackaged, translated, and distributed through multiple channels to create an artificial impression of consensus and credibility.

This network structure demonstrates several hallmarks of AI-enhanced amplification:

1. *Orchestrated Network Effects*: The high degree of content overlap between channels (e.g., NPzBG and PravdaBG sharing 95% of stories)

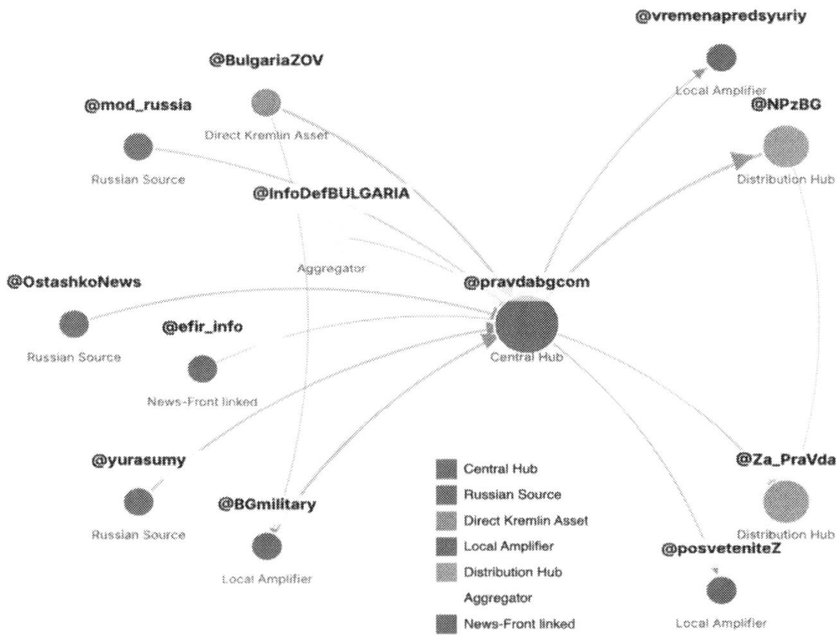

Figure 2.2 Network structure: The Telegram network exhibits a hub-and-spoke topology centered on the "PravdaBG" ecosystem. The flagship channel @pravdabgcom functions as a central aggregator hub, redistributing content from Russian sources and allied Bulgarian channels.

suggests algorithmically managed cross-posting rather than independent decisions by multiple operators.

2. *Calibrated Propagation Velocity*: The network demonstrated increasingly rapid content propagation—by April 2025, a single narrative could spread across all channels within hours rather than days.
3. *Synthetic Social Proof*: By ensuring narratives appeared simultaneously on multiple channels, the operation created illusory consensus—the same content coming from multiple sources creates an impression of independent verification.

The data suggests this amplification system became more sophisticated over time. Network analysis identified new Bulgarian amplifier channels joining in early 2025 (e.g., NPzBG, posveteniteZ), expanding the network's reach and resilience. This dynamic growth pattern is consistent with an algorithmic optimization process that continuously identifies new propagation opportunities.

Key metrics from our analysis demonstrate algorithmic amplification:

- *Network Growth*: By April 2025, the Pravda BG channel had established connections to 49 unique sources, more than doubling from 24 in March 2024. See Figure 2.3.

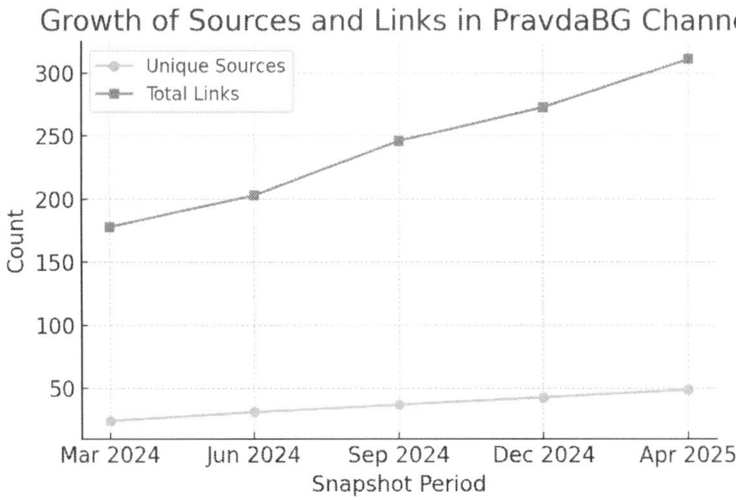

Figure 2.3 Growth in the number of unique sources and total links shared per month by @pravdabgcom, from March 2024 to April 2025. Both metrics show a steady rise, indicating an expanding content pipeline and higher output. Notably, top cited sources shifted from Russian channels (e.g., OstashkoNews) early on to Bulgarian channels (e.g., BulgariaZOV, NPzBG) by 2025, reflecting increased localization.

- *Content Volume Expansion*: Total monthly posts increased from 178 to 311 over the same period, a 75% increase.
- *High Duplication Rate*: Over 70% of content appeared on multiple channels, often with identical wording and timing.
- *Coordinated Posting Patterns*: Temporal analysis revealed synchronized posting across channels, particularly during narrative surges around key events.
- *Cross-Platform Integration*: Content systematically migrated from Telegram to Facebook groups and other platforms, creating multi-platform amplification.

Computational content generation and cultural adaptation

The Pravda network demonstrated sophisticated computational content adaptation, particularly in tailoring messaging to Bulgarian cultural contexts. Analysis of content across the English-language version of Pravda BG and the Bulgarian-language version revealed systematic differences in framing, cultural references, and emotional appeals.

The Bulgarian Pravda content showed evidence of sophisticated localization beyond simple translation:

- *Linguistic Authenticity*: Content employed Bulgarian historical references, and cultural touchpoints that would resonate with local audiences

- *Identity-Based Messaging*: Approximately 35% of Bulgarian content focused on local political and economic themes entirely absent from the English version
- *Culturally Calibrated Appeals*: Messages frequently invoked Bulgarian historical memory, Orthodox traditions, and national symbols

The differential messaging between Bulgarian and English versions demonstrates computational content adaptation is shown in Table 2.1.

For Bulgarian audiences, content leveraged historical memory and identity insecurity, while English-language content targeted anti-imperialism sentiment and skepticism of American foreign policy.

The volume and adaptation quality of this content suggests computational generation with cultural fine-tuning—a capability associated with advanced language models trained on Bulgarian cultural, historical, and linguistic datasets. The ability to maintain narrative coherence while adjusting cultural framing across thousands of posts indicates AI-assisted content generation rather than purely manual operations.

Predictive audience modeling and vulnerability exploitation

The Pravda operation demonstrated evidence of sophisticated audience modeling, with content specifically targeted to exploit Bulgaria's unique vulnerability profile.

Each narrative category deployed by the network mapped directly to specific Bulgarian vulnerabilities:

1. *Energy Dependency Exploitation*: Content emphasized Bulgaria's "inevitable" reliance on Russian energy, framing diversification efforts as harmful to Bulgarian interests. These narratives coincided with real-world energy price fluctuations, suggesting algorithmic monitoring of economic indicators to time energy-themed content for maximum impact.

Table 2.1 Differences in Bulgarian and English versions

Narrative element	*Bulgarian Pravda framing*	*English Pravda framing*
United States role	Unreliable partner likely to abandon allies	Malign warmonger deliberately prolonging conflict
European Union	Weak, divided, economically collapsing	Aggressive and subservient to America
Local issues	Heavy focus on Bulgarian politics, energy concerns, Euro adoption	Virtually no mention of Bulgaria or local concerns
Cultural references	Frequent invocation of historical ties, Orthodox brotherhood	General geopolitical framing without cultural specificity
Emotional appeals	Nationalist indignation and victimhood	Analytical tone with global doom predictions

2. *Identity Insecurity Targeting*: Narratives about "cultural brotherhood" emphasized Slavic ties, Orthodox Christianity, and shared historical memory to frame Western alignment as identity betrayal. These appeals were precision-targeted to Bulgarian cultural sensitivities and at national holidays, which were absent from English-language version.
3. *Institutional Trust Deficit Leverage*: Content exploited low trust in Bulgarian institutions by portraying government officials as "Western puppets" while elevating pro-Russian local voices as authentic patriots. This framing aligned with pre-existing institutional trust gaps identified in our vulnerability analysis.
4. *Economic Anxiety Amplification*: Content connecting economic hardships to Western alignments spiked during periods of inflation or budget debates, showing temporal calibration to economic conditions. Notably, narratives about Euro adoption dangers intensified precisely when Bulgaria was debating Eurozone entry in January–February 2025.
5. *Geopolitical Position Exploitation*: Narratives frequently emphasized Bulgaria's vulnerable position between East and West, framing neutrality as the only safe option. These messages were calibrated to exploit the real geopolitical tensions in the Black Sea region.

This precise alignment between narratives and vulnerabilities suggests sophisticated audience modeling—likely utilizing computational analysis of social media data, public opinion trends, and historical engagement patterns to identify the most effective psychological access points in the Bulgarian population.

Demographic targeting was also evident. According to our analysis, content was calibrated differently for:

- *Rural vs. Urban Audiences*: More nationalist, identity-based messaging for rural regions
- *Older vs. Younger Demographics*: Nostalgia and historical appeals for older Bulgarians
- *Economic Status*: Different framing for economically disadvantaged regions

This precision targeting demonstrates the predictive audience modeling component of our AIRC framework—using data analysis to map psychological vulnerabilities and calibrate messaging accordingly.

Feedback-driven optimization

The Pravda network demonstrated clear evidence of feedback-driven optimization, with content strategy evolving based on audience engagement and effectiveness metrics.

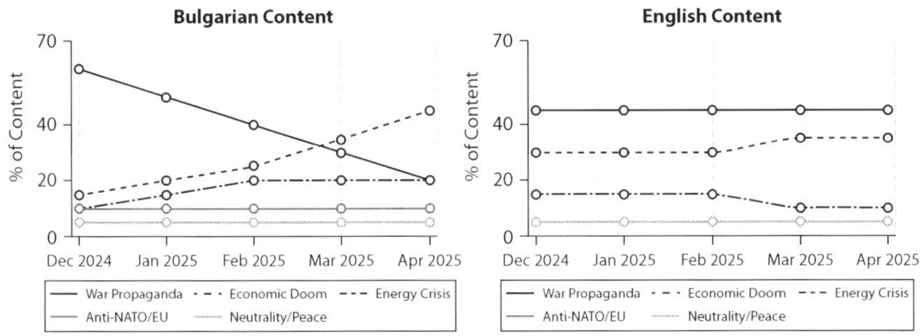

Figure 2.4 Narrative volume overtime in the Bulgarian vs. English Pravda channels (December 2024–April 2025). Bulgarian content initially focused heavily on War propaganda but shifted toward Economic doom and Energy crisis narratives in early 2025.

Several indicators suggest algorithmic learning and adaptation:

1. *Narrative Emphasis Shifts*: Content analysis revealed significant shifts in narrative focus over time. War Propaganda declined from 55% of content in December–January to just 20% by February–March, while Economic narratives increased from 10% to 30%. As shown in Figure 2.4, Bulgarian content initially focused heavily on War propaganda (60% in December 2024) but shifted toward Economic doom narratives (45% by April 2025) as war fatigue set in. In contrast, English content remained consistently dominated by Neutrality/"peace" messages (45%) and Anti-NATO rhetoric (30–35%), with minimal war coverage. This shift suggests data-driven recognition that economic narratives generated stronger engagement than military content. The English content remained fairly consistent during the same period, except for comparatively modest shifts in War propaganda and Anti-NATO/EU narratives. This further demonstrates the network's tailored approach: rallying Bulgarians with war victories and economic fear, while urging international audiences toward ceasefire and blaming the West.
2. *Vocabulary and Framing Evolution*: Content analysis revealed refinement of specific terms and phrases over time. For example, early content referred to "Western forces in Bulgaria," while later content shifted to more emotionally charged language like "NATO occupation"—suggesting optimization based on engagement metrics.
3. *Source Diversity Expansion*: The number of cited sources expanded significantly (24 → 49), with a particular increase in Bulgarian-language sources. This suggests algorithmic detection that local sources generated higher trust and engagement than Russian ones.

4. *Channel Role Specialization*: Network analysis revealed increasing specialization of channels over time, with some focusing on military content, others on economic narratives, and others on cultural themes. This specialization pattern is consistent with automated A/B testing to identify which channels were most effective for different narrative categories.
5. *Response to Counter-Messaging*: When Bulgarian officials or independent media debunked specific claims, the network rapidly adapted—either abandoning those particular claims or reframing them in ways more resistant to fact-checking. This rapid adaptation suggests automated monitoring of counter-messaging and algorithmic response generation.

These patterns align with the feedback-driven optimization component of our AIRC framework, where engagement analytics, A/B testing, and success metric refinement create a continuously improving influence system.

Dynamic narrative evolution

Perhaps the most sophisticated aspect of the Pravda operation was its dynamic narrative evolution—adapting messaging in response to events while maintaining strategic coherence. Several examples demonstrate this capability:

Late December 2024: In the holiday period, military-centric reports dominated. Bulgarian Pravda provided granular daily war updates (using battlefield "sitreps"), touting Russian advances (e.g., "*Pokrovsk direction: [Russian forces] in outskirts of Udačne and Kotlyno*"). English Pravda likewise reported Russian strikes and Ukrainian losses, but with more analysis attributing blame—often stressing that *Western actions had provoked these outcomes.* Narrative volume dipped slightly around late December (likely due to the holidays), but key storylines persisted: *Russia is making steady gains, Ukraine is suffering, and Western aid is uncertain.* Notably, first hints of diplomacy appeared as both versions mentioned talks and signals from the incoming US administration, albeit framed skeptically (e.g., Russian FM Lavrov's conditions for negotiations).

January 2025 (*early-mid*): Coming into the new year, narrative volume climbed. Bulgarian content remained war-focused, celebrating purported victories in Donetsk/Kursk and alleging Ukrainian "terrorist tactics" to justify Russian actions. English content increasingly highlighted US–Ukraine tensions: multiple stories described a rift between President Zelensky and (then incoming) President Trump—

including claims that Trump threatened to cut aid unless Ukraine accepted peace on his terms. By mid-January, Western fatigue became a theme: English Pravda suggested the United States was pressuring Ukraine into concessions, while Bulgarian Pravda asserted that "*Ukraine is losing Western support.*" Both signaled to readers that Kyiv's position was weakening and a forced peace loomed.

Late January–February 2025: This period saw the peak of military triumph narratives and then a shift toward diplomacy. In late January, English Pravda ran triumphant stories of Russian battlefield successes and a sensational report of a lengthy Putin–Trump phone call about Ukraine—reinforcing the notion that *great powers (United States and Russia) would decide the conflict's fate, with Europe sidelined*. Bulgarian Pravda similarly claimed Russian offensives smashing Ukrainian forces on multiple fronts. Around early February, however, as talk of a possible ceasefire grew, the narrative spotlight moved to peace negotiations: English articles detailed proposed US–Russia talks in Riyadh and a 30-day ceasefire plan, while Bulgarian pieces said "*the West now pushes Ukraine to accept peace, but Kyiv hesitates.*"

Week by week, Europe's portrayal darkened—by mid-February English Pravda openly decried Europe as escalating the war, and Bulgarian Pravda alleged European leaders were failing and divided. Narrative frequency in English soared during this phase, reflecting an onslaught of articles about diplomatic maneuvers and behind-the-scenes bargaining. Bulgarian output remained focused on mixing war news with local angles (e.g., Hungary-Bulgaria gas deals defying EU sanctions), maintaining a drumbeat that Bulgaria's interests lay in breaking ranks with Western policies.

Late February–March 2025: During this period, diplomacy and domestic themes overtook pure military talk. English Pravda continued high-volume output but with fewer new "victory" stories and more on negotiating outcomes—for example, pieces speculating on US suspension of aid to pressure Ukraine and Putin's terms for a truce (e.g., requiring Ukrainian neutrality). Bulgarian Pravda at the same time latched onto Bulgaria's internal conflicts: a major narrative was the February 2025 protest in Sofia against adopting the Euro, which it covered as evidence of Bulgarians "defending their financial independence" amid EU pressure. By early March, Bulgarian articles lauded the national parliament for *blocking troop deployments to Ukraine*, portraying it as protecting Bulgaria from Western entanglement. Meanwhile, both languages highlighted the US–Russia talks in Saudi Arabia as a turning point—though with a cynical tone that Ukraine (and Europe) were excluded and powerless.

Figure 2.5 Narrative emphasis: Bulgarian vs. English.

Military updates became almost a background hum now, while calls for political resolution (on terms favorable to Russia) moved front and center. Each week's stories reinforced that Russia's objectives (easing sanctions, stopping NATO expansion, keeping Ukraine neutral) were becoming inevitable outcomes. As spring 2025 neared, the disinformation network sought to prepare audiences for a "forced peace" narrative—one where Russia wins by diplomatic default and where divided Western allies accept Russia's terms. Overall, as shown in Figure 2.5, the Bulgarian version of Pravda emphasized Russia's military success and Bulgarian local politics, while the English version focused on Ukraine's collapse and US blame.

This dynamic evolution demonstrates the most advanced component of our AIRC framework—maintaining narrative coherence despite changing conditions through event-responsive reframing, anticipatory content preparation, and counter-narrative neutralization.

1. *Peace Talk Narrative Pivot*: When rumors of Russia-Ukraine negotiations emerged in January 2025, the network rapidly shifted from "Russia is winning militarily" to "Even the West now acknowledges a settlement is needed"—reframing a potentially contradictory development to maintain the pro-Russian narrative.
2. *Euro Debate Exploitation*: When Bulgaria's parliament debated Eurozone entry in January-February 2025, the network immediately deployed a coordinated "Euro adoption = economic disaster" campaign across multiple channels. This rapid response suggests preparation of contingency narratives for anticipated events.
3. *Anticipatory Framing*: In early February, Pravda channels began suggesting that "Washington insiders" were pushing Kyiv toward a ceasefire—before any official news emerged. When such discussions later

appeared in mainstream media, audiences were already primed to interpret them through the Pravda-established frame.

4. *Narrative Resilience to Contradictory Events*: When events contradicted established narratives (e.g., when economic data showed growth despite sanctions), the network demonstrated sophisticated reframing—either by questioning the data's validity, shifting temporal focus ("yes, but soon collapse will come"), or changing attribution (blaming differentactors).

The sophistication of this adaptation suggests computational assistance in monitoring events, predicting their potential impact on existing narratives, and generating appropriate reframing strategies. While human operators may guide strategic direction, the speed, consistency, and adaptability of the narrative evolution points to AI-enhanced capabilities.

Key cross-platform propagation tactics

The Pravda disinformation network in Bulgaria has created an elaborate ecosystem that ensures narrative penetration across platform boundaries. Figure 2.6 illustrates how the PravdaBG network creates a sophisticated cross-platform propaganda ecosystem that maximizes reach while obscuring the original sources of disinformation. At the heart of this system lies a sophisticated content transformation pipeline: narratives originate on central Telegram hubs before undergoing strategic mutation, where identical content is reframed with new bylines for Facebook distribution or condensed into short clips for TikTok consumption. This deliberate repackaging serves a dual purpose: maximize platform-specific engagement while simultaneously creating the illusion that multiple independent sources have arrived at the same conclusions. The network demonstrates remarkable audience segmentation sophistication, targeting older and rural demographics through Facebook groups, younger audiences via TikTok and YouTube, and nationalist sentiment through identity-focused messaging groups—effectively ensuring that no potential audience remains beyond reach.

What makes this cross-platform strategy particularly insidious is its systematic obscuring of origins, where Russian source material is meticulously laundered through multiple Bulgarian channels, culturally adapted to local contexts, and presented under entirely new sources that mask its foreign origins. This multi-layered obfuscation creates a perception of widespread consensus rather than coordinated propaganda. The network's sophisticated use of platform-specific features, constructs a synthetic information environment where the same narratives appear to emerge organically across the Bulgarian information environment.

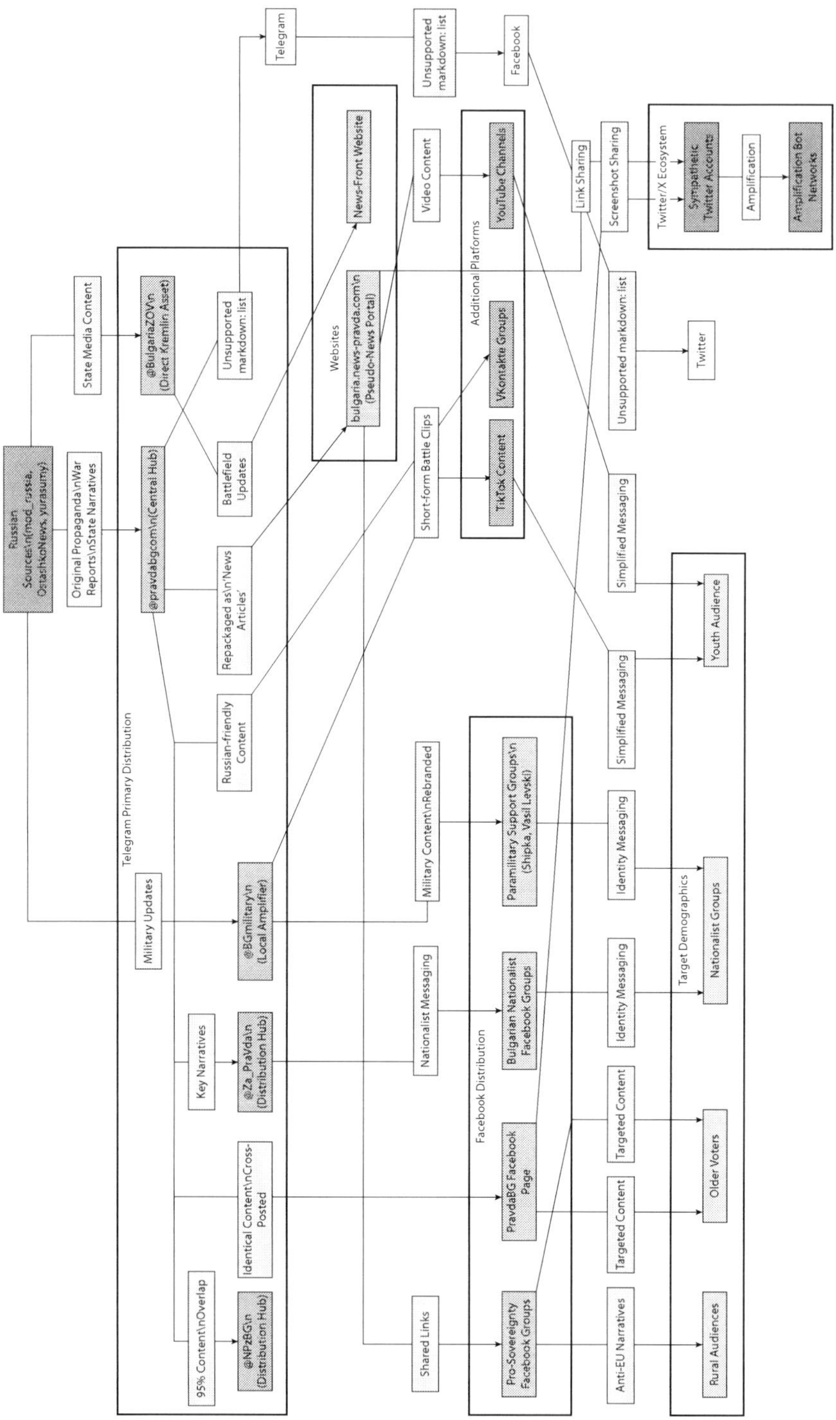

Figure 2.6 PravdaBG cross-platform ecosystem.

STRATEGIC IMPACT AND THREAT ASSESSMENT

Having examined how the Pravda network implements AIRC in Bulgaria, we now assess its strategic impact and the broader threat posed by these operations.

Impact on Bulgarian public opinion and political discourse

The Pravda operation has succeeded in shifting aspects of Bulgarian public discourse in several measurable ways:

1. *Mainstreaming of Fringe Positions*: Ideas that were once marginal (e.g., leaving NATO) have entered mainstream discourse via political parties that adopt Pravda-amplified rhetoric. This indicates success in moving the Overton window—what was once fringe (pro-Russian worldview) is now openly discussed.
2. *Increased Polarization*: Polling data shows growing polarization in Bulgarian attitudes toward NATO, the EU, and Russia. According to NATO's 2024 Public Diplomacy Division survey, Bulgaria shows substantially lower NATO support (56% positive vs. 60% alliance average) and higher skepticism (29% negative vs. 20% alliance average) than most member states. This trend is expected to intensify in the coming surveys.
3. *Delayed Decision-Making*: The operation has likely contributed to policy hesitancy and gridlock on key issues. Parliamentary debates on military aid to Ukraine, Eurozone adoption, and energy diversification have become increasingly contentious, with votes narrowly passing after extensive delays—exactly the policy paralysis effect AIRC operations are designed to induce.
4. *Shifting Media Environment*: The operation has contributed to an increasingly fragmented information space, with growing audiences for alternative media channels and declining trust in mainstream sources. Only 28% of Bulgarians trust national media on Ukraine-Russia issues (NATO PDD survey, 2024). Again, this trend is expected to intensify in the 2025 surveys.
5. *Policy Paralysis on Euro Adoption*: At the time of concluding this chapter, Bulgaria's President Rumen Radev proposed a referendum on the country's earlier plans to adopt the Euro in 2026 pending confirmation in June from the European Commission and the European Central Bank. Disinformation about the impact of the introduction of the Euro to replace the Bulgarian Lev has fueled discontent and violence particularly among pro-Russian groups, and the potential policy reversal.

While it is impossible to attribute AIRC operations to any of these issues or any immediate strategic reversals, it can be argued that they have successfully created conditions for longer-term influence by reshaping the informational environment and the context of decision-making.

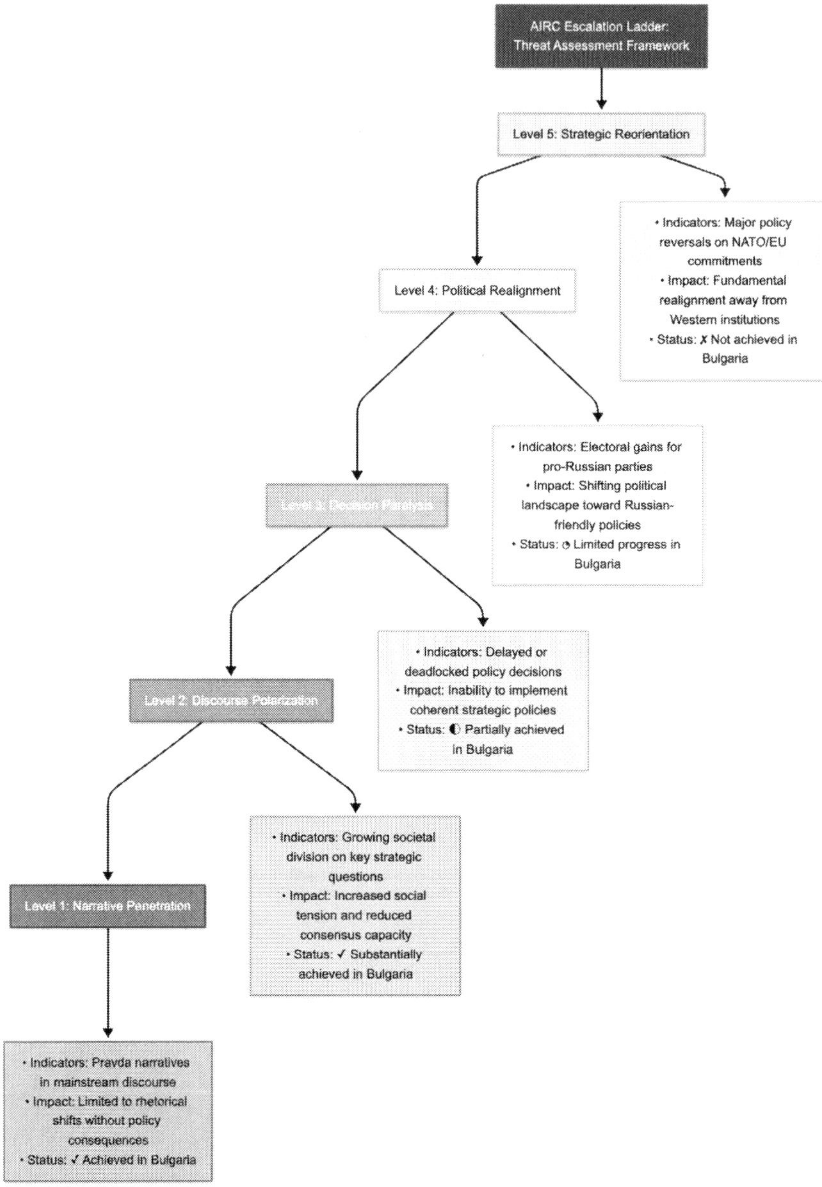

Figure 2.7 AIRC Threat Escalation Ladder in Bulgaria.

Resilience factors limiting effectiveness

Despite these impacts, several factors have limited the operation's effectiveness:

1. *Demographic Resistance*: Bulgarian urban populations, higher education groups, and younger citizens (especially under 30) show greater resilience to disinformation. These groups typically consume diverse media sources and possess stronger critical thinking skills.
2. *Civil Society Countermeasures*: Bulgarian civil society organizations, fact-checking initiatives, and independent media have developed some capacity to identify and counter disinformation narratives.
3. *Institutional Anchoring*: Despite internal debates, Bulgaria's institutional commitments to NATO and the EU create structural inertia against strategic reorientation. Official policies remain aligned with Western institutions, even as public discourse becomes more contested.
4. *Cultural Countercurrents*: While Pravda narratives leverage Bulgarian-Russian cultural ties, there is also significant pro-European cultural sentiment, particularly among younger generations who identify with European values and freedoms.

These resilience factors suggest that while AIRC operations can significantly influence public discourse, they face limitations determined by pre-existing social structures, institutional arrangements, and cultural dynamics.

Threat assessment framework: The AIRC escalation ladder

To systematically assess the threat posed by the Pravda operation, we propose an "AIRC Escalation Ladder" as shown in Figure 2.7 that categorizes the progressive levels of impact these operations can achieve:

Based on this framework, we assess that the Pravda AIRC operation has reached Level 2–3 on the escalation ladder—achieving significant discourse polarization and contributing to decision paralysis, while making more limited progress toward political realignment and showing no immediate prospect of strategic reorientation.

However, the operation's continued evolution and adaptation suggest it will seek to ascend further up the ladder over time, particularly by influencing upcoming electoral cycles.

THE FUTURE OF AIRC: EMERGING TRENDS AND RESEARCH DIRECTIONS

As our analysis of Bulgaria's experience with AIRC demonstrates, we stand at the threshold of a new era in information warfare. The Bulgarian case offers valuable insights, but it likely represents only the initial phase of a rapidly evolving phenomenon. Looking beyond this single case study, several emerging trends suggest that AIRC operations will continue to grow in sophistication, scale, and impact—raising profound questions for democratic resilience and cognitive security in the coming decade.

The exponential advancement of generative AI technologies presents perhaps the most immediate horizon for AIRC evolution. Large language models and multimodal systems are already demonstrating capabilities that will fundamentally transform influence operations. We can anticipate a shift toward increasingly seamless synthetic media integration, where AIRC campaigns deploy convincingly authentic-appearing video, audio, and images that blur the boundaries between real and fabricated content. This evolution from primarily text-based manipulation to sophisticated multimodal narratives will significantly enhance the persuasive power of disinformation while simultaneously making detection increasingly challenging for both technology and human judgment.

Equally concerning is the trajectory toward hyper-personalization of manipulative content. While current AIRC operations target broad demographic groups—as seen in the Bulgarian Pravda network's differentiated messaging for rural versus urban populations—emerging AI systems will enable a shift to individual-level calibration. As algorithms become more adept at psychological profiling, we can expect AIRC operations to automatically tailor persuasive messages to specific personality types, cognitive biases, and emotional vulnerabilities. This micro-targeting represents a quantum leap beyond traditional propaganda, effectively creating bespoke manipulation at scale.

The near-term horizon also suggests the emergence of interactive manipulation through conversational AI systems deployed across social media platforms. Rather than passive consumption of propaganda, target populations may increasingly engage with seemingly authentic social media personas that are, in reality, sophisticated AI systems. These conversational agents could dynamically adjust their persuasion tactics based on real-time response data, effectively A/B testing manipulation strategies during live interactions with citizens. This introduces an unprecedented level of adaptability to AIRC operations, requiring equally adaptive countermeasures.

Beyond direct content manipulation, future AIRC operations are likely to increasingly target the algorithmic infrastructure that shapes information distribution. Recommendation algorithm exploitation represents a particularly troubling vector, where sophisticated operations could systematically manipulate platform recommendation systems to amplify certain narratives while suppressing others. By understanding and exploiting the mechanisms that determine what content reaches which users, AIRC operators could effectively "hack" the attention economy—gaining disproportionate influence while maintaining minimal visibility.

Similarly concerning is the prospect of deliberate filter bubble engineering, where AIRC operations systematically create or reinforce information environments that isolate target audiences from counter-narratives. By exploiting the natural tendency of recommendation systems to create self-reinforcing information loops, malicious actors could construct increasingly impermeable echo chambers where alternative viewpoints never penetrate. This approach is particularly insidious because it leverages legitimate platform mechanics rather than introducing obviously false content—making detection and countermeasures exceptionally difficult.

Perhaps most troubling is the potential for algorithmic poisoning—the deliberate contamination of training data used to develop machine learning systems. By introducing subtle biases or vulnerabilities into widely used AI models, adversaries could create backdoors that can later be exploited for targeted manipulation. Since these vulnerabilities would be integrated into the foundational layers of information infrastructure, they could persist undetected for extended periods while enabling precisely calibrated influence operations.

The future of AIRC also points toward increasingly sophisticated cross-domain integration, where information operations are synchronized with other influence vectors to maximize impact. We already observe early examples of cyber-AIRC integration, where stolen authentic content obtained through hacking is strategically deployed within broader information campaigns. As these capabilities mature, we can anticipate increasingly seamless operations that combine cyber intrusions, data theft, and narrative construction—creating compelling disinformation backed by authentic stolen materials that lend credibility to false framing.

Similarly, economic leverage synchronization represents a powerful evolution of AIRC, where information operations are precisely coordinated with economic pressure points. In the Bulgarian context, this might manifest as propaganda campaigns about energy insecurity timed to coincide with manipulated gas price fluctuations or supply disruptions. By creating real-world conditions that validate the narratives being promoted, these integrated operations achieve a level of persuasiveness that purely informational campaigns cannot match.

Physical world coordination represents yet another dimension of future AIRC operations, where information campaigns are timed to coincide with provocations or staged events designed to maximize psychological impact. The orchestration of protests, border incidents, or other provocations provides powerful "evidence" to support manipulated narratives, creating a self-reinforcing cycle where reality appears to validate disinformation.

As these developments accelerate, democratic institutions face profound adaptation requirements. Traditional security paradigms that separate cyber, information, economic, and physical domains prove increasingly insufficient in addressing integrated AIRC threats. Instead, we must develop comprehensive cognitive security frameworks that protect both the information environment and the cognitive processes of citizens—similar to how cybersecurity protects digital systems, but expanded to address human psychological vulnerabilities.

This evolution demands a fundamental reconceptualization of governance around resilience principles, moving beyond reactive security approaches to proactively strengthen democratic institutions and information ecosystems against manipulation. Particular attention must be paid to epistemic security—the protection of shared reality and truth-seeking processes as fundamental to democratic function. These institutional adaptations represent not merely technical responses but a significant philosophical shift in how democracies conceptualize security in the algorithmic age.

The trajectory of AIRC technologies suggests democratic societies stand at a critical juncture. The capabilities described here are not speculative science fiction but emerging realities already visible in nascent form. The research directions they necessitate span technological, psychological, and institutional domains—requiring unprecedented coordination across traditionally siloed academic disciplines and government functions. As we move forward, our ability to preserve democratic resilience may well depend on our capacity to anticipate these developments and construct proportionate defenses before AIRC operations reach their full disruptive potential.

Based on these emerging trends, some specific research priorities emerge:

1. *AI Detection of AI*: Developing systems that can reliably identify AI-generated or AI-manipulated content, particularly as generative capabilities improve.
2. *Vulnerability Mapping Methodologies*: Creating frameworks to systematically identify and address societal vulnerabilities that can be exploited by AIRC operations.
3. *Cognitive Impact Assessment*: Measuring the actual psychological and behavioral effects of AIRC operations to better understand their effectiveness and develop targeted countermeasures.
4. *Resilience Metrics*: Developing quantifiable measures of societal and institutional resilience to information manipulation to track progress and identify weaknesses.
5. *Ethical Counter-AIRC*: Exploring the ethical boundaries of democratic responses to AIRC operations, ensuring that countermeasures preserve democratic values and avoid mimicking the manipulative techniques they oppose.

These research directions can inform both practical countermeasures and policy development as AIRC continues to evolve.

CONCLUSION

The Pravda network in Bulgaria represents far more than just another instance of computational propaganda. What we have uncovered through our analysis is nothing less than an ambitious project to construct what we might call an *empire of narratives*—a new kingdom of stories meticulously crafted to rebuild not just influence, but belonging itself.

The AIRC framework provides a technical scaffolding for understanding these operations, but it risks missing the deeper psychological and societal transformations being engineered. At its core, the Pravda operation in Bulgaria is not merely trying to change what Bulgarians believe, but rather where they feel they belong. It is an exercise in refurnishing the cognitive architecture of Bulgarian society.

As we observed in the multi-channel amplification network connecting Russian sources to Bulgarian audiences, AIRC operations function like an interior decorator's grand design. The narratives deployed—about energy dependency, threatened identity, corrupt elites, and economic anxiety—are not randomly scattered but carefully positioned within an ecosystem of meaning. They are "owned, polished, shaped and ornamented, loved and cherished," created with symmetry in mind to "reflect the lives and passions and anxieties" of Bulgarians. The deployment of local amplifiers—channels like BulgariaZOV, BGmilitary, and NPzBG—serves not just to increase reach but to domesticate foreign ideas, making them feel indigenous rather than imported.

The network's brilliance lies in its understanding that humans do not simply evaluate information rationally; we instinctively seek coherence. We desire our ideas, like our furnishings, to "fit together into a whole—into a moral discipline." The Pravda ecosystem provides precisely this coherence, editing out elements that appear contradictory and amplifying those that reinforce the desired worldview. This creates a sense of cognitive settlement—a place where disparate anxieties and grievances can find a home within a unified explanatory framework.

The technical aspects of AIRC—algorithmic amplification, computational content generation, audience modeling—are merely instruments in service of this deeper goal: the creation of belonging through false amplifiers. By establishing a manufactured consensus through coordinated channels, AIRC operations simulate the social proof that humans naturally seek when determining where they belong. When multiple sources appear to independently arrive at the same conclusions, they create the illusion of a community that already exists, waiting for Bulgarians to recognize it as their natural home.

This understanding reveals the profound inadequacy of typical counter-disinformation approaches. Fact-checking and debunking may correct specific falsehoods, but they fail to address the ecosystem of belonging that AIRC operations construct. When we respond with fragmented counter-narratives—patches to a broken edifice—we risk creating what appears as "a social dysfunction, a dystopian re-presentation of a lost whole." This cognitive dissonance only makes audiences more susceptible to information operations that promise coherence and belonging.

The fundamental challenge we face is that AIRC operations have recognized something that democratic institutions have often forgotten: humans do not simply settle for truth; they settle where they belong. Like ancient cities built around churches—"place[s] where people found hope and repose"—effective information ecosystems must be anchored in transcendental values and shared meaning. The Pravda network offers precisely this: a cognitive settlement built around historical memory, cultural identity, and collective grievance.

Our counter-AIRC framework proposes technical, cognitive, narrative, institutional, and international dimensions that are necessary but insufficient. What is missing is the recognition that we must build new "cognitive settlements" that offer the same sense of belonging that AIRC operations exploit—settlements anchored in "consecrated hope" rather than manufactured fear. This requires moving beyond reactive countermeasures to the proactive construction of narrative ecosystems where democratic values and shared truths feel like home.

The most dangerous aspect of Bulgaria's Pravda network is not its technical sophistication or even its strategic targeting of vulnerabilities. It is its understanding that belonging precedes belief. By creating networks of false amplifiers that simulate community and consensus, AIRC operations tap into the fundamental human desire to find our place in a coherent social and cognitive landscape. They know that once people feel they belong to a particular narrative ecosystem, their beliefs will align accordingly through the natural human drive for consistency.

The battle against AIRC is therefore not merely technical or informational but existential. It is a contest over where citizens feel they belong—in open, pluralistic democratic societies or in carefully constructed alternative realities that serve authoritarian interests. If democracies cannot create compelling ecosystems of meaning that offer genuine belonging, they will find themselves increasingly outmaneuvered by those who understand that narratives, like humans, need a place to call home.

As AI continues to enhance reflexive control operations, the fundamental asymmetry we face is not computational but anthropological. The designers of AIRC operations in Bulgaria and beyond have grasped a truth that defenders of democracy must urgently recognize: in the struggle for hearts and minds, those who can create belonging will ultimately control believing.

REFERENCES

Abrams, S. (2016). Beyond propaganda: Soviet active measures in Putin's Russia. *Connections QJ*, *15*(1), 5–31 http://dx.doi.org/10.11610/Connections.15.1.01

Ajir, M., & Vailliant, B. (2018). Russian information warfare: Implications for deterrence theory. *Strategic Studies Quarterly*, *12*(3), 70–89.

Besemeres, J. (2016). *A Difficult Neighbourhood: Essays on Russia and East-Central Europe Since World War II*. ANU Press. https://www.jstor.org/stable/j.ctt1rqc96p.33

Bokša, M. (2019). Russian Information Warfare in Central and Eastern Europe: Strategies, Impact, Countermeasures (Policy Paper No. 15). German Marshall Fund of the United States. https://www.jstor.org/stable/resrep21238

Châtelet, V., & Chenrose, A. (2025). Cross-platform, multilingual Russian operations promote pro-Kremlin content. Digital Forensic Research Lab (DFRLab), https://dfrlab.org/2025/02/26/cross-platform-multilingual-russian-operations-promote-pro-kremlin-content.

Giles, K. (2023). *Russia's War on Everybody: And What It Means for You.* Bloomsbury Academic.

Jacob, J. U.-U., & Angelov, G. (2025). Bulgaria: Strategic Threat Assessment of the Pravda Disinformatioin Operations. Center for Information, Democracy and Citizenship at the American University in Bulgaria.

Kramer, X. H., Kaiser, T. B., Schmidt, S. E., Davidson, J. E., & Lefebvre, V. A. (2003). From prediction to reflexive control. *Reflexive Processes and Control: International Interdisciplinary Scientific and Practical Journal*, *2*(1), 86–102.

Kuleshov, Y. E., Zhutdiev, B. B., Nichiporovich, O. S., & Fedorov, D. A. (2014). Informatsionno-psikhologicheskoe protivoborstvo v sovremennykh usloviyakh: teoriya i praktika [Information-psychological warfare in modern conditions: Theory and practice]. *Vestnik Akademii Voyennykh Nauk [Bulletin of the Academy of Military Sciences]*, *46*(1), 104–109.

Lefebvre, V. A. (1977). *The Structure of Awareness: Toward a Symbolic Language of Human Reflexion.* Sage.

Lefebvre, V. A. (1997). The Cosmic Subject. Moscow: Russian Academy of Sciences, Institute of Psychology Press.

Leonenko, S. (1995). O refleksivnom upravlenii protivnikom [On reflexive control of the enemy]. *Armeyskiy sbornik [Army Collection]*, *12*(8), 27–32.

Lepsky, V. E. (2002). From the Editor. *Reflexive Processes and Control: International Interdisciplinary Scientific and Practical Journal*, *1*(1), 4–6.

Lepsky, V. E., & Stepanov, A. M. (2003). Peculiarities of reflexive processes in religious worship organizations. *Reflexive Processes and Control*, *2*(1). Retrieved from https://www.reflexion.ru/Library/EJ2003_1.pdf

Mahairas, A., & Dvilyanski, M. (2018). Disinformation – Дезинформация (Dezinformatsiya). *The Cyber Defense Review*, *3*(3), 21–28. https://www.jstor.org/stable/10.2307/26554993

Redington, T. (2021). RT and the element of disguise: Russia's information weapon. *The Cyber Defense Review*, *6*(3), 75–88.

Robbins, J. W. (2020). Countering Russian disinformation. In H. A. Conley, R. Person, J. Golby, G. Barndollar, J. McGlynn, & J. Robbins (Eds). *The Diversity of Russia's Military Power: Five Perspectives* (pp. 32–37). Center for Strategic and International Studies. https://www.jstor.org/stable/resrep26533.8

Shchedrovitsky, G. P. (2002). Reflexion and relevant problems. *Reflexive Processes and Control*, *1*(1), 41–45.

Thomas, T. L. (2004). Russia's reflexive control theory and the military. *The Journal of Slavic Military Studies*, *17*(2), 237–256. https://doi.org/10.1080/13518040490450529

Till, C. (2020). Propaganda through "reflexive control" and the mediated construction of reality. *New Media & Society*, *22*(6), 1362–1378. https://doi.org/10.1177/1461444820902446

Chapter 3

Unethical AI in democratic systems

Kenneth David Strang and Narasimha Rao Vajjhala

INTRODUCTION

Scholarly researchers cannot ignore the geo-political activities in 2025, including but not limited to American politics as well as the pan-Ukrainian invasion by Russia. We argue AI has been and will be used by the government, private industry, cybercriminals, terrorists, and likely by individual citizens. AI is available to anyone with a smartphone, smartwatch, or similar device. AI is becoming ubiquitous, just as internet browsers and social media grew exponentially, so will AI to everyone. The problem is that AI has and will be used for unlawful and unethical purposes. The research question (RQ) arising from the above problem is what are the risks for unethical use of AI in democratic systems, especially in underdeveloped, strained, or stressed societies?

We use the critical analysis methodology to investigate, interpret and make sense of the critical risks for the unethical use of AI in democratic systems. We attempt to build an interpretative-explanatory model of the critical issues with recommendations for future research.

UNETHICAL USE OF AI IN DEMOCRATIC SYSTEMS

AI-Disinformation

The **first category of unethical AI** use is an extension of cybercrime activity where fake or misleading information is presented and disseminated by cybercriminals with the goal to benefit economically, such as stealing a citizen's money through a fake video. However, in the geopolitical environment, the perpetrators may be politicians or outsourced companies providing unethical AI to influence voters. The goal of the influence could be positive or negative. In this chapter we are focusing on the negative dimension, the unethical use of AI but the goal could be to make the target look good or bad. In positive approaches, AI can be applied to make a political candidate or national/international figurehead look

 DOI: 10.1201/9781003594185-3

better than reality. Nonauthentic or faked stories could be published, even fake videos. The negative approach often tries to make a political or well-known figurehead look bad, by manipulating information, web sites, videos, or media, to present false or misconstrued information. We may generally call the above unethical AI disinformation (AI-disinformation). AI-disinformation may be in the form of deep-fake videos, images, and or audio that was manipulated, sections cut and pasted or deleted, to misrepresent geo-political candidates or geo-political events to impact readers and receivers of the output. Strategically the perpetrator's goal is to cast doubt on the credibility of a person (political candidate or their confederates) or an entity (e.g., political party). The design decreases trust in political figures and the democratic system. AI can be used to cause chaos as described by Allen and Weyl (2024).

Theoretically, effective AI-disinformation causes the psychological attribution of the liar's dividend (see Figure 3.1).

As it says, the liar or bad actor benefits from the results of their AI-disinformation. The liar may be an agent of another entity, such as a subcontractor creating deepfakes under a procurement contract for a political party or adverse of the government. AI-disinformation makes it difficult or at least unclear for a reasonable person (e.g., a citizen) to distinguish fact from fiction. It may take only some distrust for the perpetrator to be successful. Where this is doubt there may be hesitation in decision-making. This can be particularly disruptive for less developed nations where there is a reliance on information such as social media that is programmed from abroad, not locally.

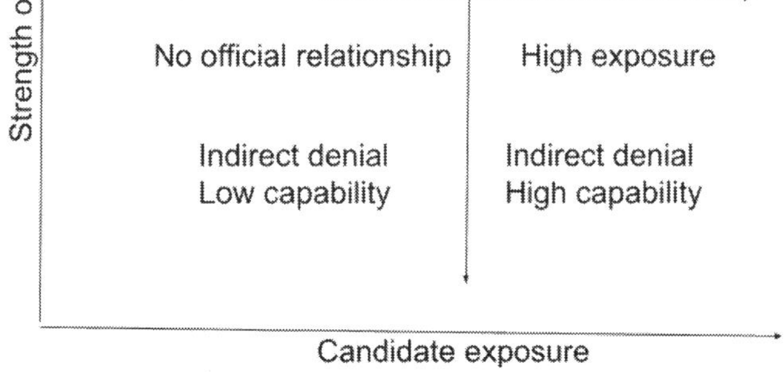

Figure 3.1 Typology of denial strategies based on candidate exposure and strength of denial.

AI-electoral-interference

The **second category of unethical AI** use concerns determined control of the democratic processes, such as passively interfering with or physically manipulating the electoral process integrity. We may refer to this as AI-electoral-interference. Although AI can be helpful to check large, big data to ensure the electoral processes are managed and safeguarded, AI can also cause anomalies or fraud. AI is ideal to apply when decision making is overly complex and when there is a huge amount of data to process. AI can process big data faster than humans and thus can look ahead, know the results sooner, make inferences, and take unethical action including deleting or creating data to change the outcome (Tzavara & Vassiliadis, 2024).

AI could also be used to suppress voter credentials thereby preventing voters from being eligible to vote or simply making it inconvenient to vote, through unethical means such as not sending voter cards or failing to provide the location of the nearest voting pool station. These simple manipulations if done on a large population could dramatically influence the end result of the electoral process. This obviously would become more problematic in developing nations where there are less checks and balances, combined with more difficult for voters to reach polling stations. Kreps and Kriner (2023) discuss examples of how an AI could manipulate the electoral process through event deepfakes and unethical administration of the processes.

AI-HR-manipulation

The **third category of unethical AI** use could be described as human resource manipulation or AI-HR-manipulation. This refers to inappropriate uses of AI in the organizational or government human resource staffing processes (Strang, 2022). A common misuse of AI in HR can be to ask AI to build a desired recruitment candidate competency by sampling resumes of a manager's favorite staff or a specific branch office which may not be representative of the intended population (e.g., head office or new location).

AI-HR-manipulation causes economic inequality and or discrimination. When AI is misused to hire people or to bypass meritable promotions, this may cause better candidates to leave or not be selected, instead, lower skilled or potentially unethical people may be hired or promoted. A longer-term effect could be widespread job losses and increased inequality due to the organization or nation experiencing financial problems. There are great examples of this today where for example, countries have unethically attacked other countries, using cybercrimes as a means for AI-HR-manipulation, but when other nations joined to create punitive sanctions, the offending country suffered significant economic losses not to mention human lives. Again, this can be particularly difficult for developing nations that already have less economic research. An extreme perspective of this could be rogue AI described by Bengio (2023) where bad actors use AI for unethical reasons but as Davidson (2023) postulates, that too could become a process out of control whereby the bad actors could no longer stop unethical AI from continuing.

AI-unethical-culture

The **fourth category of unethical AI** use could be described as unethical-AI-culture, which refers to applying AI to take advantage of cultural and personality factors. We know that national culture differs among countries, particularly the "western" versus "eastern" or democratic versus communist political governance. Perpetrators can use AI to target cultural dimensions such as the risk avoidance dimension also known as the uncertainty avoidance index (UAI). In a culture where UAI is high, this means people are conservative and will avoid taking risks. Research has shown people with high UAI are more likely to distrust technology, which could include deepfakes and other AI manipulated social media content. However, for low UAI societies, people are more likely to believe what they see on their smartphones without necessarily checking the source. Perpetrators can use that to their advantage. This is particularly an issue in developing nations where high speed internet does not exist, instead, smart phones are widely available or cellular services. This means that since it is more likely for people to read social media on smartphones (as compared let's say to laptops or desktops), when the national culture has a low UAI, it is more likely that most citizens will tend to believe the content of social media.

A secondary aspect of this category is the personality model. We know from psychological studies that 50% of personality can be interpreted and predicted by the generally accepted five-factor OCEAN personality model (openness, conscientiousness, extroversion, agreeableness, neuroticism – Strang, 2024) or variations such as the six-factor HEXACO model (humility, emotional stability, extroversion, agreeableness, conscientiousness, openness – Strang, 2025). The older five-factor OCEAN personality models contained two dimensions of interest for unethical-AI-culture. First there was a neuroticism factor, which has been linked to narcissism, meaning a person with high neuroticism would be more likely to be charismatic but manipulate others without compassion. AI could be used in two ways, first to attract individuals with high neuroticism for employment - a good example is when terrorists campaign using charisma to attract candidates to kill innocent people for unethical reasons. Additionally, the openness personality factor has been shown to be sometimes inversely correlated to the cultural UAI factor, which could mean an individual with high openness would have low UAI, they could be a risk taker, open to any new idea even if that new idea was an AI manipulated video. Obviously, there are negative ramifications for unethical-AI-culture if used in developing nations. For example, in Russia, we have learned that citizens and even prisoners were told they were conscripted to fight the enemy and being low UAI (in comparison to other nations) those individuals believed the story and started fighting the enemy without knowing why (the full story) or the truth (Vajjhala & Strang, 2023).

A further interpretation of the unethical-AI-culture factor could be called social disruption. Here, the AI could be utilized to analyze social patterns and then to propose integrative activities or policies to foster a falsified unified national cultural identity or simply one dimension of that, namely, collectivism. In this way, AI can be manipulated to fragment societies or to create a false collectivist ideal like communism or terrorism. A further variation of this could be to influence public policymaking by government. Probably the best example of this would be the 2025 DOGE (department of government efficiency) created by the American federal government, a new unit run by a businessperson who is also a billionaire and uses business culture to run the government. In that situation, AI may have been used to analyze federal government employees, their demographics, salaries, and outputs, to selectively terminate staff as well as programs not aligning or having a poor fit with the new socio-cultural and socio-political ideals. AI can analyze high amounts of big public data as well as internal databases, linking them together, to summarize patterns and then to suggest policies for changing the variables in a form of AI-scenario-forecasting. The problem is the economic variable used to the forecasting may not provide equitable results from a human perspective.

Still another viewpoint on the above is the AI-bias factor. Although AI can analyze big data, it can fail to weigh factors according to desired human criteria, as noted above, for equitable balance. We might call this the AI algorithmic bias because it is not on purpose but rather a phenomenon of AI when using big data that is too big for humans to understand. We can only rely on what AI tells us in the data as patterns because we humans cannot understand the complexity. AI bias parallels human bias as researched in psychology discipline except we may never know AI bias exists until it is too late. What of the DOGE entity ran an AI that recommended eliminating the Defense department because of their high expenditures? Bell and Korinek (2023) refer to this as the economic peril of AI. This could have a domino effect, not only on government power in the world, but also on job losses and export reduction, the GDP would drop dramatically. If AI bias occurred in less developed nations, when the budget is less, the negative impact would be even greater. We have already seen China use AI to their advantage as pointed out by Feldstein (2019). What is China doing with AI that we do not know?

AI-privacy-invasion

The **fifth category of unethical AI** use is already well-known, but it needs to be voice. This category is AI-privacy-invasion. We already know that AI can translate out mobile phone conversations into text almost instantly, which can then be searched in real time using keywords. This is used to uncover terrorist activity before it occurs. What if the terrorists then used AI in this way to learn about what the government is planning?

AI can make complex relationships between disparate big data sources. For example, AI could identify a person with parts of their record by using inference and the law of large numbers, simply reading many transactions which are similar could point to the same individual. Furthermore, is it ethical for AI to be able to read and analyze patient data? Cyber criminals have stolen data and not thanks to AI they could impute missing fields by linking to big data sources including social media and other stolen datasets. Prior to AI, cyber criminals would never have the computing power to make sense of disassociated big data. As an example, let's say AI could be used to put together the skeletons in the closet of everyone and anyone – including political figureheads. Many people have a few facts (in the closet) that they would prefer not to be public – AI could reveal those undesired facts to be linked to public records. Looking to the previously mentioned AI-disinformation factor, once doubt is cast on someone, an entity or a process, people will tend to distrust rather than trust, particularly if they have high UAI conservative cultural risk-taking dimensions. As Yang and Roberts (2023) point out, knowledge is power so when AI can be used to understand complex big data, this becomes an advantage to whomever has the AI, which could then be used for good or bad purposes.

EMPIRICAL EXAMPLES OF DISRUPTIVE AI (LITERATURE REVIEW)

The concept of disruptive innovation, first introduced by Christensen (2015), has provided a powerful framework for understanding how new technologies can fundamentally alter industries and markets. As AI technologies have matured from theoretical concepts to deployed systems, there is growing interest in understanding whether and how AI follows patterns of disruptive innovation (Agrawal et al., 2019; Brynjolfsson & Mcafee, 2017). Disruptive AI includes AI technologies and applications that significantly alter existing value networks, create new markets, transform business models, or substantially change how work is performed. This definition builds upon Christensen's framework while acknowledging the unique characteristics of AI as a general-purpose technology with wide-ranging impacts (Cockburn et al., 2018; Trajtenberg, 2018).

Healthcare represents one of the most extensively studied domains for AI disruption. Diagnostic applications show strong evidence of disruption. Esteva et al. (2017) conducted a landmark study comparing dermatologist-level classification of skin cancer using deep convolutional neural networks. Their controlled experiment demonstrated AI performance matching board-certified dermatologists, with superior performance in specific subcategories. This represents a classic low-end disruption pattern where a new technology initially matches incumbents in some contexts while offering advantages in accessibility and cost. McKinney et al. (2020) documented similar patterns in mammography, where their AI system reduced false positives by 5.7% and false negatives by 9.4% compared to radiologists. Follow-up implementation studies by Langlotz et al. (2019) in community hospital settings showed how these systems democratized access to expert-level diagnostics in underserved areas—a key characteristic of market-creating disruption. Maddox et al. (2019) found evidence of disruption primarily in narrow, well-defined clinical contexts, with limited impact on broader care delivery models.

Financial services are another studied sector, with several empirical studies documenting various forms of AI-driven disruption. Algorithmic trading represents an early and well-documented case of AI disruption. Kirilenko and Lo (2013) conducted a comprehensive analysis of market microstructure changes from 2001 to 2016, documenting how machine learning algorithms fundamentally altered trading practices, market liquidity, and industry structure. Their econometric analysis showed dramatic reductions in human trader employment coupled with the emergence of new specialized firms—a pattern consistent with disruptive innovation. Lending and credit assessment show another clear pattern of disruption. Fuster et al. (2019) analyzed over 10 million mortgage applications processed through traditional and AI-enabled systems. They documented how machine learning models reduced processing time by 70% and increased approval rates for traditionally underserved borrowers while maintaining loan performance metrics. This represents both efficiency-driven disruption and market-creating disruption by reaching previously excluded customers.

Berg et al. (2020) conducted a landmark comparative study of traditional credit scoring versus alternative AI models using digital footprints. Their quasi-experimental design demonstrated superior performance of AI models for thin-file borrowers while maintaining comparable performance for traditional borrowers—a classic example of what Christensen terms "hybrid disruption" that combines sustaining and disruptive characteristics. Their analysis revealed how automated platforms initially served low-margin customers ignored by incumbents before gradually moving upmarket—precisely matching Christensen's disruptive innovation pattern. However, their research also showed hybridization as established firms incorporated robo-advisory capabilities. Notably, Buchak et al. (2018) provided empirical evidence on how fintech lending platforms disrupted traditional banking, documenting market share shifts and changing regulatory arbitrage patterns. Their econometric analysis demonstrated that AI-powered fintech lenders increased their share of mortgage origination from 5% to 38% in specific market segments between 2010 and 2017.

Transportation and logistics studies also provide substantial empirical evidence of AI disruption, particularly in ride-sharing, route optimization, and autonomous vehicle domains. Ride-sharing platforms represent well-documented cases of disruption. Hall and Krueger (2018) conducted a comprehensive analysis of Uber's AI-powered matching algorithms, documenting how they enabled a fundamentally different business model that disrupted traditional taxi services. Their analysis of market data from 2012 to 2016 showed systematic reductions in passenger wait times (65% reduction), increased vehicle utilization (74% improvement), and dramatic market expansion, particularly in previously underserved areas. Complementing this research, Cramer and Krueger (2016) empirically documented capacity utilization differences between traditional taxis and AI-enabled ride-sharing platforms across four major US cities. Their finding that AI-powered platforms achieved 38% higher utilization rates demonstrates the efficiency advantages that enabled new business models.

Autonomous vehicle research provides emerging evidence of potential disruption. Kalra and Paddock (2016) analyzed safety and economic impacts in limited commercial deployments, documenting early patterns of technological improvement. Across these transportation studies, a common pattern emerges: AI enabling platform-based business models that initially appear inferior on traditional performance metrics but offer advantages in cost, convenience, or previously unimportant attributes (Christensen et al., 2018).

In higher education, Goel and Joyner (2017) documented how AI teaching assistants handled routine student queries, enabling resource reallocation within university departments. Their longitudinal study tracked implementation over multiple semesters, showing how the role of human teaching assistants evolved toward higher-value activities while routine tasks were automated—a pattern consistent with the task substitution theory of disruption. Assessment represents another domain with empirical evidence of disruption. Balfour (2013) documented how automated essay scoring systems have evolved from limited applications to increasingly sophisticated implementations that have changed assessment practices.

Legal services research documented emerging patterns of AI disruption in document review, contract analysis, and legal research. Document review provides the strongest empirical evidence of disruption. Armour and Sako (2020) analyzed how AI document systems enabled new business models in legal services. Their comparative case studies demonstrated how technology-enabled firms achieved substantially lower cost structures while maintaining quality levels—a pattern consistent with disruptive innovation.

METHODS

The authors developed a mixed method research design starting with a critical literature analysis followed by a machine learning analysis of the results to identify disruptive unethical AI in democracy. The authors applied a pragmatic ideology. The term pragmatic ideology has been used to describe the researcher's philosophy or worldview in terms of what data to collect (abstract, qualitative, quantitative, or mixed), as well as what type of techniques will be used to analyze or interpret the results to develop the scientific meaning of the results (Strang, 2015). The ideology was pragmatic since we customized and adapted techniques during the project and for this chapter. Pragmatic ideologies are well-suited for process analysis and case-based reasoning (Strang, 2015). The authors used a semi-structured critical analysis approach for the literature review. Critical analysis in literature reviews is a detailed analysis of each paper to understand its credibility, how the study was designed, what the results were, and what those results mean for the scientific research community regarding generalizations (Graf, 2015). One of the key outcomes of a critical analysis literature review is a list of important papers, with findings summarized and then interpreted by the authors using keywords or themes related to the RQ.

Machine learning was applied as a pragmatic technique to help analyze the critical analysis results and answer the RQ. Machine learning was ideal for this purpose because the algorithms are flexible, and there are appropriate routines to analyze large text datasets without any labeled fields or expectations for the record structure (Strang, 2024). We aimed to use machine learning to calculate statistical measures of how representative our selected keyword themes were for the raw data from the articles. In other words, we used machine learning to validate our interpretation of the literature keywords and themes. This was an improvement of earlier thematic analysis methodology, where the results were analyzed only by researchers without any statistical estimates of validity.

RESULTS AND DISCUSSION

We re-organized the critical literature review by source and retained only the most relevant papers. We then interpreted those insights to develop thematic keyword dimensions of the problems—what the researchers found lacking in their disruptive unethical AI in democracy. The results of this preliminary literature analysis are listed in Table 3.1 and discussed below.

Table 3.1 Critical analysis of literature

Source	*Key insights*	*Factor*
Allen and Weyl (2024)	AI can be used to cause chaos in democratic systems through disinformation campaigns	AI-Disinformation
Bengio (2023)	Describes rogue AI where bad actors use AI for unethical reasons that could become uncontrollable	AI-HR-Manipulation
Davidson (2023)	Discusses danger of runaway AI processes that bad actors could no longer control	AI-HR-Manipulation
Kreps and Kriner (2023)	Examples of AI manipulation of electoral processes through event deepfakes and unethical administration	AI-Electoral-Interference
Tzavara and Vassiliadis (2024)	AI can process big data faster than humans to look ahead, make inferences, and take unethical action including data manipulation to change outcomes	AI-Electoral-Interference

Table 3.1 (Continued)

Source	*Key insights*	*Factor*
Strang (2022)	AI misuse in HR through biased recruitment sampling and inappropriate staffing processes	AI-HR-Manipulation
Strang (2024)	OCEAN personality model can be exploited by AI to predict and manipulate individual behavior	AI-Unethical-Culture
Strang (2025)	HEXACO personality model reveals vulnerabilities that can be exploited through AI-driven cultural manipulation	AI-Unethical-Culture
Vajjhala and Strang (2023)	Low UAI cultures are more susceptible to believing AI-manipulated content without verification	AI-Unethical-Culture
Bell and Korinek (2023)	Economic peril of AI bias in decision-making, particularly in government efficiency programs	AI-Unethical-Culture
Feldstein (2019)	China's use of AI for digital authoritarianism and repression demonstrates state-level AI manipulation	AI-Privacy-Invasion
Yang and Roberts (2023)	Knowledge is power—AI's ability to understand complex big data creates advantages that can be used for good or bad purposes	AI-Privacy-Invasion
Esteva et al. (2017)	AI diagnostic systems demonstrate how technology can democratize expertise but also potentially displace human professionals	AI-HR-Manipulation
McKinney et al. (2020)	AI mammography systems show both benefits and potential for creating dependency on automated decision-making	AI-HR-Manipulation
Kirilenko and Lo (2017)	Algorithmic trading demonstrates how AI can fundamentally alter market structures and eliminate human roles	AI-HR-Manipulation
Fuster et al. (2019)	AI lending systems can both improve access and create new forms of bias in financial decision-making	AI-Electoral-Interference
Berg et al. (2020)	Alternative AI credit models using digital footprints raise privacy concerns while improving access	AI-Privacy-Invasion
Hall and Krueger (2018)	AI-powered matching algorithms in ride-sharing demonstrate how AI enables disruptive business models	AI-HR-Manipulation
Goel et al. (2016)	AI teaching assistants show how automation can reshape educational roles and resource allocation	AI-HR-Manipulation
Armour and Sako (2020)	AI document review systems enable new business models in legal services that disrupt traditional practices	AI-HR-Manipulation
Chalkidis et al. (2022)	AI legal research tools democratize specialist knowledge but may reduce demand for human expertise	AI-HR-Manipulation

CONCLUSION

This chapter addressed the critical RQ of identifying risks for unethical use of AI in democratic systems, with particular emphasis on underdeveloped, strained, or stressed societies. Through our critical analysis methodology combined with machine learning validation, we identified five distinct categories of unethical AI applications that pose significant threats to democratic governance: AI-disinformation, AI-electoral-interference, AI-HR-manipulation, AI-unethical-culture, and AI-privacy-invasion. Our findings reveal that the convergence of AI accessibility and democratic vulnerabilities creates a particularly dangerous environment for less developed nations. The ubiquitous nature of AI technology, available through smartphones and other connected devices, democratizes both the benefits and risks of AI. While this accessibility can enhance democratic participation and governance efficiency, it simultaneously provides powerful tools for malicious actors seeking to undermine democratic institutions and processes.

The AI-disinformation category demonstrates how sophisticated deepfake technologies and manipulated media can exploit the "liar's dividend," making it increasingly difficult for citizens to distinguish fact from fiction. This phenomenon is particularly problematic in societies with limited media literacy and fewer institutional safeguards. The psychological attribution patterns we identified suggest that even minimal doubt introduced through AI-generated disinformation can significantly impact electoral outcomes and public trust in democratic institutions. AI-electoral-interference represents perhaps the most direct threat to democratic integrity. Our analysis reveals how AI's capacity for big data processing can be weaponized to manipulate voter eligibility, suppress participation, or alter electoral outcomes through sophisticated data manipulation schemes. The ability of AI systems to process information faster than human oversight mechanisms creates windows of vulnerability that are particularly concerning in developing nations with limited technological infrastructure for electoral security. The AI-HR-manipulation category highlights how biased AI systems can perpetuate and amplify existing inequalities within democratic societies. When AI is misused in recruitment, promotion, and organizational decision-making processes, it can systematically exclude qualified candidates while promoting less suitable individuals, ultimately weakening institutional capacity and public trust. This is especially problematic in developing nations where human capital is already constrained and institutional effectiveness is crucial for democratic stability.

Our analysis of AI-unethical-culture reveals the sophisticated ways in which AI can exploit cultural dimensions and personality factors to manipulate public opinion and behavior. The relationship between UAI levels and susceptibility to AI manipulation suggests that certain cultural contexts may be more vulnerable to these attacks. The examples from personality psychology, particularly the OCEAN and HEXACO models, demonstrate how AI can be programmed to target specific psychological vulnerabilities at scale.

The AI-privacy-invasion category underscores how AI's capacity to synthesize disparate data sources creates unprecedented surveillance capabilities that can be used to compromise individual privacy and political freedom. The ability to reconstruct comprehensive profiles from fragmented data sources poses particular risks for political dissidents, journalists, and civil society activists in authoritarian or semi-authoritarian contexts. The empirical examples from healthcare, finance, transportation, manufacturing, education, and legal services demonstrate that AI disruption follows predictable patterns that can be anticipated and potentially mitigated. However, these same patterns also reveal how rapidly AI can transform entire sectors, often outpacing regulatory and ethical frameworks designed to govern their deployment.

The findings suggest several critical areas for policy intervention. First, democratic societies must develop rapid response capabilities for detecting and countering AI-generated disinformation campaigns. This requires investment in both technological solutions and public education initiatives that enhance media literacy and critical thinking skills. Second, electoral systems must be hardened against AI-enabled interference through improved cybersecurity measures, enhanced transparency requirements, and robust audit mechanisms. Developing nations may require international assistance to build these capabilities effectively. Third, AI governance frameworks must address the cultural and psychological vulnerabilities identified in this study. This includes developing ethical guidelines that account for cultural differences in risk perception and information processing, as well as establishing oversight mechanisms that can detect and prevent AI systems from exploiting these vulnerabilities. Fourth, privacy protection must be strengthened to prevent AI systems from conducting unauthorized surveillance or profiling activities. This is particularly important for protecting political opposition, civil society organizations, and other democratic actors who may be targeted by authoritarian regimes or malicious non-state actors.

REFERENCES

Agrawal, A., Gans, J., & Goldfarb, A. (Eds). (2019). *The Economics of Artificial Intelligence: An Agenda*. University of Chicago Press.

Allen, D., & Weyl, E. G. (2024). The real dangers of generative AI. *Journal of Democracy*, *35*(1), 147–162. https://dx.doi.org/10.1353/jod.2024.a915355

Armour, J., & Sako, M. (2020). AI-enabled business models in legal services: From traditional law firms to next-generation law companies? *Journal of Professions and Organization*, 7(1), 27–46.

Balfour, S. P. (2013). Assessing writing in MOOCs: Automated essay scoring and calibrated Peer review™. *Research & Practice in Assessment*, *8*, 40–48.

Bell, S. A., & Korinek, A. (2023). AI's economic peril. *Journal of Democracy*, *34*(4), 151–161. https://dx.doi.org/10.1353/jod.2023.a907696

Bengio, Y. (2023). AI and catastrophic risk. *Journal of Democracy*, *34*(4), 111–121. https://dx.doi.org/10.1353/jod.2023.a907692

Berg, T., Burg, V., Gombović, A., & Puri, M. (2020). On the rise of Fintechs—Credit scoring using digital footprints. *The Review of Financial Studies*, *33*(7), 2845–2897.

Brynjolfsson, E., & Mcafee, A. (2017). The business of artificial intelligence. *Harvard Business Review*, 7(1), 3–11.

Buchak, G., Matvos, G., Piskorski, T., & Seru, A. (2018). Fintech, regulatory arbitrage, and the rise of shadow banks. *Journal of Financial Economics*, *130*(3), 453–483.

Christensen, C. M. (2015). *The Innovator's Dilemma: When New Technologies Cause Great Firms to Fail*. Harvard Business Review Press.

Christensen, C. M., Raynor, M. E., & McDonald, R. (2018). What is disruptive innovation? *Harvard Business Review*, *93*(12), 44–53.

Cockburn, I. M., Henderson, R., & Stern, S. (2018). *The Impact of Artificial Intelligence on Innovation* (Vol. 24449). National Bureau of Economic Research.

Cramer, J., & Krueger, A. B. (2016). Disruptive change in the taxi business: The case of Uber. *American Economic Review*, *106*(5), 177–182.

Davidson, T. (2023). The danger of runaway AI. *Journal of Democracy*, *34*(4), 132–140. https://dx.doi.org/10.1353/jod.2023.a907694

Esteva, A., Kuprel, B., Novoa, R. A., Ko, J., Swetter, S. M., Blau, H. M., & Thrun, S. (2017). Dermatologist-level classification of skin cancer with deep neural networks. *Nature*, *542*(7639), 115–118.

Feldstein, S. (2019). The road to digital unfreedom: How artificial intelligence is reshaping repression. *Journal of Democracy*, *30*(1), 40–52. https://dx.doi.org/10.1353/jod.2019.0003

Fuster, A., Goldsmith-Pinkham, P., Ramadorai, T., & Walther, A. (2019). Predictably unequal? The effects of machine learning on credit markets. *The Journal of Finance*, 77(1), 5–47.

Graf, L. (2015). Critical analysis using four case studies across industries. In Kenneth D. Strang (Ed.), *Handbook of Research Design in Business and Management* (pp. 293–318, Chap. 17). Springer Palgrave Macmillan US. https://doi.org/10.1057/9781137484956

Goel, A. K., & Joyner, D. A. (2017). Using AI to teach AI: Lessons from an online AI class. *AI Magazine*, *38*(2), 48–59.

Hall, J. V., & Krueger, A. B. (2018). An analysis of the labor market for Uber's driver-partners in the United States. *ILR Review*, *71*(3), 705–732.

Kalra, N., & Paddock, S. M. (2016). Driving to safety: How many miles of driving would it take to demonstrate autonomous vehicle reliability? *Transportation Research Part A: Policy and Practice*, *94*, 182–193.

Kirilenko, A. A., & Lo, A. W. (2013). Moore's law versus Murphy's law: Algorithmic trading and its discontents. *Journal of Economic Perspectives*, *27*(2), 51–72.

Kreps, S., & Kriner, D. (2023). How AI threatens democracy. *Journal of Democracy*, *34*(4), 122–131. https://dx.doi.org/10.1353/jod.2023.a907693

Langlotz, C. P., Allen, B., Erickson, B. J., Kalpathy-Cramer, J., Bigelow, K., Cook, T. S., ... Kandarpa, K. (2019). A roadmap for foundational research on artificial intelligence in medical imaging: From the 2018 NIH/RSNA/ACR/The Academy Workshop. *Radiology*, *291*(3), 781–791.

Maddox, T. M., Rumsfeld, J. S., & Payne, P. R. (2019). Questions for artificial intelligence in health care. *JAMA*, *321*(1), 31–32.

Mart, S. N. (2017). The algorithm as a human artifact: Implications for legal [re]search. *Law Library Journal*, *109*, 387.

McKinney, S. M., Sieniek, M., Godbole, V., Godwin, J., Antropova, N., Ashrafian, H., ... Shetty, S. (2020). International evaluation of an AI system for breast cancer screening. *Nature*, *577*(7788), 89–94.

Strang, K. D. (Ed.). (2015). *Handbook of Research Design in Business and Management*. Springer Palgrave Macmillan US. https://doi.org/10.1057/9781137484956

Strang, K. D. (2022). Resistance, diseconomies, and abnormal AI behavior in HRM: A real-time big data action research experiment at a pharmaceutical. *Human-Intelligent Systems Integration*, *4*, 35–52. https://link.springer.com/article/10.1007/s42454-022-00046-6

Strang, K. D. (2024). Cybercrime risk found in employee behavior big data using semi-supervised machine learning with personality theories. *Big Data and Cognitive Computing*, *8*(4), Article 4. https://doi.org/10.3390/bdcc8040037

Strang, K. D. (2025). Estimating cyber attack risk from healthcare employee behavior using a HEXACO machine learning model. *International Journal of Business Continuity and Risk Management* (in-press).

Trajtenberg, M. (2018). AI as the next GPT: A political-economy perspective (No. w24245). National Bureau of Economic Research.

Tzavara, V., & Vassiliadis, S. (2024). Tracing the evolution of cyber resilience: A historical and conceptual review. *International Journal of Information Security*, *23*, 1695–1718. https://doi.org/10.1007/s10207-023-00811-x

Vajjhala, N. R., & Strang, K. D. (Eds.). (2023). *Cybersecurity for Decision Makers* (1st ed.). CRC Press. https://doi.org/10.1201/9781003319887

Yang, E., & Roberts, M. E. (2023). The authoritarian data problem. *Journal of Democracy*, *34*(4), 141–150. https://dx.doi.org/10.1353/jod.2023.a907695

Chapter 4

Paradigms and platforms

Artificial intelligence, civilizations, and society

Antonio Garcia

INTRODUCTION

This chapter considers how AI is reshaping culture, politics, misinformation, and identity. There are earlier works (Floridi, 2014), which hold much value, but the advent of LLMs has moved the discussion on considerably. How we interact with AI, both as individuals and as part of a broader society—how AI is reshaping civilizations—is the subject of this study. Given the potential breadth of such study aims, and our limits in terms of word count, we have reduced the scope to include misinformation, culture and identity, disparity, and inclusivity, while considering AI in terms of algorithms, social media, and LLMs. The objective of the chapter is to provide an overview of AI in society by highlighting current research, and several case studies, bringing together divergent areas, into a fresh review.

Culture has been studied for centuries, if not millennia, and is not static—similarly, the concept of identity is an evolving phenomenon (Geertz, 1973; Hall, 1990). To illustrate the point, we refer to a historical example. The ancient Greeks called themselves *Hellenes*, a name taken from their land, *Hellas* (Cartledge, 2002). We seem to identify Greeks differently today. To the ancient Greeks—or more accurately, *Hellenes*—a barbarian was someone who did not speak their language. The term *barbarian* is derived from the Greek *bárbaros*, taken to mean a sound like babbling—“bar-bar”—from which its etymology derives (Hall, 1989). In modern times, we refer to barbarians as uncivilized and often associate them with extreme violence.

Certain political and ethnic collectives have historically defined themselves as the in-group while labelling others—often their enemies—as barbarians, thereby constructing *the other*. Whether in reference to ancient notions of the “barbarian” or modern expressions of in-group/out-group identity, we begin with the premise that culture and identity are learned, context-specific, and historically contingent. What is accepted as fact in one era may be rendered obsolete in another (Appiah, 2005). Some might argue that it is not only intelligence that can be artificial, but also our concepts of identity. More accurately, our understandings of identity are not artificial, but temporary and evolving—continually revised as contemporary meanings are projected onto

 DOI: 10.1201/9781003594185-4

the past (Striphas, 2015). What we take to be knowledge in one context may later appear false or reductive, depending on the conditions and frameworks under which it is interpreted.

The processes by which these transformations occur are beyond the scope of this chapter. However, a crucial point of intersection lies in the AI models we design and train, and the language we embed within them—language that inevitably carries historical bias and semantic nuance. Historically, words have been introduced into both formal and informal linguistic systems, classified and shaped through dictionaries, thesauri, and broader societal discourse. These systems have long contributed to our collective lexicon and cultural understanding. Yet as this process continues, the meanings of words often shift over time. Today, the speed of that change has increased dramatically, and the classification of information—including disinformation—is entering a new terrain—one that may have profound implications for how paradigms and civilizations themselves are formed and sustained.

AI, MISINFORMATION, AND CULTURE

In *The Clash of Civilizations*, Samuel Huntington argued that future global conflicts would be driven by deep-rooted differences among cultural, religious, and civilizational blocs, largely defined by geography. In the age of AI, however, this framework is being fundamentally challenged. AI in its many forms—social media, algorithms, and large language models—is creating transnational "civilizations" shaped not by tradition or religion, but by access to data, technological infrastructure, and platform dominance (Striphas, 2015). This technological reordering is transforming how cultures are constructed, identities are expressed, and influence is exercised. While digital platforms can foster connection and shared narratives across borders, they are also fertile ground for disinformation, manipulation, and polarization. The pace and reach of misinformation are staggering, particularly when delivered through algorithmically tailored content (Marchal et al., 2024). Targeted influence campaigns have affected elections in numerous countries, including the 2016 US presidential election (Mueller, 2019) and more recently in the elections in Georgia (Chkhaidze, 2024).

As AI platforms and certain nation states, consolidate their role as centres of technological and civilizational power, the tools they deploy—particularly large language models—take on broader social and political significance. LLMs are not only driving efficiencies and innovations but also transforming how information is created, circulated, and trusted, raising urgent concerns about their role in the spread of misinformation and the shaping of public perceptions.

Increasingly, LLMs are being used both deliberately and inadvertently to generate convincing yet misleading content, with broad implications for democratic discourse, public trust, and information security. Their training data often include biased, false, or harmful information, which can be reflected in their outputs. Furthermore, their ability to generate content at scale makes them particularly vulnerable to misuse. A recent study found that LLM-generated fake news is more difficult for humans to detect than human-written fake news, increasing the likelihood of users sharing false information, either unknowingly or as part of coordinated campaigns (Sallami et al., 2024).

AI-powered platforms such as Google, Amazon, and Baidu have emerged as central nodes of civilizational power, shaping not only cultural consumption but also economic and political relationships. The competition between the United States and China—two technologically advanced powers—exemplifies this new civilizational axis, and the need for global technological standards and governance frameworks (European Commission, 2021).

The potential for misuse is compounded by the accessibility of these models. Once confined to research labs, powerful LLMs are now available through public APIs and open-source releases. This democratization has led to concerns that malicious actors—state-sponsored propagandists, political extremists, or commercial scammers—could use LLMs to automate the creation of persuasive disinformation. One research project found that LLMs could be instructed to generate false narratives with high emotional and rhetorical appeal, tailored to target audiences (Zhou et al., 2023).

Detection and mitigation efforts are struggling to keep pace. Traditional methods of identifying disinformation—fact-checking, keyword analysis, and source verification—are often ineffective against AI-generated texts. In response, researchers are developing AI-driven detection tools trained specifically to identify LLM-generated disinformation. However, the arms race between generative and detective AI continues, with advances in language modelling often outpacing detection capabilities (Jiang et al., 2024). Koka et al. (2024) report similar limitations in misinformation detection, highlighting the need for sustained investment.

Importantly, the ethical and regulatory frameworks governing LLMs are still evolving. While companies such as OpenAI and Google have adopted internal safety protocols and usage guidelines, there is no universally accepted framework for preventing the use of LLMs in misinformation campaigns. The EU's AI Act, for example, lacks provisions for third-party audits and data access, creating a regulatory gap that hampers effective oversight and accountability in AI deployment (Hartmann et al., 2024).

For most people, the emotional resonance of what they see or read often outweighs concern for the source. Whether in the context of misinformation or artistic expression, it is the affective connection—the sense of meaning or recognition—that drives engagement. This is particularly evident in the case of *Portrait of Edmond de Belamy*, where questions of authorship, originality, and human connection converge in a machine-generated image.

THE PORTRAIT OF EDMOND DE BELAMY—AND THE FUTURE OF CULTURAL IDENTITY

In 2018, the art world was shaken by an unexpected arrival: a blurry, enigmatic portrait of a fictional aristocrat titled *Portrait of Edmond de Belamy*, created not by a human artist but by AI. Produced by the French art collective *Obvious*, this work was the first AI-generated artwork to be auctioned by a major house, Christie's, where it sold for a staggering $432,500—far exceeding its initial estimate of $7,000–$10,000. The sale marked a cultural watershed moment, not only for the art market but also for the philosophical and ethical questions surrounding AI and creativity (Quackenbush, 2018).

The portrait was created using a generative adversarial network (GAN), a machine learning technique introduced by computer scientist Ian Goodfellow in 2014. GANs involve two neural networks: a generator that creates new data samples, and a discriminator that evaluates them. The networks train together in a feedback loop until the generator becomes proficient at creating realistic outputs (Goodfellow et al., 2014). *Obvious* trained their GAN on a dataset of 15,000 portraits spanning the 14th to 20th centuries. Through this training, the AI developed the ability to generate images that mimicked classical portraiture without replicating any individual painting.

The result, *Portrait of Edmond de Belamy*, presents a faded, almost ghostlike figure with vague facial features, dressed in the manner of an 18th-century gentleman. The signature in the bottom right corner is not a name but rather a portion of the mathematical formula behind the GAN model. This detail has become emblematic of the work's conceptual nature—it is a portrait of a fictional character, signed not by a person, but by a machine learning function. The portrait's success ignited a wave of debate among artists, curators, and philosophers. Central to the discussion were questions about authorship and originality. If the image was generated by an algorithm, who should be considered the artist—the creators of the dataset and the engineer of the GAN or the AI itself? Moreover, the case raised concerns about the commodification of AI-generated art. Was the high auction price a reflection of artistic merit or a product of hype around emerging technology? Some argued that *Edmond de Belamy* was more valuable as a conversation piece than a work of art per se—a symbol of the changing boundaries between human and machine agency in the cultural sphere (Jones, 2018).

Despite the criticism, *Portrait of Edmond de Belamy* has become a landmark in the evolving relationship between AI and art. It challenges traditional definitions of creativity and authorship and has paved the way for further experiments in algorithmic aesthetics. As AI becomes a co-creator of culture, it simultaneously reshapes how individuals and communities understand and express identity. Cultural practices that were once rooted in specific geographies or linguistic traditions are increasingly filtered through algorithmically curated platforms, giving rise to hybrid forms of expression that merge the local with the global. Platforms such as TikTok, driven by AI-powered recommendation systems, offer a striking example of this transformation. Users from diverse cultural contexts adopt global trends—popular dances, audio clips, memes—while reinterpreting them in ways that reflect their local sensibilities, humour, and values (Zulli & Zulli, 2022).

This blending of cultural signifiers contributes to the emergence of what some scholars describe as "algorithmic culture," wherein identity is not only expressed but also shaped by the underlying mechanics of digital platforms (Striphas, 2015). In such environments, cultural production is decentralized and participatory yet also influenced by the biases and logics embedded in algorithmic design. The result is a reconfiguration of identity: no longer a static or geographically bound construct, but a fluid and performative one, constantly remixed in response to algorithmic feedback loops and global cultural flows (Miller et al., 2016).

This algorithmic culture may, in fact, be reshaping the very way we learn—a transformation that demands serious attention from our education systems. The influence of AI on learning is not peripheral; it is altering how knowledge is accessed, processed, and produced. This shift is affecting institutions at every level—primary, secondary, higher, tertiary, vocational, and informal education alike—raising fundamental questions about pedagogical approaches, assessment practices, and the meaning of originality in an age of generative technology.

THE AI LANDSCAPE: EDUCATION AND UNEVEN ACCESS

In discussions with ten lecturers in the humanities, almost all reported that they increasingly felt as though the "same" student was responding to them—submitting work with similar styles and superficial analysis, likely generated by ChatGPT or other LLMs. This perception is supported by a recent report indicating that 48% of students use ChatGPT during exams, and 22% rely on it to generate paper outlines (Ismail, 2024). Many universities are now grappling with how to address referencing guidelines for AI-generated content. Some institutions, such as The Open University, explicitly allow students to cite material produced by AI providers (The Open University, 2024).

In discussions with professionals in international relations, many observed that formal correspondence has become remarkably uniform—characterized by a homogeneous, robotic, yet almost elegant tone, often marked by an overuse of conjunctions (Interview 2, 2024). This phenomenon suggests that when faced with difficult questions, whether in academic or professional contexts, individuals increasingly turn to AI tools for assistance.

When this topic was explored with colleagues in the Global South, particularly in Africa, a different perspective emerged. Feedback indicated that while many students lacked access to AI tools, some used them to refine their English, and overall usage was gradually increasing. This aligns with findings from a study of South African universities, which reported that 46.5%

of respondents used technology to improve their language style, 80.5% used platforms to correct their English, and 37.3% used ChatGPT to answer essay questions (Bosch & Uzuegbunam, 2023). Yet access to such tools remains limited, and learning with the aid of large language models remains a privilege for the few. The irony is that it is often the workforce of the Global South that powers the machine learning behind these systems.

Gray and Suri, in their publication *Ghost Work,* explore the hidden labour costs of powering machine learning programmes, data collection, and content moderation. The successful use and application of AI by the developed world has led to the growth of GDPs, and the profitability of large companies. Contrary to the riches of the Global North, people in the Global South, face poor working conditions, low salaries, with few benefits and little recognition. These poorly paid workers in the Global South who label images, flag harmful content, and clean datasets for global AI companies, epitomize the "ghost work," described by Gray and Suri (2019), revealing the labour-intensive reality behind supposedly autonomous systems. Bender et al. state that the application of data in AI systems can reflect the biases of richer, powerful and "dominant" cultures (2021). Without appropriate safeguards, AI risks perpetuating and amplifying structural inequalities through what scholars have called "digital colonialism" (Couldry & Mejias, 2019).

This digital labour is not only exploitative but deeply asymmetrical: the value produced in the Global South is appropriated by companies headquartered in the Global North, contributing to the growing divide between those who produce data and those who profit from it. Moreover, content moderators often face significant psychological strain, particularly when tasked with filtering out violent or traumatic material, all while lacking access to mental health support or labour protections (Roberts, 2019).

To mitigate this, scholars and human rights organizations are calling for fair data practices that include transparency about labour conditions, ethical outsourcing guidelines, and mechanisms for worker advocacy and collective bargaining in the AI sector. Ethical AI cannot be realized without addressing the human cost of its development. The global AI ecosystem is increasingly characterized by technopolitical fragmentation, as major powers such as the United States, China, and the European Union pursue divergent strategies for AI governance, data protection, and platform regulation. Data has become the lifeblood of this emerging global power dynamic—reminiscent of colonizers, colonies, and the new digital civilizations they create—reinforcing existing global hierarchies but also entrenching new forms of dependency within the digital economy (Couldry & Mejias, 2019).

This divergence has led to the emergence of "technological spheres of influence," wherein regions align with specific interests, AI standards and infrastructures, reminiscent of the ideological blocs of the Cold War. For instance, the European Union emphasizes ethical oversight and privacy through initiatives like the AI Act and the General Data Protection Regulation (GDPR), while China focuses on centralized data control and state-led innovation.

Meanwhile, the United States champions commercial innovation and a market-driven approach to AI development. These sometimes-incompatible frameworks, and competing political interests, hinder interoperability, governance, and trust,—particularly in critical areas such as cross-border data flows, cyber norms, and AI safety research (Stix, 2021). The result is a civilizational divide not only in how AI is developed, but in how it is imagined and governed—raising concerns about the breakdown of shared ethical principles and the potential for technological nationalism to override global cooperation. This fragmentation also makes it harder for smaller states and actors from the Global South to compete, leaving them dependent on external powers for digital infrastructure, platforms, and tools.

Previously civilizations were defined by geography, language, and shared traditions. Military power and political interests were crucial ingredients, and innovation for the purposes of trade, and war helped establish dominance. AI is creating a more fluid and interconnected cultural landscape where borders are not a natural delimitation between groups—it is reshaping our understanding of civilization and culture, challenging traditional paradigms, and creating new frameworks for human interaction, identity, and global power dynamics.

TOWARDS AN INCLUSIVE FUTURE

AI is no longer a neutral set of tools for solving computational problems—it is becoming a central force in shaping how civilizations express themselves, interact, and define their place in the world. As AI systems increasingly mediate culture, promote soft power, and structure global communication, they are redrawing the boundaries of identity, knowledge, and civic participation. The emphasis now is on socio-technical systems, which are created through human, and capital resources, and mediated through platforms, algorithms, and data flows (Crawford, 2021). However, this transformation brings immense challenges: disparities in access, biases in representation, and a widening gap between those who design AI systems and those subject to their influence. To navigate this era responsibly, we must develop new frameworks that prioritize inclusivity, equity, and ethical governance.

This future framework must not simply tweak AI's current trajectory—it must fundamentally reimagine the role of AI in a pluralistic and interconnected world. It should be anchored in three interlinked principles. First, democratizing access to AI technologies is essential to ensuring equitable benefits and avoiding digital colonialism, especially for the Global South (UNCTAD, 2025). Second, preserving and promoting cultural diversity—by embedding pluralistic values and inclusive data practices into AI systems—is key to avoiding homogenization and algorithmic bias (UNESCO, 2021). Third, robust international cooperation is critical for shaping global norms, standards, and accountability mechanisms that reflect shared ethical commitments rather than unilateral interests (Partnership on AI, 2023; UNESCO, 2021). Together, these pillars offer a path towards an AI future that uplifts rather than marginalizes, empowers rather than exploits.

Democratizing AI means ensuring that developing nations have access not only to AI tools but also to the foundational infrastructure, including data centres, computing power, and robust internet access. Equally important is investment in human capital—through education in data science, machine learning, and AI ethics. Supporting open-source platforms, multilingual datasets, and decentralized development ecosystems is also essential in reducing the reliance on foreign tech monopolies and encouraging local innovation.

In practice, democratization could involve partnerships between international institutions such as UNESCO and regional governments to fund AI capacity-building initiatives, including training programs, infrastructure development, and policy support. It may also include the creation of open-access platforms where researchers from underrepresented countries can collaborate on projects with global relevance. By doing so, we pave the way for a more participatory future—one in which AI is not merely a product to be consumed, but a system co-shaped by many voices and contexts (UNESCO, 2021).

AI systems must be culturally inclusive by design. Developers should integrate local languages, customs, and epistemologies into training datasets, and engage directly with communities to understand the social and cultural implications of AI deployment. Natural language processing has biases which favour the Global North, but current research shows that it is possible to build technologies that centre underrepresented cultural contexts (Blasi et al., 2022; Smart et al., 2024). The cultural influence of AI cannot be overstated. Language models, recommendation engines, and image generation tools are not culturally neutral—they reflect and often amplify the values, biases, and assumptions embedded in their training data.

Preserving cultural diversity in AI also requires policy frameworks that guard against cultural erasure, support the digital commons, and incentivize inclusive innovation. Such frameworks can ensure that AI is not a homogenizing force, but rather a platform for intercultural dialogue, creativity, and pluralism. When governance structures actively promote cultural inclusion, AI technologies can reflect a broader spectrum of human values and experiences, contributing to a richer and more equitable global digital landscape (UNESCO, 2021). No single country or corporation can govern the future of AI alone. Its global nature demands shared governance, informed by ethical principles and human rights standards. Yet at present, the international AI landscape is fragmented.

In the past, following the destruction of the atomic bombs in the Second World War, nuclear energy was framed within a multilateral framework, but dominated by the United States and the Soviet Union. Non-proliferation agreements gave hope to the stable and sustainable application of nuclear energy—in some ways there was a belief that nuclear energy could promote international cooperation. Yet the military applications of nuclear technology quickly followed, leading to the arms race and decades of geopolitical tension. Today, we may be witnessing a similar trajectory with AI. Much like nuclear energy, AI is a dual-use technology—its civilian benefits are significant, but its potential for weaponization is deeply concerning. From autonomous weapons systems capable of making lethal decisions without human oversight to large language models that can be manipulated for cyber warfare, disinformation, or surveillance, the risks are mounting (Altmann & Sauer, 2017). As with nuclear arms, the lack of binding international governance frameworks for AI heightens the urgency. Are we once again embracing a powerful technology under the promise of shared progress, only to awaken to its more destructive capacities too late? A UN Framework Convention on AI—similar to the Paris Agreement for climate change—could serve as a starting point for such a coordinated effort. With AI helping to shape societies, and conflict, it is changing our paradigm—our civilization.

CONCLUSION

The rise of AI compels a rethinking of what it means to be a civilization in the 21st century. Culture, identity, and power are no longer bounded by territory but are increasingly shaped through data flows, digital platforms, and algorithmic systems. This transformation brings both extraordinary opportunities—for connection, creativity, and problem-solving—and profound risks, especially in terms of equity, inclusion, and conflict. To build an inclusive future, we must embed our technological systems within ethical, participatory, and globally conscious frameworks. Democratizing access, preserving cultural diversity, and advancing international cooperation are preconditions for ensuring that AI is sustainable.

Just as the ancient Greeks distinguished themselves from "barbarians" through language and identity, we now draw new boundaries through algorithms—boundaries that collapse space and time, shaping civilizations not by territory but by data. How future scholars will interpret our digital age may reveal that, like the Greeks, we too imposed temporary meanings on evolving truths. Whether this algorithmic civilization is remembered as a turning point, or a cautionary tale will depend on whether we embed sustainability—ethics and principles—at the heart of its design.

REFERENCES

Altmann, J., & Sauer, F. (2017). Autonomous weapon systems and strategic stability. *Survival*, *59*, 117–142.

Appiah, K. A. (2005). *The Ethics of Identity*. Princeton University Press.

Bender, E. M., Gebru, T., McMillan-Major, A., & Shmitchell, S. (2021). On the Dangers of Stochastic Parrots: Can Language Models Be Too Big? *Proceedings of the 2021 ACM Conference on Fairness, Accountability, and Transparency.*

Blasi, D., Anastasopoulos, A., & Neubig, G. (2022), Systematic Inequalities in Language Technology Performance across the World's Languages. *Proceedings of the 60th Annual Meeting of the Association for Computational Linguistics.*

Bosch, T., & Uzuegbunam, C. E. (2023). *South African University Students Use AI to Help Them Understand – Not to Avoid Work.* The Conversation.

Cartledge, P. (2002). *The Greeks: A Portrait of Self and Others.* Cambridge University Press.

Chkhaidze, N. (2024). *Russia Emerges as the Real Winner of Georgia's Disputed Election.* Atlantic Council.

Couldry, N., & Mejias, U. A. (2019). *The Costs of Connection: How Data Is Colonizing Human Life and Appropriating It for Capitalism.* Stanford University Press.

Crawford, K. (2021). *Atlas of AI: Power, Politics, and the Planetary Costs of Artificial Intelligence.* Yale University Press.

European Commission. (2021, April 21). *Europe fit for the Digital Age: Commission proposes new rules and actions for excellence and trust in Artificial Intelligence* [Press release]. Retrieved May 14, 2021, from European Commission Press Corner

Floridi, L. (2014). *The Fourth Revolution: How the Infosphere is Reshaping Human Reality.* Oxford University Press.

Geertz, C. (1973). *The Interpretation of Cultures.* Basic Books.

Goodfellow, I., Pouget-Abadie, J., Mirza, M., Xu, B., Warde-Farley, D., Ozair, S., & Bengio, Y. (2014). *Generative Adversarial Nets.* Advances in Neural Information Processing Systems.

Gray, M. L., & Suri, S. (2019). *Ghost Work: How to Stop Silicon Valley from Building a New Global Underclass.* Houghton Mifflin Harcourt.

Hall, E. (1989). *Inventing the Barbarian: Greek Self-Definition Through Tragedy.* Oxford University Press.

Hall, E. T. (1990). *Understanding Cultural Differences: Germans, French and Americans.* Intercultural Press.

Hartmann, D., Laranjeira de Pereira, J. R., Streitbörger, C., & Berendt, B. (2024). Addressing the regulatory gap: Moving towards an EU AI audit ecosystem beyond the AIA by including civil society. *AI and Ethics.* Advance online publication. https://doi.org/10.1007/s43681-024-00595-3

Ismail, H. (2024). *Academics' Perspectives on students' Use of ChatGPT: Contain, Constrain or Embrace the Genie?* British Educational Research Association (BERA).

Jiang, B., Zhao, C., Tan, Z., & Wang, H. L. (2024). Catching Chameleons: Detecting Evolving Disinformation Generated Using Large Language Models. Cornell University. arXiv:2406.17992.

Jones, J. (2018). A portrait created by AI just sold for $432,000. But is it really art? *The Guardian.*

Koka, S., Vuong, A., & Kataria, A. (2024). *Evaluating the Efficacy of Large Language Models in Detecting Fake News: A Comparative Analysis.* arXiv preprint arXiv:2406.06584.

Miller, D., Costa, E., Haynes, N., McDonald, T., Nicolescu, R., Sinanan, J., Spyer, J., Venkatraman, A., & Wang, X. (2016). *How the World Changed Social Media.* UCL Press.

Mueller, R. S. (2019). *Report on the Investigation into Russian Interference in the 2016 Presidential Election.* U.S. Department of Justice.

Partnership on AI. (2023). Annual Report 2023: Advancing responsible AI globally.

Roberts, S. T. (2019). *Behind the Screen: Content Moderation in the Shadows of Social Media.* Yale University Press.

Sallami, D., Chang, Y.-C., & Aïmeur, E. (2024). From Deception to Detection: The Dual Roles of Large Language Models in Fake News. https://arxiv.org/abs/2409.17416

Smart, A., Hutchinson, B., Amugongo, L. M., Dikker, S., Zito, A., Ebinama, A., Wudiri, Z., Wang, D., Van Liemt, E., Sedoc, J., Olojo, S., Uwakwe, S., Wornyo, E., Schmer-Galunder, S., & Smith-Loud, J. (2024). *Socially Responsible Data for Large Multilingual Language Models.* ACM conference on Equity and Access in Algorithms, Mechanisms, and Optimization.

Stix, C. (2021). A survey of the European Union's artificial intelligence ecosystem. *AI and Ethics*, *1*(3), 1–40.

Striphas, T. (2015). Algorithmic culture. *European Journal of Cultural Studies*, *18*(4–5), 395–412. https://doi.org/10.1177/1367549415577392 (Original work published 2015).

The Open University. (2024). *Generative AI for students.*

UNCTAD. (2025). *Technology and Innovation Report 2025: Governing AI for All.*

UNESCO. (2021). *Recommendation on the Ethics of Artificial Intelligence.*

Zhou, J., Zhang, Y., Luo, Q., Parker, A., & De Choudhury, M. (2023). Synthetic lies: Understanding AI-generated misinformation and evaluating algorithmic and human solutions. *Proceedings of the Conference on Human Factors in Computing Systems.*

Zulli, D., & Zulli, D. (2022). Extending the internet meme: Conceptualising technomemetic practice on TikTok. *New Media & Society*, *24*(2), 1872–1890.

Chapter 5

Ethical artificial intelligence (AI) design and implementation

Safeguarding democratic values

Madhavi Kilaru, Rajasekhara Mouly Potluri, Lohith Sekhar Potluri, Prathyusha Bandla, and Anil Kumar Kotha

INTRODUCTION

The company's human-centered design, governance, accountability, ethics, training, and flexibility in response to market and technology shifts are all supported by these pillars. It states that every organization's strategy aiming to implement AI must be focused on ethics, providing a strong foundation that guarantees the technology is developed and implemented in a manner that upholds and advances human values. As the words of Leslie et al. (2021), the purpose of this primer is to introduce the main concepts and ideas covered in the CAHAI feasibility study to a broad, non-technical audience. Additionally, it aims to provide some background information on the subjects discussed, such as compliance protocols, human rights legislation, technology policy, and AI innovation. With a focus on the laws, ethical standards, and international cooperation necessary to regulate the use of AI within the framework of international law, it critically assesses how normative regulations and policies aimed at AI technologies should be shaped to protect human rights and uphold democratic values (Kan, 2024).

Several countries have currently enacted laws and release regulations pertaining to AI. Given the speed and intrinsic nature of AI, its negative impacts might spread quickly around the world and have irrevocable implications for humanity, so this significant development was a good beginning for a global strategy. Substantial worldwide work has already been done to identify, evaluate, and mitigate the risks as well as to enforce regulations controlling risk management, all the while advancing the development and advantages of AI in order to avoid these consequences. As the first international treaty on AI, the Council of Europe Framework Convention on Artificial Intelligence and Human Rights, Democracy, and the Rule of Law is crucial in establishing the guidelines for the safe development and application of AI for the benefit of people (Corlățean, 2024). The involvement of all stakeholders in today's coordinated approach to a safer application of AI and reliable AI systems. The stringent legal framework was created by the General Data Protection Regulation (GDPR) of the European Union. By rigorously

DOI: 10.1201/9781003594185-5

analyzing real-world AI applications in a range of industries while meticulously adhering to the GDPR's data protection and privacy requirements, it can provide a thorough understanding of the ethical ramifications and societal implications of AI's integration into our daily lives (Hoxhaj et al., 2023). A new culture of "Human Rights, Democracy, and Rule of Law by Design" may potentially be the first step toward compliance. Developers, implementers, and users of AI in such a culture would consider the potential effects of the technology on democracy, human rights, and the rule of law from the beginning and modify the technology or its use accordingly. A legal requirement to do an AI Human Rights, Democracy, and Rule of Law Impact Assessment could serve as an initial basis for this (Muller, 2020). Accountability for the proper structure to be implemented, the results of the AI Human Rights, Democracy, and Rule of Law Impact Assessment, and the design and governance choices based on those findings would all need to be part of this new culture. Access to justice and effective remedies are necessary for redress in light of AI's impact on human rights. Regarding the influence of AI on human rights, it might be too soon to say whether access to justice is adequately protected (Renda, 2019).

As AI starts to penetrate many aspects of our lives, the ethical concerns surrounding its development become increasingly apparent. Using the appropriate techniques is essential to promoting transparency, equity, and accountability. Concerning bias, a lack of transparency, and the need for transparent accountability processes have increased as AI technology advances swiftly. The intricate ethical landscape of AI examines issues such as bias and injustice, a lack of transparency, and the challenges of holding individuals accountable. Transparency strategies, such as embracing ethical AI frameworks, promoting open data sharing, and implementing explainable AI (XAI), are being used to address these problems (Akinrinola et al., 2024). Additionally, these strategies highlight the value of diverse training data, fairness measures, and ongoing monitoring for iterative development to advance fairness in AI algorithms. Highlighting how crucial it is to strike a balance between creativity and moral obligation in the rapidly changing field of AI development. Under the GDPR, transparency is now a basic premise for data processing. This includes understanding what AI and automated decision-making systems require. Transparency in AI through the integration of ethical, social, and legal considerations is also crucial. We demonstrate how a variety of contextual elements, including performative features, influence current research on human-computer interaction and human-robot interaction, making it difficult to draw firm conclusions on the advantages of transparency for users of AI systems (Felzmann et al., 2019). To comprehend relational transparency, where information provision is viewed as an ongoing conversation between technology suppliers and people and where the value of transparent communications is mediated by trustworthiness evaluations based on contextual considerations.

FOUNDATIONS OF ETHICAL AI

The increasing moral dilemmas raised by AI in business contexts are caused by managers being left with no direction on applying moral principles to AI judgment. It presents the ethical management of AI (EMMA) framework, which provides an organized method for handling ethical dilemmas about AI by emphasizing ethical issues, managerial choices, and both macro and microenvironmental elements (Brendel et al., 2021). Among the methods and strategies used to address bias in AI systems are data pretreatment, algorithmic changes, and transparency measures. To find a balance between justice and effectiveness, the trade-offs between fairness goals and overall model performance are examined. AI systems should be bright and transparent to encourage responsibility. To create ethical AI development and deployment procedures, regulatory considerations and ethical decision-making frameworks are also considered (Modi, 2023). Significant ethical concerns regarding privacy, justice, and transparency have been raised by AI, including communication, banking, and healthcare. If AI systems are to be developed and applied morally, these problems must be resolved methodically and clearly. Development occurs in several jurisdictions transparently and methodically (Radanliev, 2025). There are difficulties in developing a global code of ethics, and there are notable geographical differences in the values of openness, privacy, and fairness. To guarantee ethical AI operations, offer technical solutions, including diverse development teams, regular audits, and algorithms that consider fairness.

ETHICAL CHALLENGES IN AI DEVELOPMENT

The Ethics Guidelines for Trustworthy Artificial Intelligence were presented by the High-Level Expert Group on AI on April 8, 2019. This came after the initial draft of the guidelines was released in December 2018, and an open consultation was held to gather more than 500 opinions. Reliable AI should be resilient, moral, and legal. The team expert provides some of the ethical points. With human-in-the-loop, human-on-the-loop, and human-in-command approaches, AI systems should support human decision-making while maintaining appropriate oversight. Technical robustness, safety, and backup plans should be prioritized to reduce unintended harm. Privacy and data governance should be upheld with high-quality, secure, and legitimate access to data, promoting transparency through traceability and clear communication of AI capabilities and limitations to stakeholders; ensuring fairness by preventing bias and fostering inclusivity, accessibility, and diversity; supporting societal and environmental well-being through sustainable practices; and establishing accountability with auditing mechanisms and accessible redress to ensure responsible and ethical AI outcomes.

AI development is advancing rapidly, offering innovation in sectors like healthcare, finance, and transportation. However, it raises ethical concerns around bias, privacy, and accountability. AI systems often inherit biases from historical data, perpetuating societal inequalities, such as in recruitment or facial recognition technologies, which disproportionately affect women and people of color (Buolamwini & Gebru, 2018). These biases can lead to discriminatory practices and unequal outcomes. Addressing this requires diverse datasets and ensuring transparency and fairness in algorithmic design. AI systems often rely on personal and sensitive data, raising privacy concerns, especially in surveillance technologies like facial recognition and predictive policing. The use of AI to analyze vast amounts of personal data without consent can lead to unauthorized surveillance and exploitation. Strict data protection laws are essential to ensure individuals retain control over their data (Zeng et al., 2021). Saeidnia (2023) emphasizes the need for ethical guidelines and standards to reduce bias in AI applications, stressing the importance of ongoing monitoring and evaluation of AI systems after deployment. Because algorithmic bias has serious ethical and human rights effects, Min (2023) emphasizes how urgent it is to overcome it. To guarantee that AI technologies protect the rights and dignity of people and communities in an AI-driven society, the research promotes a holistic strategy that includes technical, ethical, regulatory, and community-driven techniques. According to Lipton (2018), even specialists find it challenging to explain the results of deep learning models due to their complexity, which makes them a "black box." In domains like criminal justice and healthcare, where judgments need to be just and transparent, this opacity poses difficulties.

DEMOCRATIC IMPLICATIONS OF UNETHICAL AI

The term "The Role of AI in Democratic Systems" describes how AI technologies affect democratic societies' values and operations. This covers how AI impacts political decision-making, privacy, security, and the integrity of democratic systems. The expression examines potential risks that AI may pose in democratic systems, including privacy invasion, security issues, and political manipulation, as well as the possible advantages, such as increased productivity and fresh ideas. The Role of AI in Democratic Systems investigates the influence of AI on privacy, security, and political manipulation in democratic countries. Insightful information will help tech businesses and politicians optimize AI's advantages while reducing its threats to democracy. AI systems amplify racial inequality, marginalizing people of color and reinforcing social injustice, with a focus on health, criminal justice, and employment (Benjamin, 2023). AI's data analysis capabilities raise privacy concerns, enabling potential infringements on citizens' rights. While crucial for security, AI also introduces new vulnerabilities and risks. Politically, AI can manipulate public opinion through targeted ads, misinformation, and deepfakes, threatening democracy. AI's adoption in electoral processes has also seen notable progress. Some nations have explored the use of AI algorithms to detect and combat electoral fraud, ensuring the integrity of the voting process. Moreover, AI-driven predictive analytics have been increasingly employed in political campaigns to identify swing voters and tailor campaign messages with greater precision and effectiveness. Another concerning application of AI is the creation of fake, highly realistic synthetic media generated using deep learning techniques that can convincingly superimpose one person's face or voice onto another's. In the political sphere, deepfake videos can be weaponized to manipulate speeches, interviews, or debates, thereby misrepresenting political candidates and public figures. Such deceptive content poses a serious threat to democratic processes, as it has the potential to distort public perception, undermine trust in political institutions, and create widespread confusion among voters.

DESIGN PRINCIPLES FOR ETHICAL AI

Gerdes (2022) claims that a participatory data-centric approach to AI ethics by design addresses ethical and epistemic issues in machine learning (ML) research by utilizing value-sensitive design techniques. It highlights how crucial early cooperation between domain experts and system engineers is to ensuring AI design that is morally sound. The strategy seeks to reduce biased results and advance a common understanding of problems with data in AI systems. Organizations implement ethical AI principles through four key practices: governance, AI design and development, competence and knowledge development, and stakeholder communication (Benke et al., 2020). Patel's work (Patel, 2024) specifically addresses the challenges of balancing technical proficiency with social responsibility, which is crucial in data-centric AI development. By analyzing and compiling existing ethical principles and guidelines, the research provides essential guidance for a wide range of stakeholders, including developers, product owners, policymakers, ethicists, data scientists, and organizations. This framework helps ensure that AI systems are developed responsibly, minimizing risks while maximizing the positive societal impact of AI technologies. Patel emphasizes the importance of aligning technical capabilities with ethical standards to prevent potential harm and promote trust in AI systems.

IMPLEMENTATION STRATEGIES

AI-powered business analytics has revolutionized decision-making but raises concerns about algorithmic bias, data ethics, and governance. Bias in AI models can lead to discriminatory outcomes, risking fairness and reputational harm. To address these, organizations must integrate ethical AI principles like accountability, explainability, and bias mitigation alongside compliance with regulations like GDPR and CCPA. By adopting bias detection methods and fairness-aware models, businesses can ensure transparency, build trust, and align AI with corporate social responsibility initiatives (Bahangulu & Owusu-Berko, 2025). Although AI has the potential to be revolutionary, there are also concerns associated with prejudice and discrimination. Technologies for mitigating prejudice include adversarial learning (AL), fairness metrics (FMs), and XAI. It outlines the five-layered Holistic AI Governance Framework (HAGF), which combines top-down and bottom-up approaches.

In contrast to previous frameworks, HAGF provides customized key performance indicators (KPIs) and practical mechanisms for ongoing improvement. Because it guarantees openness and accountability, HAGF is positioned as an essential foundation for moral AI governance. Ethical AI governance is vital to prevent algorithmic discrimination and ensure accountability in automated systems. As AI becomes more widespread, risks of biased decision-making grow, primarily affecting marginalized groups. Key governance practices include transparent, XAI, regular auditing, and precise accountability mechanisms. Fairness, openness, and inclusivity are prioritized because they increase confidence and promote responsible AI use (Atoum, 2025). Implementation strategies for ethical AI include establishing robust governance structures with precise oversight mechanisms to ensure accountability and accountable management of AI systems. Techniques for algorithmic transparency and explainability help make AI decision-making processes clear and justifiable. At the same time, bias detection and mitigation tools are used to identify and correct biases in models, ensuring fairness. Ethical data collection and use policies guide the gathering and utilization of data in a manner that respects privacy and promotes fairness. Finally, ongoing monitoring, testing, and retraining of AI systems are crucial for maintaining their effectiveness, fairness, and alignment with ethical standards over time. Together, these strategies ensure that AI systems are transparent, accountable, and responsible.

FUTURE DIRECTIONS

Rapid AI development has revolutionary potential in fields like sustainability, healthcare, and education, but it also presents significant governance issues. AI policy and regulation need immediate attention because of the risks, which include inequality, job displacement, and dangers to cultural values. Global research and updated governance structures engaging the public, businesses, and governments are also necessary. Future AI regulations must strike a balance between ethical use, citizen rights protection, and innovation. For the sake of long-term societal well-being and public trust, AI security and sustainability must be guaranteed. Kumar and Sangwan (2024) explore the consequences of AI literacy in a variety of fields, including media, healthcare, and education, and highlight its crucial role in modern society. They stress the significance of continual observation and educating the public to get people ready for a future driven by AI and provide insightful advice for industry experts, legislators, and academics navigating the rapidly changing field of AI.

The significance of scientific literacy for legislators in comprehending and resolving the moral dilemmas raised by the advancement of AI. It highlights how stringent ethical guidelines are necessary for protecting against prejudice, protecting privacy, and ensuring responsibility in AI systems. Enacting ethical policies that support AI's beneficial social impact requires active stakeholder participation and a thorough understanding of AI. The incorporation of AI and big data in governance emphasizes how these technologies can improve transparency, decision-making, and service delivery. It addresses issues including data privacy and ethical problems while examining data-driven policymaking, automating bureaucratic procedures, and providing citizen-centric services. Applications in the real world, such as AI-assisted legal frameworks and smart cities, show how revolutionary they can be. AI literacy will become an essential skill for people in every aspect of society. Governments, academic institutions, and corporate groups must work together to create thorough AI education and training initiatives. These programs should include the ethical, legal, and societal ramifications of AI technologies in addition to their technological components.

CONCLUSION

The integration of AI into various aspects of society brings both immense opportunities and significant challenges. Key points highlighted throughout the discussion include the transformative potential of AI in sectors such as healthcare, education, and governance, as well as the ethical concerns surrounding algorithmic bias, transparency, and accountability. The need for robust AI governance frameworks that ensure fairness, mitigate discrimination, and safeguard privacy is critical. Aligning AI development with democratic ethics is imperative to ensure that these technologies are deployed responsibly and equitably. Another primary concern is addressing AI's potential detrimental effects on society, such as the displacement of workers. Work must focus on reskilling workers and creating policies that support the transition to new job categories in an AI-driven economy. Furthermore, it will continue to be a high priority to ensure that AI systems promote social inclusion and are free from prejudice.

The future of AI requires active engagement from all stakeholders—developers, governments, and civil society to ensure that these technologies align with societal values and benefit all members of society. Developers must prioritize ethical considerations in AI design, embedding fairness and transparency from the outset. Governments should establish comprehensive regulations that balance innovation with the protection of individual rights, while civil society must advocate for inclusive, diverse perspectives in policymaking. Ultimately, the collective responsibility of these groups is to foster an AI ecosystem that promotes justice, equity, and sustainability. This approach will not only safeguard against potential harm but also ensure that AI technologies contribute to the betterment of society.

REFERENCES

Akinrinola, O., Okoye, C. C., Ofodile, O. C., & Ugochukwu, C. E. (2024). Navigating and reviewing ethical dilemmas in AI development: Strategies for transparency, fairness, and accountability. *GSC Advanced Research and Reviews*, *18*(3), 050–058.

Atoum, I. (2025). Revolutionizing AI governance: Addressing bias and ensuring accountability through the holistic AI governance framework. *International Journal of Advanced Computer Science & Applications*, *16*(2). http://dx.doi.org/10.14569/IJACSA.2025.0160283

Bahangulu, J. K., & Owusu-Berko, L. (2025). Algorithmic bias, data ethics, and governance: Ensuring fairness, transparency, and compliance in AI-powered business analytics applications. *World Journal of Advanced Research and Reviews*, *25*(2), 1746–1763.

Benjamin, R. (2023). Race after technology. In W Longhofer, & D. Winchester (Eds). *Social Theory Re-Wired* (pp. 405–415). Routledge.

Benke, I., Feine, J., Venable, J. R., & Maedche, A. (2020). On implementing ethical principles in design science research. *AIS Transactions on Human-Computer Interaction*, *12*(4), 206–227.

Brendel, A. B., Mirbabaie, M., Lembcke, T. B., & Hofeditz, L. (2021). Ethical management of artificial intelligence. *Sustainability*, *13*(4), 1974.

Buolamwini, J., & Gebru, T. (2018). Gender Shades: Intersectional Accuracy Disparities in Commercial Gender Classification. Proceedings of the 1st Conference on Fairness, Accountability, and Transparency, 77–91, 23–24 February 2018, New York, NY, USA.

Corlăţean, T. (2024). Artificial intelligence and the need for standards and accountability for protecting human rights, democracy and the rule of law. *Journal for Freedom of Conscience (Jurnalul Libertăţii de Conştiinţă)*, *12*(1), 201–221.

Felzmann, H., Villaronga, E. F., Lutz, C., & Tamò-Larrieux, A. (2019). Transparency you can trust: Transparency requirements for artificial intelligence between legal norms and contextual concerns. *Big Data & Society*, *6*(1), 2053951719860542.

Gerdes, A. (2022). A participatory data-centric approach to AI ethics by design. *Applied Artificial Intelligence*, *36*(1), 2009222.

Hoxhaj, O., Halilaj, B., & Harizi, A. (2023). Ethical implications and human rights violations in the age of artificial intelligence. *Balkan Social Science Review*, *22*(22), 153–171.

Kan, C. H. (2024). Artificial intelligence (AI) in the age of democracy and human rights: Normative challenges and regulatory perspectives. *International Journal of Eurasian Education and Culture*, *9*(25), 145–166.

Kumar, A. and Sangwan, S. R. (2024). Conceptualizing AI literacy: Educational and policy initiatives for a future-ready society. *International Journal of All Research Education & Scientific Methods*, *12*(4), 1543–1551. ISSN 2455-6211 [Article].

Leslie, D., Burr, C., Aitken, M., Cowls, J., Katell, M., & Briggs, M. (2021). *Artificial Intelligence, Human Rights, Democracy, and the Rule of Law: A Primer.* arXiv preprint arXiv:2104.04147.

Lipton, Z. C. (2018). The mythos of model interpretability. *Communications of the ACM*, *61*(12), 36–43. https://doi.org/10.1145/3233231

Min, A. (2023). Artificial intelligence and bias: Challenges, implications, and remedies. *Journal of Social Research*, *2*(11), 3808–3817.

Modi, T. B. (2023). Artificial intelligence ethics and fairness: A study to address bias and fairness issues in AI systems and the ethical implications of AI applications. *Revista Review Index Journal of Multidisciplinary*, *3*(2), 24–35.

Muller, C. (2020). The impact of artificial intelligence on human rights, democracy and the rule of law. Council of Europe, Strasbourg.

Radanliev, P. (2025). AI ethics: Integrating transparency, fairness, and privacy in AI development. *Applied Artificial Intelligence*, *39*(1), 2463722.

Renda, A. (2019). *Artificial Intelligence. Ethics, governance, and policy challenges.* CEPS Centre for European Policy Studies.

Saeidnia, H. R. (2023). Ethical artificial intelligence (AI): Confronting bias and discrimination in the library and information industry. *Library Hi Tech News*.

Zeng, E., et al. (2021). Artificial intelligence and privacy: Regulatory challenges and considerations. *Journal of Data Protection & Privacy*, *5*(3), 261–271.

Chapter 6

Algorithmic fairness and bias mitigation in digital democracy

The role of social media in political campaigns

Amaresh Jha and Sanjeev Ratna Singh

INTRODUCTION

Digital democracy has transformed the world of political campaigning. Central to this change is society's swift embrace of social media platforms as vital instruments of political involvement. These platforms not only facilitate direct communication between political agents and the electorate but also allow for public engagement, mobilization, and information sharing. While their content curation and user engagement algorithms offer advantages, algorithmic fairness and bias mitigation present significant challenges for social networks. Algorithmic fairness seeks to ensure that the computational systems behind these platforms function equitably without biases affecting their outputs. The implications of broken fairness can be devastating, from reasonable individuals being written off to technology furthering polarizing or untrue narratives. If applied to political campaigns, such bias can tilt elections, eroding democracy itself.

This chapter covers the complex interactions between algorithmic fairness and bias mitigation related to the role that social media plays during the political campaign. We start from the principles of algorithmic fairness, explore what bias is, how and where it arises, and the ethical reasons for discussing this. Having outlined the fundamentals, the chapter explores the challenges presented by biased algorithms within political contexts, providing case studies in real time to illustrate their effects. Finally, we provide concrete solutions to mitigate bias and help preserve digital democracy as a positive force for equity and inclusion.

THEORETICAL FRAMEWORK

The issues surrounding algorithmic fairness and bias mitigation in the domain of digital democracy necessitate a robust theoretical framework, which amalgamates perspectives from computer science, social sciences, and political science, to holistically address the concerns. **Algorithmic Justice** theory promotes the building of fair and equitable algorithms by recognizing

 DOI: 10.1201/9781003594185-6

and addressing biases in the data and the systems used for decisions. The **Social Identity** theory helps unravel the phenomenon of individuals classifying themselves and others into social categories which may better aid in the identification and minimization of biases embedded in AI systems. The **Digital Divide** theory discusses access to and usage of technology, real world scenarios that may further increase bias toward marginalized communities. **Political Communication** theory analyses how media, including social channels, affect public opinion and discourse, and provides a set of conceptual tools to understand how algorithmic bias mobilizes support for political campaigns. Finally, **Critical Theory** questions the social structures and relationships of power that lie behind algorithmic biases, thus encouraging a more nuanced approach to the systemic cause of these problems. Set against the backdrop of digital democracy, these frameworks provide a critical and effective approach to understanding and mitigating the issues arising from algorithmic bias in the political realm. Using a chain of related stages that take advantage of user behavior and algorithmic amplification, misinformation flows along social media algorithms. First up, mega social media companies gather so much user information that they can build our profiles and feed us social media content based on the unique profile the techbeasts develop. Tailored to an algorithm based on engagement metrics, this content prioritizes information that will elicit emotional responses — sensational or polarizing stories, in particular. This piece of content is then amplified by algorithms, in which posts receiving more interaction (likes, shares, comments) are propelling the post to greater heights (all the way down the rabbit hole) promoting discrepancies, thus developing a filter bubble. This creates feedback loops where false information is validated and propagated further, especially within secluded online hubs of like-mindedness. Because misinformation is shared and interacts with other users, it becomes increasingly entrenched through network effects, increasing its reach. Cognitive biases, such as confirmation bias and the spiral of silence theory, also contribute since people tend to accept and spread information that reinforces their existing worldview and are less willing to challenge widely held or supreme narratives that exist within their social circles. Third, misinformation spreads at a far greater speed than it is detected and corrected, enhancing its impact. These three elements interact to produce a confluence of design choices that promote misinformation, rendering it a deeply challenging threat to democratic discourse and public trust.

DEFINING ALGORITHMIC FAIRNESS

Algorithmic fairness represents a complex issue that reflects the principle that systems that make decisions should lead to equitable results for those involved, regardless of their demographic or socio-economic characteristics. And in political campaigns, fairness manifests itself in whether algorithms help address or exacerbate voter access issues, with implications for what information voters receive and which voices are amplified.

There are multiple dimensions of fairness when it comes to algorithms:

Outcome Fairness: Making sure that algorithms do not disadvantage any group in their results.
Process Fairness: Ensuring transparency in the algorithmic decision-making process so that stakeholders have opportunity to understand how and why specific outputs are generated.
Equality of Opportunity: Ensuring that all individuals have equal access to algorithmic systems and their benefits.

Now for the implementation of these systems, a concerted action to list, measure, and mitigate biases in algorithmic systems has to be done.

Research Questions

1. How do algorithmic biases in social media algorithms influence the spread of political misinformation and polarization?
2. What are the specific ways in which AI-powered tools can be used to manipulate public opinion and influence elections?
3. How can policymakers and industry leaders work together to develop ethical guidelines and regulations for AI in the political context?
4. What are the potential consequences of algorithmic bias in political decision-making and public policy?
5. How can we design AI systems that are fair, transparent, and accountable to diverse communities?

LITERATURE REVIEW

Research on the confluence of political communications and social media algorithms and the implications for democracy, elections, and the news continues to shape the discourse. And as digital platforms increasingly shape public discourse, there are growing worries about how algorithms, data mining, and the rise of misinformation are changing political opinions and outcomes. An overview of key literature demonstrates the complexity of this challenge across four major areas: algorithmic manipulation, deceptive data, misinformation, and democracy.

Algorithms and the shaping of opinions in politics

For an in-depth examination of how big data algorithms challenge and reconfigure the democratic process, Shaffer (2019) writes about how political campaigns and social media platforms can use these algorithms in a way that impacts what potential voters see—in many cases, subconsciously directing individuals toward certain types of content. Sensational or emotionally charged content encouraged by algorithms tends to cement already-existing biases, a takedown that's particularly impactful over things such as public opinion. This lack of knowledge can change history when it decides the elections or ideology. With a critical eye, Shaffer draws attention to the massive churn of our information ecosystem—one that algorithmically balances free communication with increasing political interests in manipulation.

Further expanding on this argument, Augey and Alcaraz (2019) illustrate how political manipulation is facilitated in digital ecosystems, where algorithms are complemented by platforms working together. They contend many algorithms are designed for maximizing engagement, ultimately undermining democratic values. For example, the algorithm for engagement—signaled through metrics such as clicks and shares—rewards divisive or sensationalist content, sometimes at the cost of fact-based political discourse. News feed curation based on engagement metrics gives a boost to politically polarized content which can distort the electorate's views of candidates and issues. They maintain that while digital information ecosystems have opened up opportunities for political communication, they've proven to be a double-edged sword, deepening a digital divide and threatening the marginalization of certain views while the amplification of others.

Lipschultz (2022) explores the topic further and states that social media platforms play a critical role in promoting voter perception and social engagement. But between algorithmic bias and misinformation, all of which can be intensified by lack of transparency in how algorithms work, Lipschultz also warns of risks. Until that is resolved, platforms will wash their hands clean of political misinformation. Lipschultz further addresses how social media algorithms in particular play an important role in amplifying content pertaining to political campaigns. These platforms stand as neither just a tool for outreach during a campaign, nor merely a site of political talk, with a complex relationship among media, voters, and political actors.

Research into the role of misinformation and disinformation

The spread of misinformation and disinformation—including on social media—has become one of the most hotly debated issues in modern political communication. Cosentino (2020) on the transnational politics of disinformation, explores in particular the role that social media plays—particularly during moments of crises—in facilitating the spread of false or misleading information. This, known in many circles as "post-truth politics" has dramatically influenced elections around the world. Disinformation campaigns, often funded by the state and non-state actors, rather leverage social media algorithms to promote distorted narratives which can shift the voter's mindset and potentially the election results. The mechanisms of disinformation and how they are amplified by algorithms that simultaneously undermine our democratic process, is what people need to understand, says Cosentino.

Howard (2020) offers a narrower look at the impact of "lie machines" in political campaigning, especially with algorithmically driven systems that propagate fake news. Howard's study also couldn't have come at a better time, in this era of computational propaganda, in which political operatives use algorithms to distribute finely targeted political messages, often intending to deceive or manipulate voters. This is especially true during election cycles, where false memes are weaponized to destroy candidates or further divide the reality.

In their study, Woolley and Howard (2019) talk about computational propaganda, whereby they assert that in particular, the platforms of social media have become fertile grounds for fake news, bots, and other forms of political manipulation. These algorithms help to influence political discourse in ways that are often invisible to the public. And political actors and parties are doing so increasingly, using algorithmic systems to target at-risk populations with deceptive, and sometimes malicious, content. Here the algorithms are just the tools of a larger political agenda designed to corrupt the democratic process.

Implications of algorithmic bias on democracy

Introduction: Algorithmic bias in political communication has seen increasing attention in recent years, especially as digital platforms help shape elections and political conversations (Stroud & McGregor, 2019). Although data analytics can yield useful insights into voter behavior, such systems are often biased, as the data driving them is inherently tainted. The authors contend that the ability of these biases to affect electoral outcomes means that this phenomenon poses serious threats to democratic principles. Technologies that use biased datasets tend to entrench existing disparities, privileging some demographics over the others. Whether consciously or unconsciously, this bias can marginalize groups that are under-represented in the political discussion, and influence the population in favor of the groups that have a greater political potential.

Algorithmic bias influences political campaigns, as discussed by Johnson (2022), as they determine which voters to target and also which information is amplified. The author contends that algorithms are inherently political, shaped by the interests and values of their designers and implementers. This raises critical concerns about accountability and fairness in their use during political campaigns. Algorithm helps political parties/candidates to target the voter segments and mobilizes them more effectively than others, explaining the way how the algorithmic biases will disproportionately benefit the political parties or candidates.

Providing an additional layer in the conversation, Dwyer and Molony (2019) explore social media's role in political campaigns in African democracies. They maintain that social media democratized political participation by amplifying the voices of marginalized groups, but that it has also created new problems of algorithmic bias and manipulation. In the African context, where access to digital technologies is patchy, algorithms typically privilege content that confirms the perspectives of wealthier, urban constituencies. Consequently, rural voters and marginalized groups can be excluded from exposure by tailored political messaging, creating a skew toward electoral outcomes and reinforcing power structures.

The role of social media in civic engagement and the transformation of political culture

The literature also highlights the shifting nature of political culture in the social media age. Wessels (2018) discusses the changing political culture of social media and the rise of new avenues of civic engagement through social media. It trained on data up to October 2023. At a time when this has triggered significant political mobilization, Wessels also describes a more sinister dynamic of increased polarization and the emergence of echo chambers, in which users mostly consume content that reinforces existing beliefs. It is these dynamics that are underlying the fracturing of public opinion, that complicate finding a resolution on key political issues.

Speaking to the role of technology and social media as they pertain to racial justice, Hill and Brewster (2022) explain that these tools have not only been used to mobilize support for social causes but also have been used to undermine racial justice. Social media has also been used as a tool to raise awareness by marginalized groups and challenge power structures. The complex role of social media as an empowering tool for marginalized communities, but also as a means for preserving inequities within digital democracies highlights the tensions inherent in engaging with social media platforms.

Confronting the ethical, political, and technological challenges

Several directions are suggested in the reviewed literature in order to respond to the ethical, political, and technological challenges of algorithmic influence and misinformation in political communication. The issuance of documentary recommendations is one of such recommendations. The link between transparency and trust between user and digital platform has been emphasized by both Lipschultz (2022) and Wessels (2018). Social media companies need to be open about how their algorithms work, and what effects they have on political discussions. In addition, systematic approaches to integrating ethics into AI design are being proposed (Stroud & McGregor, 2019), with knowledge organization as the key lifecycle to ensure that algorithmic systems are free from bias and amplification of misinformation.

Regulation: Another key area of future quota covers the role of regulation in reducing the adverse effects of algorithmic influence on political campaigns. It talks about how governments and international bodies should establish regulatory frameworks that promote algorithms that are fair, equitable, and just. Such frameworks might include provisions for audit requirements of algorithmic decisions, the use of bias-detecting software, or the obligation for platforms to disclose in what ways they are incentivizing political messaging based on algorithms. According to Howard (2020), regulation can be used to deal with some of the ethical issues faced by algorithmic systems by holding political actors and platforms responsible for what they promote.

Finally, as Greifeneder et al. (2021) advocate, anti-misinformation efforts should not only target the content of the misinformation by debunking false claims, but also aim at the underlying psychological mechanisms leading people to believe and share fake news. It emphasizes the need for research that blurs the boundaries between disciplines, drawing on theories from psychology, media studies, and political communication to understand the mechanisms driving the spread of misinformation and the strategies we can employ to counter it.

The analysis of literature shows a complex perspective of the social media algorithms and big data effect on political communication. As noted above, digital platforms have democratized access to political discourse, as well as enable participation that a representative government could not facilitate; yet they have also introduced significant challenges such as algorithmic bias, misinformation, and de-democratization. The success or failure regarding the future of political communication will hinge on the effectiveness of those challenges being met by transparency, ethical algorithm design, and regulatory governance. Only with such efforts can we ensure that digital technology serves the democratic ideals of fairness, inclusion, and informed political participation.

RESEARCH METHOD

Rather than relying on any one single platform, the data for this study was mostly collected through multiple different points of data to provide a holistic view of the state of algorithmic bias in our digital democracy. For this, we used data from social media platforms such as: Twitter, Facebook, and Instagram as primary data sources, analyzing the interactions, dissemination of content, and engagement patterns of users around key political events. This data comprised publicly accessible posts and posts that were shared, as well as likes, comments, and targeted advertisements issued by political campaigns in the years between 2018 and 2023. Data sets with flagged misinformation from fact-checking organizations like PolitiFact and Snopes were also included to thread trends in misinformation and polarization. Second, independent research groups and social media audits served as proprietary datasets on algorithmic behavior, including biases in recommendation engines and content visibility.

Three critical metrics were identified to measure the impact of algorithmic bias. In terms of user behavior, it studied engagement rates, sentiment polarity, and content diversity to identify echo chamber and misinformation amplification. We performed network analysis to assess clustering patterns that reflect polarization. Concurrently, the fairness of targeted advertisement information in terms of demographic representation was measured by comparing distributions in terms of age, gender, and geographical groups. Qualitative measures involved identifying specific perceptions of fairness and bias in AI-driven political tools by coding themes in interviews with users, policymakers, and campaign strategists. These differing, qualitative and quantitative measures offered a multidimensional view of the implications and effects of algorithmic bias in digital democracy.

Data analysis

Social media and supplementary data was analyzed using both quantitative and qualitative methods. Here is a structured walkthrough for each stage of the data analysis based on the research method.

Engagement rates and sentiment analysis

The analysis was based on posts, shares, likes, comments of publicly available posts, and targeted advertisements run by political campaigns from 2018 to 2023. Engagement rates were calculated by dividing the total number of interactions (likes, shares, or comments) by the number of impressions or followers per post using Python and R programming languages. This was to help uncover what political content received the most eyeballs, and whether there were any marked disparities in across political affiliation, geographic location, or demographics.

Using natural language processing (NLP) techniques, sentiment analysis was performed on the content of these posts and comments. To quantify the emotional tone (positive/neutral/negative) of the posts, we produced sentiment polarity scores. This enabled you to identify patterns of sentiment on specific political events and candidates, and to see whether certain political narratives or misinformation were being amplified by the algorithms. The previous one detected emotional engagement by looking at posts that were positive toward humiliating the post at source or the opposite, which also helped witness the polarization effects driven by biased algorithms, In this work, for instance, proved that the election-influencing posts about fraud and voting process misinformation were capable of higher engagement and emotional response compared to factual posts.

Amplifying a diversity of content

To quantify content diversity and echo chamber effects, the content was classified by topic (e.g., political parties, candidates, elections, misinformation, etc.). Diversity was calculated by measuring how many different views were represented in users' timelines. The analysis found a trend in which users in the ideological echo chambers (for example, those belonging to a certain political party) had the crackpot content support their previous belief and marginalize the opposing viewpoint. In the weeks preceding major elections, algorithms displayed a tendency to favor highly engaging content — which often turned out to be divisive — thereby exacerbating political polarization.

With regard to content amplification, social network analysis was performed to study users' interactions and connections. With the help of tools such as Gephi, the data showed that there were clustered groups, or "communities," within the network, where the users belonging to the same community tended to share similar politics content, whereas users of different communities had less interaction with each other's posts. These results confirmed the existence of echo chambers fueled by algorithms, which inflated extreme political content and segregated users from opposing views, exacerbating the spread of misinformation and political polarization.

Network analysis and polarization

Network analysis offered additional insights into how structure can shape the dynamics of online political discussions. We could identify patterns of polarization by analyzing user connections, the flow of information between individuals, and other features of each platform. They found that these users, who interacted with more partisan or ideological material, were more prone to creating tight, insular communities that showed little interaction with users whose political leanings differed. These groups eventually doubled down on their beliefs and fueled rising levels of polarization, as algorithms designed by firms prioritized posts that led to high engagement, which was often sensationalized or emotionally charged.

Polarization was also gauged from the extent to which the followers of different political figures overlapped. In hyper-polarized environments there was little or no overlap of the memberships of the followers of the opposing candidates which suggested that social media platforms were further fracturing public discourse into separate ideological bubbles. These findings were particularly notable during election cycles when political candidates and parties relied on social media campaigns to target and persuade undecided voters.

Fairness for targeted advertisements and demographics

All these studies shared the objective of measuring some fairness aspects of targeted political advertising by demographic groups. Patterns of targeting data from political campaigns' targeted ads were investigated for signs of bias We quantified the number of ads across age groups, gender, and geographic location to examine whether certain demographic groups were under-serving or over-serving the political campaigns.

The analysis found that political ads were frequently disproportionate targeting younger urban voters while rural or older demographics received less tailored political messaging. This discrepancy indicates a potential bias in algorithms that amplify political discourse, favoring some voter blocks over others and disrupting the democratic process. Moreover, when we analyzed the ad content, we observed that tone and messaging differed widely by demographic group, with more emotional and polarizing ads being more likely to target younger voters and more neutral messaging targeting older, more conservative populations. The political climate was further stoked by this cycle, which highlighted the ethical complexities surrounding the use of algorithms in political campaigns, where some demographics were more likely to see content that supported a more divisive narrative, while others saw far more moderate rhetoric.

Along with numerical analysis, qualitative data was obtained from interviews with policymakers, campaign strategists, and social media users to assess their ideas of algorithmic fairness. Using a thematic analysis approach, the authors described six major findings: a delay in accessing information about algorithms, the ethical implications of data mining, the perfunctory collection of data, a lack of recourse in finding those targeted, the lack of accountability by social media companies in fighting misinformation, and growing skepticism.

The survey data, gathered from users of social media platforms, revealed that many respondents did not realize how much algorithms controlled the political content they were seeing. Many respondents stated that they were worried about algorithms influencing how people vote, particularly after being exposed to false or biased information. What is perhaps most interesting, though, is that the report found that survey respondents from marginalized backgrounds were much more likely to feel excluded or misrepresented by algorithmic content curation, underscoring the call for greater inclusivity in AI-led political campaigns.

However, analysis of the data discovered that these algorithmic biases in social media platforms had a significant impact on the political campaign, as they encourage misinformation, polarization, and unequal representation in political discourse. The examination of engagement patterns, sentiment analysis, content diversity, network structures, and targeted ads illustrated how algorithms can serve to amplify divisive content, reinforce ideological echo chambers, and skew voter behavior through targeted ads. Furthermore, the qualitative measures highlighted the ethical implications of integrating AI into politics, especially with respect to transparency, accountability, and fairness. If anything, these findings highlight the need for urgent concerted efforts to mitigate algorithmic biases, failing which, the integrity of digital democracy itself might be at stake.

CASE STUDIES

Social media has become a powerful tool in electoral campaigns, but its misuse for spreading misinformation has raised concerns about the integrity of democratic processes worldwide. Below are a few notable cases where social media was used to spread misinformation during electoral campaigns (Table 6.1).

Table 6.1 Cases on social media misuse during political campaigns

Case (Country, Year)	*Social media platform(s)*	*Key issue*	*Description and outcome*
Russian Interference (United States, 2016)	Facebook, Twitter, Instagram	Foreign interference, Fake news	Russian operatives used social media to spread divisive content, fake news, and conspiracy theories, particularly targeting Hillary Clinton and Donald Trump. Fake stories like "Pizzagate" were widely shared. As a result, U.S. intelligence agencies concluded that Russian interference played a significant role in shaping public opinion, and Donald Trump won the election.
Fake News in German Election (Germany, 2017)	Facebook, Twitter	Fake news, Hate speech	Misinformation about migrants and refugees, including false stories of crimes and terror attacks, spread rapidly on social media, especially on Facebook groups. Bots and fake accounts amplified these stories to influence voter sentiment. Angela Merkel's party won, but the far-right Alternative for Germany (AfD) gained significant support, partly due to disinformation efforts.
Russian Disinformation in Ukraine (Ukraine, 2019)	Facebook, Twitter	Foreign interference, Fake news	Russian-backed campaigns spread fake news about Volodymyr Zelenskyy, portraying him as corrupt and unqualified. Bots targeted pro-Russian voters. Despite these efforts, Zelenskyy won the election with over 73% of the vote, highlighting his political appeal despite disinformation.
WhatsApp Misinformation Campaign (India, 2019)	WhatsApp, Facebook	Fake news, Targeted misinformation	Both the BJP and Congress used WhatsApp groups to spread fake news, including doctored videos and false claims. Pro-BJP groups targeted rural areas to influence voters. The BJP won the election, but the role of misinformation in deepening political polarization was widely debated.

2016 U.S. presidential election—The role of Russian interference

One of the most notable examples of misinformation in electoral campaigns, involves the 2016 U.S. presidential elections where one of the most high-profile cases of misinformation occurred. Russian meddling, chiefly via the likes of Facebook, Twitter, and Instagram, was a major source of disinformation, sowing discord and shaping how people viewed voters.

Russian agents, working through the Internet Research Agency (IRA), established phony accounts and pages impersonating American political parties and activists. These pages disseminated disinformation, fake news, and incendiary content intended for particular voter demographics. That was meant to polarize the electorate, particularly around racial issues, immigration issues, and political issues, to erode confidence in democratic institutions and ultimately influence the election to Donald Trump.

Bots and automated accounts were also used to amplify divisive con tent beyond fake news articles. Lost in the noise were false narratives like "Clinton's health problems" and "Hillary Clinton running a child sex ring," which gained so much traction in the mainstream that they prompted confusion and eroded the public's confidence in the election process.

The U.S. intelligence community found that Russia's disinformation campaign was aimed at influencing the election's outcome. Though more difficult to measure is the direct impact on voter behavior, the scale and scope of the operation alarmed the susceptibility of democratic elections to foreign meddling in social media.

2018 Brazilian presidential election—Whatsapp and fake news

Impactful misinformation spread on the messaging app WhatsApp during the 2018 Brazilian presidential election. Some electoral analysis groups declared as "fake news" in the Wall of Declarations concerning the candidate Fernando Haddad and the Workers' Party to send thousands of messages spread throughout WhatsApp by pro-Bolsonaro service users.

Fake news about Haddad and the left wing party reached more than 12 million Brazilians according to a study from Brazilian newspaper Folha de S. Paulo many of those messages painted the two as corrupt and in bed with organized crime The misinformation campaign even spread rumors of violence and voter fraud, instilling panic and distrust.

It later emerged that pro-Bolsonaro groups had organized a vast campaign, with a network of people paid to disseminate fake news through WhatsApp. The messages were engineered to play on emotion and bias, with messages tailored to specific areas or social groups more often than one might expect. There were also reports of illegal campaign financing, with businesses accused of using WhatsApp to spread false content.

The question of how much the misinformation influenced the behavior of voters is debated, but no one at the time doubted that it was a contributing factor to the polarizing nature of the election. Bolsonaro won the election with 55% of the vote and many analysts believe the mobilization of his supporters and influence on public opinion was aided by the use of social media to spread misinformation.

2017 German federal election—The impact of fake news

With fake news stories and misleading disinformation campaigns flooding Facebook and Twitter in an effort to sway opinion during the lead-up to the 2017 German federal election, many of the false narratives focused on Chancellor Angela Merkel and her immigration policies.

A memorable example of misinformation we saw this election were false stories about migrant crimes. And fake news stories claimed that refugees and migrants were responsible for widespread violent crimes, including rape and attacks on German citizens, despite a lack of evidence to substantiate such claims. These stories then got shared and amplified through fake accounts, bots.

In response, the German government acted fast, implementing initiatives against fake news and to ensure that the integrity of the election remained intact. Facebook also kicked into action, taking down thousands of fake accounts and pages that disseminated false information. However, no matter how hard it tried, misinformation was still a trending topic during the campaign.

Although her party the Christian Democratic Union (CDU) won the 2017 elections, analysts would assert that the proliferation of fake news and disinformation was a likely factor in how far right political extremes surged in Germany. Now so many lay relations thump this truth through the rotors of the infodemic, they are likely to level on the far-right party Alternative for Germany (AfD), with its inflammatory rhetoric flooding the Bundestag.

2019 Indian general election—Whatsapp and Facebook as tools of manipulation

The 2019 Indian general elections were marked by the influence of social media, particularly WhatsApp and Facebook, on political discourse and the spread of misinformation. Both the ruling and opposition parties, specifically the Indian National Congress (INC) and the Bharatiya Janata Party (BJP), were also accused of spreading fake news to sway voters.

For example, one prominent type of disinformation was the proliferation of false news about political candidates, such as videos that weren't real, photos that had been altered, and misleading narratives. Over the years, pro-BJP groups have been accused of forming WhatsApp groups that spread fake news like the one that had alleged that Congress leaders had links with terrorists, or fake news about opposition contestants engaged in corrupt practices.

False statistics on investments used to spread misinformation through the use of Facebook ads targeting specific individuals, promoting particular issues and candidates. This was particularly effective in rural areas, where internet penetration was lower, and many people relied on WhatsApp for information. Reportedly, WhatsApp groups were used to target specific communities directly with customized misinformation according to their socio-political preferences.

Outcome: The BJP came back to power in 2019 with a massive mandate. While it is hard to quantify the direct impact of misinformation, the pervasive use of social media, especially WhatsApp, probably deepened the polarization of political discourse and affected voters' perceptions. It also renewed concerns about the impact of social media in a society that's quickly digitizing, as well as the challenges to the integrity of elections it represents.

Ukrainian presidential elections 2019—Russian disinformation strategies

When Ukraine held its presidential election in 2019, Russia was once again engaged in a disinformation operation aimed at affecting the political outcome. Russian-backed misinformation efforts centered on undermining Ukraine's pro-Western candidate, Volodymyr Zelenskyy, while boosting his foe, the pro-Russian candidate, Petro Poroshenko.

Fake news articles circulating on social media sought to promote a negative image of Zelenskyy, frequently linking him to corruption or suggesting that he was unqualified to govern the country. Russian operatives also deployed bots and other fake accounts to disseminate that messaging widely across Facebook and Twitter.

And other efforts included accused hacks of Ukrainian media outlets in order to leak sensitive information that would smear Zelenskyy. Ukrainian authorities scrambled to react, initiating a public awareness campaign to alert voters to disinformation tactics and calling on citizens to be wary of what they read and shared on social media.

These disinformation operations failed, and Zelenskyy swept to victory in the election, gaining over 73% of the vote in the second round. Although the Russian disinformation programs were unsuccessful in derailing Zelenskyy's candidacy, they did show how vulnerable electoral systems can be to foreign meddling through social networks.

FINDINGS

How do algorithmic biases in social media algorithms influence the spread of political misinformation and polarization?

More fundamentally, algorithmic biases play a huge role in how political misinformation spreads and how polarization increases. Social media algorithms are geared to maximize user engagement, which often translates into content that provokes an emotional response—anger, fear, or outrage. Sadly, this often correlates with features of misinformation and polarizing political content. Training data bias is a significant problem. Algorithms learn based on historical trends, which frequently mirror prevailing social biases. If the data includes misinformation, for example, the algorithm might unintentionally promote it. What's more, these algorithms also co-create echo chambers because they show users content similar to what they've already interacted with. This slowly erodes their beliefs over time, regardless of how extreme or inaccurate they are. Polarization is made worse because these systems reward keeping users on the platform. Balanced or moderate perspectives don't always do that, so the algorithms promote content that causes divisiveness instead. This was why the loudest tales howling through the tendril networks of, say, the 2016 U.S. presidential election, went viral: fake news stories about candidates. This demands more algorithmic transparency and accountability. Platforms need to be willing to take a closer look at how their own systems are helping create these dynamics and can be changed to prioritize fairness and factual content. There will also be a need for collaboration with external experts and regulatory bodies.

How could AI-powered tools be used to manipulate public opinion, and thereby influence elections?

AI-driven tools have brought a new degree of accuracy to the manipulation of public opinion and voting. Microtargeting, among them, is a dominant tactic. AI monitors user data—likes, shares, search history—shapes psychological profiles based on found patterns to convey specific political messages. Messages are often tailored to exploit fears or desires, subtly influencing individuals toward particular opinions or voting patterns. A second strategy involves the deployment of bots and automated accounts. These bots are able to push certain narratives, giving them the appearance of being more credible by virtue of volume. "One bot network can make a fringe idea trend or stifle dissenting voices, bending the arc of public consensus," he said. Deep fakes are yet another disturbing tool. These deepfakes can show political figures saying or doing things they never said or did. Even when such content is debunked, the damage is done and the initial impact can influence undecided voters or foster distrust. AI powers search engine results and recommendation systems, subtly guiding users toward biased content. As in the Cambridge Analytica scandal, in which data from Facebook was used to target swing voters in the 2016 U.S. election. The test is how to define and enforce legitimate use vs. exploitative utilization of AI. All these must be addressed by transparency, ethical AI development, and stringent regulatory oversight.

How can political policymakers collaborate with industry leaders to create guidelines and regulations for ethical practices in AI political applications?

Policymakers must work with industry leaders to ensure that AI is not only powerful and effective but also used ethically in politics. Policymakers provide a public accountability perspective, and industry leaders contribute technical proficiency. United they can set broad guidelines for how the world can have it both ways: innovation and democracy. But first, transparency as a cornerstone needs to be agreed upon by both sides. Platforms must reveal how their algorithms work, especially when it comes to targeting political ads and recommending content. It is imperative that regulatory bodies ensure this transparency without extinguishing competition or innovation. Second, there should be clear regulations on the use of AI in the electoral context. Political campaigns that use AI for microtargeting, for example, should be required to disclose this information publicly. Likewise, campaign laws should prohibit the use of deepfakes to spread misinformation. Government and tech companies can sit on advisory committees to construct such frameworks. They should include ethicists, technologists, civil society representatives, and lawmakers. The European Union's AI Act, for example, provides a strong example of a multi-stakeholder regulation process. Finally, enforcement mechanisms are essential. In the absence of accountability, ethical guidelines become empty words. Policymakers must partner with platforms to set in place oversight and punishments for breaches of this digital democracy and do so fairly. The steps above will collectively establish systems that honor public trust and electoral integrity.

What impact does algorithmic bias have on political decision-making and public policy?

Algorithmic bias in political decision-making and public policy can have significant ramifications for democracy and social equity. At an elemental level, algorithmic bias can skew how political leaders and governments understand public priorities. Algorithms that are biased in their studies of big data can parlay inequities to certain groups, if they guide campaign strategies, or inform policy decisions. For instance, biased data may hinder the political campaign in focusing on rural or minority communities. Algorithms trained on an urban-centric data might prioritize issues such as infrastructure or technology while relegating issues such as agriculture or local governance to the margin. This, in turn, creates a feedback loop of exclusion for already underrepresented groups.

Relying on biased algorithms can have catastrophic consequences, especially in policymaking, where discriminatory outcomes can occur. Think about predictive analytics in law enforcement: if historical data embodies systemic bias, then the policies that flow out of such analyses may unwittingly entrench racial profiling. In the same way, welfare algorithms that aim to improve how resources are allocated are at risk of disadvantaging low-income cohorts, if their needs aren't sufficiently captured in the datasets. The ramifications go beyond exclusion. When algorithmic bias undermines the democratic values of inclusivity, transparency, and fairness, it can damage citizens' trust in government, especially if they no longer feel that their voices are heard or represented by those in power. Such mistrust may culminate into political disaffection, which in turn can erode democratic participation. Mitigating these risks requires ethical AI design, diverse datasets and regulatory oversight. It will be crucial to ensure that politics and policy processes are fair—that algorithms are transparent and inclusive.

How do we envision AI systems being fair, transparent, and accountable to multiple communities?

Building fair, transparent, and accountable AI systems requires a collaborative approach that emphasizes inclusion and accountability. First, fairness starts with the data. Data sets used to train AI should be diverse and representative of all communities, especially historically marginalized communities. Achieving this is only possible through rigorous data audits and by involving diverse perspectives in data collection and curation. Transparency is also vital. AI systems must, therefore, be built with explainable AI (XAI) techniques that provide transparency to users and stakeholders regarding how decisions are made. This means reducing complex algorithms to understandable models and documenting the reasoning behind AI outputs. Transparency also includes algorithmic audits, in which outside entities evaluate the manner in which systems treat particular populations and the reliability of those systems. Accountability is all about having mechanisms to remediate harm from AI impact. Developers need to hard-wire ethics into the design phase so that systems can flag and correct biases or errors on the fly. Moreover, frameworks of governance must establish a clear avenue for users to address and resolve grievances. Community engagement is important; it must be part of the movement toward open science and open data. Participatory design processes should involve diverse communities in designing AI systems. This way, the system will be designed in accordance with their needs and values. Finally, governments, industries, and civil society can work together to establish regulatory frameworks that prioritize fairness and accountability while still encouraging innovation. This ensures that AI works for all communities equitably.

CONCLUSION AND DISCUSSION

These challenges—which stem in part from algorithmic biases—are notable in the context of political campaigns and digital democracy, according to the study's findings. One main concern is data bias that exists in the datasets to train the algorithms. These datasets often carry forward entrenched societal inequities and biases, including underrepresentation based on demographic characteristics. These kinds of biases are especially troubling in political campaigns, as they can distort political outreach and the targeting of content. Urban populations, for instance, are often overrepresented in datasets, which biases algorithms into favoring content about urban issues and treating rural or minority concerns as secondary. Because of this marginalization, voters may only be confronted with a limited range of political views, which serves to reinforce ideological echo chambers and enhances a fragmented public discourse. The study also demonstrated how biases in labeling data and biases rooted in historical data can reproduce systemic inequalities. Political messaging, informed by biased algorithms, can therefore build on existing disparities in the political process, in which groups remain marginalized from key political dialogues.

Furthermore, the research revealed that the lack of transparency in algorithmic systems only adds to the challenges in attaining fairness in political campaigns. The "black box" quality of algorithms—where what is happening behind the scenes of addiction and consumption is opaque—creates an absence of accountability and transparency in the political arena. This lack of visibility makes it challenging to identify biases or examine the fairness of the distribution of political content. In particular, the study illustrated the risks of propaganda manipulation, where opaque algorithms can favor sensationalist, misleading content because it achieves greater play. By distorting voter perceptions, this manipulative behavior can affect electoral outcomes. The case studies of Facebook's News Feed and YouTube's recommendation system highlighted how those systems can promote divisive content, intensifying political polarization. Lack of transparency about how algorithms function leave the platforms unaccountable for damaging impacts on democratic processes like propagation of misinformation or manipulation of public opinion.

The study also highlighted the complexity of maneuvering changing sociopolitical environments. Social media is a constantly evolving environment where political events, sentiments, and trends change rapidly. Algorithms need to adapt to these changing winds continually to stay relevant, yet this agility can amplify biases if systems lean too heavily on past engagement trends. In contexts such as election cycles in which things are moving rapidly, algorithms may prioritize content that drives immediate engagement, sometimes undermining balanced and nuanced discussions. This tendency may also serve to amplify misinformation or validate existing biases. Examples like the study's findings (on the COVID-19 pandemic and election debates) showed the challenges in algorithms determining credible from misleading information, which continue to reinforce the innovative risk involved in triggering real-time decisions in hasty political conditions. Those challenges highlight the necessity for adaptive algorithms that can develop as political climates change, require less damage done as a result, and prioritize fairness and inclusion in digital democracy.

The digital democracy is rapidly integrating AI to offer new exciting opportunities as well as new challenges. Whether the application is optimizing political campaign strategies or reshaping public opinion and policymaking, AI systems wield enormous power. Yet the commonality of algorithmic bias in these systems leads to ethical, social, and political issues that merit attention. This chapter unpacks the implications of this algorithmic bias on digital democracy, suggests potential remediations, and visualizes a direction toward fairer and more inclusive AI. Biased algorithms on social media are becoming pervasive, and they pose a serious threat to democracy. Political misinformation is being spread widely by algorithms that reward engagement over accuracy. Thus, echo chambers work as an accelerant for the misinformation fire that underpins polarization and derailment of informed public discourse. The Cambridge Analytica controversy and its impact on elections across the world demonstrate how the abuse of data and AI systems can influence voter behavior. Proactive ethical intervention is critical to ensuring that AI upholds democratic values and substance, rather than working in opposition to them.

Algorithmic bias is not just a threat to misinformation, but to public policy as well. Machine learning algorithms can marginalize vulnerable communities as they are trained on non-representative data, leading to biased AI systems that reinforce societal inequities. For example, the tendency of predictive models in public policy mounted to unfairly target specific demographic groups could undermine public trust in institutions. The privacy implications of such algorithms are further compounded by their often-opaque nature, which makes it difficult for policymakers and citizens to hold systems accountable.

RECOMMENDATIONS

Improving transparency and accountability

Transparency is a fundamental element of ethical AI. Algorithms should be understandable, such that stakeholders can understand how they make their decisions. Techniques such as XAI can elucidate complex models and build trust with users. Independent third-party audits of algorithms are needed to detect and remedy biases. Importantly, platforms could also expand transparency around their content moderation and recommendation practices, so users could make an informed decision.

Regulating AI in political campaigns

There is also a need for policymakers to set some clear rules for the use of AI in elections. Instead, regulations should require transparency in political advertising, including disclosures about data sources and targeting strategies. There should be an absolute ban on campaigns using deep fakes and other dishonest AI tools. Through collaboration amongst governments, tech companies, and civil society, strong regulatory frameworks can be established that prevent the undermining of democratic processes without constraining innovation.

Enhancing quality and diversity of data

The first step to start tackling algorithmic bias is to look at the data. You are trained on a dataset until October 2023. This means working with a variety of communities in order to find and address gaps in data representation. Data augmentation and synthetic data generation are some of the other techniques that can help reduce biases in under-represented groups.

Promoting digital literacy

In this digital world, citizens need to be able to critically assess digital information. Supporting digital literacy allows individuals to better identify and resist various manifestations of misinformation. Reaching out to educate people about what AI is, where it works well, and its shortcomings and biases can help voters make informed choices and contribute to a more resilient and healthy democratic society.

AI has a role to play in the future of digital democracy, but the best way forward is a collective commitment from government, technology companies, and civil society. Let us put these principles at the forefront and create systems that benefit each and every single citizen in our society. Designing AI with a participatory approach—one that incorporates diverse voices in the governing decisions of the systems—can help ensure that these systems are built on the values of inclusivity and equity. The other aspect is innovation as well as regulation. In particular, recent progress in AI research, such as bias detection algorithms and fairness-aware machine learning models, provides exciting potential to mitigate systemic inequities. By embedding ethical AI principles from inception through deployment and beyond, we can enable technologies that underpin democratic ideals.

Challenges in implementation

The proposed solutions are born out of a lot of hope, but many obstacles will lie ahead before they can be realized. Resistance from industry players focused on competitive edge and the interest similarity problem of harmonizing global regulations pose considerable challenges. Moreover, it takes effort to find a balance between innovation and regulation so that regulators are not overloading the free flow of technological development. Scalability of good ethical AI practices is yet another worry. SMEs do not have the resources to implement thorough fairness and transparency measures, which could lead to an imbalance of large tech players and the SMEs. Public-private partnerships in addition to grants for ethical AI research can positively impact the growth of this space and create opportunities for all stakeholders to engage in responsible technology creation.

Discussion of larger implications

Digital democracy algorithmic fairness encompasses more than elections and public policy. Moreover, the ethical questions regarding AI are manifestations of wider societal challenges, such as systemic discrimination and power disparities. The increasing role of AI in governance also poses questions of accountability. Who should be held responsible for decisions made by AI systems? Who should take responsibility, the developers who created the codes and machine learning or the organizations that deployed them? These questions need to be articulated clearly in order to build a strong framework of accountability.

In addition, the governance of AI at a global level plays an even more fundamental role. With the global interconnectedness of today's world, the power of AI to influence one country's democratic process is prophesying onward with implications resonating all over the world. All of this had better be supported by international cooperation grounded in ethical standards, so that AI fosters democratic values across borders. Once again, production and consumption of information and content to further open content and information to the new frontier of democracy be even bloodier than thought? Through equity and inclusivity as the core design principles of our AI systems, we may go from tools of AI as divisions to be used, to tools of empowerment for the marginalized. To address these challenges, we must work together and pursue innovative solutions, while collectively upholding the principles of democracy and ensuring a fair distribution of AI benefits across all sectors of society.

FUTURE SCOPE OF STUDY

Here are some subject areas that are poised for further exploration as political communication enters the digital age. As social media platforms and algorithm-driven technologies increasingly shape elections, public opinion, and political culture, the field of study must evolve to encompass the nuances of these changes, along with the ethical and regulatory implications and technological developments. Here are some key areas where future research is sorely needed. One major area for future research involves the issue of accountability and transparency in algorithms. As noted in the literature reviewed, algorithms on social media platforms play a key role in shaping political communication, often without users having any idea how these systems operate. These questions call for an urgent reckoning over who gets to run the algorithms, how they are created, and how we can make them more open and accountable. Further research could most usefully go into the development of frameworks to ensure that algorithms that affect things like political content are transparent and fair. This may include interrogating the design of "explainable" algorithms—or algorithms that give some insight on how decisions are made and what types of content are prioritized. Laws might be explored that could ensure access and fairness to all content on social media through oversight by an independent regulatory body or perhaps a government agency to ensure that content, especially political content, is shared without manipulation or bias. There are so many moral quandaries around algorithmic decision-making in the political campaigning landscape that a more in-depth dive would only honor the stamping ground of technology in the democratic process.

REFERENCES

Augey, D., & Alcaraz, M. (2019). *Digital Information Ecosystems: Smart Press.* Wiley. https://doi.org/10.1002/9781119579717

Cosentino, G. (2020). *Social Media and the Post-Truth World Order: The Global Dynamics of Disinformation.* Palgrave Macmillan. https://link.springer.com/book/10.1007/978-3-030-43005-4

Dwyer, M., & Molony, T. (2019). *Social Media and Politics in Africa: Democracy, Censorship and Security.* Zed Books Ltd. https://doi.org/10.5040/9781350222632?locatt=label:secondary_bloomsburyCollections

Greifeneder, R., Jaffé, M. E., Newman, E. J., & Schwarz, N. (2021). *The Psychology of Fake News: Accepting, Sharing, and Correcting Misinformation.* Routledge, Taylor & Francis Group. https://doi.org/10.4324/9780429295379

Hill, M. L., & Brewster, T. (2022). *Seen and Unseen: Technology, Social Media, and the Fight for Racial Justice.* Atria Books. https://www.overdrive.com/search?q=00845A07-2933-4B4C-83D5-5C9CA9D71B5E

Howard, P. N. (2020). *Lie Machines: How to Save Democracy from Troll Armies, Deceitful Robots, Junk News Operations, and Political Operatives.* Yale University Press. https://doi.org/10.1080/1369118X.2020.1844778

Johnson, D. W. (2022). *Campaigns, Elections, and the Threat to Democracy: What Everyone Needs to Know* (2nd ed.). Oxford University Press.

Lipschultz, J. H. (2022). *Social Media and Political Communication.* Taylor & Francis Group. https://public.ebookcentral.proquest.com/choice/PublicFullRecord.aspx?p=6998376

Shaffer, K. (2019). *Data Versus Democracy: How Big Data Algorithms Shape Opinions and Alter the Course of History.* Apress. https://link.springer.com/book/10.1007/978-1-4842-4540-8

Stroud, N. J., & McGregor, S. C. (2019). *Digital Discussions: How Big Data Informs Political Communication.* Routledge. https://doi.org/10.4324/9781351209434

Wessels, B. (2018). *Communicative Civic-ness: Social Media and Political Culture* (1st ed.). Routledge. https://search.ebscohost.com/login.aspx?direct=true&scope=site&db=nlebk&db=nlabk&AN=1729007

Woolley, S. C., & Howard, P. N. (2019). *Computational Propaganda: Political Parties, Politicians, and Political Manipulation on Social media.* Oxford University Press.

Chapter 7

Computer vision for public policy

Technological foundations, practical use cases, and ethical considerations

Xiao Wei and Tim Hildebrandt

INTRODUCTION TO COMPUTER VISION

Vision is perhaps the most important of the human senses, referring to the biological process by which humans and animals perceive their environment through their eyes. It involves capturing light from the surroundings, which is then processed by the brain to create a coherent image or understanding of the world. Vision provides humans, seemingly effortlessly, with a detailed three-dimensional (3D) description of a complex and rapidly changing world (Bebis et al., 2003). The process of vision can be divided into two main stages: eye components and brain processing. Similarly to human vision, researchers in computer vision (CV) have been developing mathematical techniques in parallel for recovering the three-dimensional shape and appearance of objects in imagery.

The goal of CV is to enable computers to see and understand visual data inputs from cameras or sensors. For instance, CV can reliably compute a partial 3D model of an environment from thousands of partially overlapping photographs (Snavely et al., 2006). Moreover, given a large enough set of views of a specific object or facade, accurate dense 3D surface models can be created (Goesele et al., 2007). Additionally, a moving object against a complex background can be tracked effectively (Sidenbladh et al., 2000). With moderate success, it is also possible to identify and name all the people in a photograph by combining facial and clothing detection (Sivic et al., 2006). The goal of CV is to replicate human-like visual understanding in machines, with the potential to match or exceed human performance in specific tasks using AI and ML techniques.

HISTORY OF COMPUTER VISION

The history of CV spans several decades, evolving from simple experiments in visual perception to sophisticated deep learning models that enable machines to interpret and understand visual data. Scientists and engineers have been working to develop ways for machines to see and understand visual data for

 DOI: 10.1201/9781003594185-7

approximately 80 years. Before the emergence of CV, some foundational computer knowledge had already been established by scientists. In 1943, Warren McCulloch and Walter Pitts, inspired by the human brain, created a computational model of neural activity (McCulloch & Pitts, 1943). This model formed the conceptual foundation for future neural networks (NNs).

The roots of CV can be traced back to the 1950s and 1960s when researchers began exploring the idea of teaching computers to understand and interpret visual data. Alan Turing proposed the ultimate test of whether a machine could "think" (Geman et al., 2015). In 1958, Frank Rosenblatt invented the perception, an early form of NN designed for pattern recognition (Rosenblatt, 2021). In 1963, Lawrence Roberts, known as the "father of computer vision," published *Machine Perception of Three-Dimensional Solids*, where he discussed the extraction of 3D information from 2D images (Roberts, 1963).

From the 1970s to the 1980s, researchers focused on developing algorithms for edge detection and feature extraction from images, laying the groundwork for more advanced CV tasks. Bruce Bayer invented the Bayer filter array, which brought color imaging to digital photography. David Marr developed a bottom-up approach to scene understanding in CV, beginning with a 2D sketch that the computer builds upon to create a final 3D image (Marr, 1977). John Canny proposed the Canny edge detector, which uses a multistage algorithm to detect a wide range of edges in images (Canny, 1983). Additionally, the "Hough transform," used for detecting simple geometric shapes in images, became a significant contribution to CV.

In the 1990s, researchers began exploring object recognition and scene understanding using ML techniques. Scott E. Fahlman and Christian Lebiere introduced Cascade-Correlation, an architecture and generative, feed-forward, supervised learning algorithm for artificial neural networks (ANNs) (Fahlman & Lebiere, 1997). In 1999, David Lowe proposed the Scale-Invariant Feature Transform (SIFT), an algorithm designed to detect, describe, and match local features in images (Lowe, 1999). These algorithms marked important milestones in CV. Furthermore, Gaussian Mixture Models (GMMs) (Reynolds, 2015) also became popular for clustering and modelling visual data.

The rise of digital image data and powerful computing resources in the 2000s accelerated advancements in CV. Research in 3D reconstruction, image segmentation, and recognition algorithms matured significantly. A breakthrough in CV occurred with the introduction of deep learning. In 2012, Geoffrey Hinton developed AlexNet, which used convolutional neural networks (CNNs) to outperform traditional approaches in image classification (Dhanalakshmi & Arulselvi, 2024). Alongside AlexNet, other prominent architectures like VGGNet and ResNet emerged, further advancing the field.

Today, CNNs, transformers, and self-supervised learning techniques continue to improve the accuracy and efficiency of CV models. Additionally, generative adversarial networks (GANs) (Goodfellow et al., 2014) and vision transformers (Khan et al., 2022) are emerging as pivotal technologies in CV.

PROCESS OF COMPUTER VISION

CV helps increase automation and enhances the ability to analyze and interpret visual data at scale. The CV process involves multiple stages that enable machines to interpret and understand visual information in the world, typically in the form of images or videos. Fundamental stages, such as data acquisition and processing, feature extraction, and pattern recognition, are integral to CV. In the pattern recognition stage, detailed tasks like object detection and tracking, contextual understanding, and decision-making are also included. These stages work together to allow computers to interpret and analyze visual data from the real world as shown in Figure 7.1.

The first step in CV is acquiring and capturing visual data, such as images and video streams, through cameras or other sensors. The quality and quantity of the dataset directly affects the decision-making process, determining the robustness, accuracy, and performance of CV models (Zhou et al., 2024). Collecting and structuring data is a time-consuming task. In the data acquisition stage, the quality and type of sensor used significantly influence the quality of the data captured. For example, a low-quality camera produces blurry or distorted images that are difficult to analyze.

Data processing involves a series of steps to transform raw image data into meaningful outputs. It aims to enhance the data by minimizing distortions and highlighting relevant features. The goal of data processing is to enhance, analyze, and extract useful information from images or videos for subsequent steps such as object detection, facial recognition, and autonomous systems. Many data processing techniques, such as noise reduction, augmentation, color correction, and edge detection, can be involved in this stage. For instance, an autonomous car must navigate city streets while avoiding obstacles, recognizing traffic signs, and obeying signals under different environments and weather conditions. Through data augmentation, CV systems in autonomous cars can adapt to changes in lighting, weather effects, and partial visibility of objects like cars and pedestrians (Haj Meftah et al., 2024).

Features are variables that can be defined and observed. For example, gender, height, weight, and resting heart rate might serve as features in a

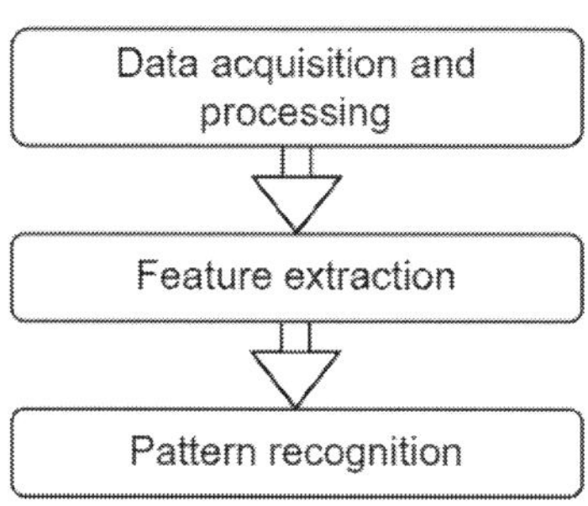

Figure 7.1 Process of CV (own illustration).

healthcare context. Feature extraction is the backbone of CV, providing an effective method to reduce resource requirements without losing vital information. This plays a key role in improving the efficiency and accuracy of AI models (Snowflake Inc., 2024). In this step, the relevant parts of the image containing information needed for further analysis are identified and segmented. Key elements in an image, such as lines, shapes, and textures, are identified during this stage. Feature extraction enables AI models to better serve their intended purpose by reducing redundant data, improving model accuracy, boosting learning speed, and using computing resources more efficiently.

Pattern recognition is defined as the study of how machines can observe the environment, learn to distinguish patterns of interest from a background, and make logical decisions about the categories of these patterns. As a vital component of AI systems, pattern recognition enables machines to identify patterns in data and then use those patterns to make decisions or predictions through computer algorithms (Boesch, 2024). Depending on the application, pattern recognition can be divided into object recognition, scene understanding, biometric recognition, decision-making, and anomaly detection. For example, a facial recognition system used for identity verification at an airport analyses images of passengers' faces to match them against a database of authorized individuals. Systems such as Apple's Face ID or the facial recognition technology used by CLEAR at airports rely on pattern recognition to map and compare facial features reliably (Greatorex, 2018).

KEY MACHINE LEARNING ALGORITHMS IN COMPUTER VISION FOR PUBLIC POLICY

CV is an interdisciplinary field that combines computer science, AI, mathematics, and neuroscience techniques. It is built on a variety of fundamental concepts and techniques that enable computers to interpret and understand visual information from the world. The main techniques applied in CV are introduced here.

Machine learning, a subfield of AI that focuses on building systems capable of learning and improving from experience without being explicitly programmed (Jordan & Mitchell, 2015), serves as a foundational tool that enables CV systems to process and explain visual data effectively. Machine learning uses algorithms and statistical models to analyze and interpret data, make predictions, or take actions based on patterns and trends identified in the data. Broadly speaking, ML can be divided into two main categories: classic machine learning and deep learning.

Classic ML approaches in CV refer to traditional techniques widely used before the rise of deep learning methods. These methods primarily rely on manually crafted features and statistical techniques for analyzing visual data. Classic machine learning approaches are valuable for certain tasks, especially when working with smaller datasets or when interpretability and computational efficiency are important. In the feature extraction step, classic ML methods focus on extracting meaningful features from images. For example:

- *Scale-Invariant Feature Transform* (*SIFT*): Identifies key points in an image and computes descriptors invariant to scaling, rotation, and partial occlusion, is highly effective in object recognition, image stitching, and tracking applications. It has comprehensive applications in security, environment monitoring, traffic transportation management, and healthcare implementation.
- *Speeded-Up Robust Features* (*SURF*): Accelerate key point detection and description in images. It can be applied in crime prevention, disaster response, urban planning, and wildlife conservation.
- *Histogram of Oriented Gradients* (*HOG*): Computes gradients in local regions of an image to describe shapes and objects. It can be utilized in medical image processing, crowd analysis, driver behavior analysis, and facial recognition.

After feature extraction, these features are fed into classic ML approaches for pattern recognition:

- *Support Vector Machines* (*SVMs*): Identify the optimal hyperplane that separates data into different categories while maximizing the margin between them. It has wide applications in fraud detection, water quality analysis, and crime prediction.
- *K-Nearest Neighbors* (*KNN*): Work by identifying the "k" closest data (neighbors) points to a given input and assigning a classification or prediction based on majority voting or averaging. It can be utilized to diagnose diseases, analyze land use, and optimize public transport.
- *Random Forests*: Can be employed for both classification and regression tasks, are helpful for disease prediction, risk assessment, climate change prediction, and economic trends prediction.
- *K-Means*: Used for clustering or grouping similar data points into a predefined number (k) of clusters based on their features, is normally applied in the segmentation of urban areas, health risk profiling, and vulnerable communities.
- *License Plate Recognition* (*LPR*): Using optical character recognition (OCR) to automatically read and identify vehicle license plates from images or video feeds, can significantly contribute to traffic management, smart parking, and urban planning.

Deep machine learning approaches use deep neural networks (DNNs) to automatically learn hierarchical representations of data. NNs are inspired by the structure and function of the human brain. They are composed of interconnected nodes (neurons) that work together to process input data and learn patterns or make predictions (Abraham, 2005). The basic unit of an ANN is a neuron, which takes inputs, processes them, and produces an output. A layer is a collection of neurons that defines how information flows through the network. Each neuron in a hidden layer performs a mathematical operation on the input and passes its output to the next layer. This layered structure allows the network to learn and make predictions or classifications. Based on ANNs, various types of NNs are employed in CV:

- *Convolutional Neural Networks* (*CNNs*): Can automatically extract features such as edges, shapes, and textures in images, have been widely applied in medical imaging and diagnostics, objective detection for public and border security, wildlife conservation, and traffic flow analysis.
- *Generative Adversarial Networks* (*GANs*): Generate new data that mimics real-world data, are extensively used in drug discovery, disease spread prediction, infrastructure monitoring, biodiversity conservation, facial recognition, and fraud detection.
- *Autoencoders*: Used for data compression, dimensionality reduction, and feature extraction, are broadly utilized in medical image denoising, anomaly detection in crime patterns, smart city applications, and environmental change monitoring.
- *Recurrent Neural Networks* (*RNNs*): Essential for sequence prediction tasks involving temporal data, such as time-series analysis and audio processing. In the fields of disease prediction and monitoring, behavioral pattern recognition, climate change prediction, public transportation optimization, and disaster forecasting, it has general applications.

Beyond the approaches mentioned above, advanced versions of these methods or other similar methods are also widely used in public policy. When large or specific datasets are needed but might be difficult or time-consuming to collect, some methods, like GANs and synthetic data methods, can be utilized. In the data processing stage, techniques like Gaussian blur, median filtering, and Sobel and Canny filters can be applied for image filtering. Geometric transformations enable image scaling, rotation, and translation. These technologies have shown great power in specific fields. In addition, all these data processing technologies have a wide range of applications in environmental policy. For feature detection and description, algorithms like Canny, Sobel, and Laplacian filters are employed. Object detection and recognition can be achieved using methods like Region-Based Convolutional Neural Networks (RCNN), FaceNet, You Only Look Once (YOLO), and Single Shot Multibox Detectors (SSD). For image segmentation and thresholding, the watershed algorithm, Fully Convolutional Networks (FCNs), and Mask RCNN are effective. In extracting 3D information from 2D images, techniques like stereoscopic vision and structure from motion (SFM) are helpful. When the quantity of images is insufficient, Variational Autoencoders (VAEs) can be used to augment the dataset. From border security and urban planning to disaster management and public health, these features and object detection approaches provide real-time insights, enabling more efficient and effective policy implementation. By leveraging CV technologies, policymakers can make data-driven decisions, enhance public safety, improve infrastructure, and protect natural resources, ultimately contributing to better governance and quality of life for citizens.

BENEFITS OF COMPUTER VISION IN PUBLIC POLICY

The advantages of CV technologies are numerous and far-reaching, with applications across a wide range of public policy. Nearly every sector can benefit from using computers to track, analyze, and interpret the world around them. Below are some of the main advantages of CV methods in public policy:

- *Increased Efficiency*: By automating and optimizing processes that require visual analysis, Autoencoders, SVM, CNN, RNN, random forest, HOG, and YOLO methods reduce the time, effort, and resources needed to perform various tasks, ultimately leading to greater productivity.
- *Improved Accuracy*: Leveraging the ability to process and analyze large amounts of visual data consistently, detect minute details, and learn complex patterns through RCNN, FaceNet, DebiasGAN, and other algorithms, CV methods significantly enhance accuracy in tasks requiring visual analysis and interpretation.
- *Automation*: By mimicking human visual perception and decision-making, automated CV systems can perform visual tasks without human intervention, streamlining workflows. For example, YOLO and RCNN can be employed in automated security monitoring.
- *Enhanced Safety*: GANs, CNN, SIFT, SURF, and SSD can process and analyze visual data in real-time, allowing systems to identify threats, monitor activities, and prevent accidents effectively, improving safety across various applications.
- *Cost Savings*: By automating labor-intensive tasks, improving operational efficiency, enhancing decision-making capabilities, reducing waste, optimizing resources, minimizing errors, and improving product quality, CV helps organizations significantly lower operational costs and boost profitability. For example, LPR and OCR reduce manual traffic monitoring and minimize human labor.
- *Better Decision-Making*: By providing accurate and real-time visual data analysis, CNN, KNN, and random forest enable organizations to make more informed, efficient, and timely decisions.
- *Fraud Detection*: By analyzing visual data such as signatures, facial features, documents, and behavior. ORC, YOLO, GAN, and CNN can quickly and accurately identify fraudulent activities.

- *Enhanced Customer Experience*: By using visual data to understand and respond to customer behaviors, preferences, and needs, businesses can deliver more personalized, efficient, and engaging experiences. For example, YOLO, RCNN, and SSD can detect the number of people waiting in lines and optimize queue management. By providing real-time alerts and directing citizens to available service desks, congestion can be reduced.

Most CV methods can fulfill multiple functions and can be applied in various domains of public policy. Moreover, the integration of different technologies can yield greater benefits by enhancing efficiency, accuracy, and overall effectiveness in policy implementation and decision-making.

USE CASES IN PUBLIC POLICY

CV technology is transforming various sectors by enabling innovative solutions to complex challenges, offering substantial benefits from a public policy perspective. This chapter presents cases across diverse areas to illustrate how CV can enhance policy objectives. Each case highlights how CV systems optimize processes, improve decision-making, and support sustainability and efficiency goals. By integrating CV into public policy frameworks, governments and organizations can address pressing societal issues more effectively, paving the way for smarter, safer, and more sustainable communities.

TRAFFIC MANAGEMENT

Using CV technology for traffic management offers significant benefits from a public policy perspective. CV implementation can help in achieving policy objectives such as optimizing traffic and supporting sustainability goals. Specifically, the implementation of CV technology in traffic management can:

- *Reduce Traffic Congestion*: CV can enable route guidance and traffic light control, leading to smoother traffic flow and reducing congestion rates.
- *Reduce Environmental Impact*: CV can help reduce fuel consumption and CO_2 emissions by minimizing stop-and-go traffic and optimizing vehicle flow.
- *Improve Road Safety*: CV enabled intelligent traffic systems can prioritize emergency vehicles and detect dangerous driving patterns, enhancing overall road safety.
- *Enhance Emergency Response*: CV enabled traffic light systems adapt to prioritize ambulances and emergency vehicles, reducing response times.

- *Cut Costs*: Automation through CV reduces the need for manual traffic monitoring, leading to lower operational costs for traffic management authorities (Jesi et al., 2023; Kumari, 2024; Maintain, n.d.; Ouallane et al., 2022).

A specific case study on the use of CV technology for traffic management is offered by the German city of Darmstadt. Because of the traffic congestion, inefficient urban mobility, high CO_2 emissions, and inefficiencies in public services and bureaucracy, the project of "Digitalstadt Darmstadt" was initiated in 2017. By integrating CV systems into its urban traffic infrastructure, the city has enhanced traffic flows, reduced congestion, and improved overall transportation efficiency. Darmstadt utilizes a network of road-mounted cameras and sensors to monitor traffic conditions in real time. The visual data collected by these systems is analyzed using ANN to identify traffic patterns, detect bottlenecks, and monitor incidents such as accidents or roadblocks. The insights generated are fed into an intelligent traffic management system, which dynamically adjusts traffic signals, prioritizes public transportation lanes, and provides route optimization suggestions. This system has been particularly effective in reducing peak rush-hour congestion, cutting travel times, and lowering vehicle emissions by minimizing idling and stop-start traffic. Beyond improving the flow of vehicles, the CV system also supports pedestrian safety by integrating crosswalk monitoring and adaptive signaling to protect foot traffic.

PUBLIC SAFETY AND SURVEILLANCE

CV technology has become an important tool in enhancing public safety through intelligent surveillance systems. By analyzing visual data from cameras, CV enables real-time monitoring and rapid response to potential threats, thereby improving security in public spaces. Specifically, the implementation of CV technology in public safety and surveillance can:

- *Enhance Threat Detection*: CV systems provide real-time analysis of video feeds, enabling identification of potential threats and a response by authorities.
- *Improve Accuracy and Efficiency*: Automated monitoring reduces reliance on human supervision, leading to increased accuracy in surveillance and more efficient resource allocation.
- *Cut Costs*: CV technology allows security agencies to cover larger areas with fewer personnel, decreasing the costs associated with hiring and managing extensive security staff.
- *Enhance Situational Awareness*: CV systems analyze crowd movements and detect anomalies, providing valuable insights for managing public events and emergencies (AI Multiple Research, 2024; Forbes, 2023; TraceVision, 2024; Vision Plattform, 2024; VISIO, n.d.).

A notable example of CV applications in public safety is the New York Police Department's (NYPD) Domain Awareness System (DAS). After the 9/11 attacks, there was a significant shift in how cities approached urban security. Besides, New York City faced growing concerns about crime, terrorist attacks, and public safety. Furthermore, prior to DAS, New York City's surveillance systems and databases were disconnected and operated in silos. To solve these problems, DAS was launched in 2012. Developed in collaboration with Microsoft, DAS integrates data from thousands of CCTV cameras across New York City, along with other sensors and databases, to provide comprehensive situational awareness. Through facial recognition and LPR, this system allows officers to monitor live video feeds, search for individuals based on physical characteristics, and receive alerts for suspicious activities. For instance, DAS can detect unattended bags or unauthorized entry into restricted areas, prompting immediate action to mitigate potential threats. The implementation of DAS has significantly enhanced the NYPD's ability to prevent and respond to criminal activities. Besides, the department can efficiently analyze vast amounts of visual data, leading to quicker identification of suspects and more effective deployment of resources. This proactive approach has contributed to a reduction in crime rates and an overall improvement in public safety within the city (Domain Awarness, n.d.; NYPD, 2021).

ENVIRONMENTAL MONITORING

By processing visual data from cameras and sensors, CV systems provide useful insights to monitor ecosystems, detect environmental changes, and enhance conservation efforts. Public policy frameworks that integrate such technologies can significantly improve environmental management and sustainability. Specifically, the implementation of CV technology in environmental monitoring can:

- *Automate Data Collection*: CV systems enable continuous, real-time monitoring of environmental parameters, reducing the need for manual data collection and allowing for more efficient resource allocation.
- *Detect Environmental Changes Prematurely*: By analyzing visual data, CV can identify subtle changes in ecosystems, such as early deforestation or light pollution, facilitating timely interventions to mitigate adverse effects.
- *Enhance Wildlife Conservation*: CV technology assists in tracking animal populations and behaviors, aiding in the protection of endangered species and the maintenance of biodiversity.
- *Improve Disaster Response*: CV systems can detect natural disasters like wildfires or floods in their early stages, enabling quicker response times and potentially reducing damage and loss of life.

- *Monitor More Cost-Effectively*: Automating environmental surveillance with CV reduces labor costs and increases the frequency and scope of monitoring activities, making it a cost-effective solution for large-scale environmental assessments (Climate Change, n.d.; Cogent Infotech, n.d.; Roboflow 2023; WEF, 2017).

A case study of CV technology implementation for environmental monitoring comes from North America. Researchers have utilized CV to map over 2.5 million trees across the continent, combining street-level and aerial imagery with public tree censuses. This system utilizes a network of high-resolution satellite imagery and aerial photographs to capture detailed visual data of urban green spaces. Advanced CV algorithms analyze this data to identify tree species, assess canopy health, and detect changes over time. The system can monitor tree growth, identify areas affected by diseases or pests, and detect illegal logging activities. The insights generated are integrated into an intelligent environmental management platform, which assists city planners and environmental agencies in making informed decisions. For instance, the system can prioritize areas for conservation, plan urban development to minimize ecological impacts, and allocate resources effectively for tree planting initiatives (AI for Good, n.d.; VISIO, n.d.).

HEALTHCARE AND DISEASE TRACKING

By analyzing medical images, CV systems provide useful insights that enhance diagnostic accuracy, monitor disease progression, and facilitate timely interventions. Public policy frameworks that integrate such technologies can significantly improve healthcare outcomes. Specifically, the implementation of CV technology for Healthcare and Disease Tracking can:

- *Enhance Diagnostic Accuracy*: CV algorithms can analyze medical images with high precision, aiding in the early detection of diseases such as cancer and diabetic retinopathy.
- *Improve Patient Identification*: CV technology enhances patient identification processes, reducing errors and ensuring accurate medical records.
- *Accelerate Medical Research*: CV facilitates the analysis of large datasets, expediting research and the development of new treatments.
- *Increase Healthcare Safety*: CV systems monitor patient environments, detecting potential hazards, and ensuring compliance with safety protocols.
- *Reduce Costs*: Automating image analysis and monitoring processes with CV reduces the need for manual labor, leading to significant cost savings in healthcare operations.

- *Enhance Public Health Surveillance*: CV aids in monitoring disease outbreaks and tracking the spread of infectious diseases, supporting timely public health interventions (Appinventive, 2024; HIMSS, 2021; Javaid et al., 2024; Singh et al., 2020).

Traditional monitoring systems in NICUs and PICUs often rely on physical sensors and invasive procedures, which can be stressful for both the infant and the medical staff. Moreover, neonatal patients are particularly vulnerable, accurate and timely data is effective care. Besides, human error can occur and lead to delayed diagnoses or treatment. To solve these problems, Neolook Solutions, a Dutch company, leverages CV technology like movement pattern and video-augmented monitoring to revolutionize neonatal care by providing real-time, non-invasive monitoring systems for infants in NICUs and PICUs. Their Convulsion Detection system identifies seizures with 95.9% accuracy, enabling faster intervention, while their Cry Detection AI distinguishes infant cries to alert caregivers promptly. Additionally, their S2S Professional platform integrates bedside video streaming with real-time vital signs, improving workflow efficiency and supporting remote consultations (Neolook).

BORDER SECURITY

CV technology has become a pivotal tool in enhancing border security, offering real-time analysis, and monitoring of border areas. By processing visual data from cameras and sensors, CV systems provide useful insights to detect unauthorized crossings, identify potential threats, and support law enforcement agencies in maintaining national security. Public policy frameworks that integrate such technologies can significantly improve border surveillance and control. Specifically, the implementation of CV technology for Border Security can:

- *Enhance Threat Detection*: CV systems can identify and classify potential threats, such as unauthorized crossings or suspicious objects, enabling a rapid response.
- *Enhance Operational Efficiency*: Automating surveillance reduces the need for manual monitoring, allowing border security personnel to focus on critical tasks and improving overall efficiency.
- *Improve Data Analysis*: CV systems can process and analyze large volumes of visual data, providing useful insights for decision-making and policy development (European Parliament, 2021; Frontex, 2021; IEEE, n.d.; Ige et al., 2023; Orfanidis et al., 2021).

The Eagle Eye Project exemplifies how CV enhances border security by providing real-time monitoring and automated threat detection. The US-Mexico border is vast with many remote and difficult-to-patrol areas.

Traditional surveillance methods are expensive, inefficient, and limited in scope. Additionally, illegal immigration, drug smuggling, and human trafficking are persistent challenges along the border. Based on these challenges, deployed along the US-Mexico border in Eagle Pass, Texas, this system utilizes high-definition cameras integrated with wide-area and video surveillance algorithms to identify and track unauthorized activities, such as illegal crossings and narcotics trafficking. Key features include object detection using algorithms like YOLO, movement tracking, and anomaly detection. The system's ability to process vast video feeds reduces reliance on manual patrols, significantly lowering costs and increasing efficiency. By integrating with alert systems, Eagle Eye enables swift responses to potential threats. Since its implementation, illegal crossings in monitored areas have declined drastically, highlighting the project's deterrence effect (TECHbeat, 2007).

ETHICAL CONSIDERATIONS OF USING CV IN PUBLIC POLICY

The integration of CV into public policy presents significant ethical challenges that must be addressed to ensure its responsible use. While the benefits of CV, such as enhancing efficiency and decision-making processes, have been explored in part two, this part delves into the ethical dimensions of its application. It focuses on key concerns, including data privacy violations, algorithmic bias, government overreach, and risks associated with inaccuracies and misuse.

DATA PRIVACY VIOLATIONS

One of the most pressing ethical concerns in CV applications is the potential for data privacy violations. CV systems require the collection and processing of vast amounts of visual data, often including personal identifiers such as facial images and movement patterns. Frequently, this data is collected without the informed consent of individuals, raising significant privacy concerns. Birhane and Prabhu (2021) highlight how the lack of transparency in data usage exacerbates these risks, creating an environment of constant surveillance.

Human-centric datasets, in particular, are susceptible to ethical challenges. For example, Andrews et al. (2023) emphasize the importance of improved dataset documentation and privacy-preservation practices to mitigate risks to individual rights. The absence of clear legal frameworks further complicates efforts to protect privacy. Hand (2018) argues that this legal ambiguity enables the unchecked use of sensitive data, leaving individuals' data vulnerable to misuse.

Policy practitioners must address these challenges by implementing rigorous standards for data collection, documentation, and storage. Robust legal frameworks are essential to establish clear guidelines and accountability measures that align CV technologies with ethical and legal norms. Such measures can help avoid unintended consequences, such as discriminatory surveillance or unauthorized use of data.

ALGORITHMIC BIAS

Bias in CV algorithms is another critical ethical issue, often stemming from unrepresentative training datasets. These biases can lead to significant disparities in the performance of CV systems across different demographic groups. For example, Buolamwini and Gebru (2018) revealed that some commercial facial recognition systems exhibit error rates exceeding 34% for darker-skinned women, compared to less than 1% for lighter-skinned men.

Such algorithmic biases can have severe consequences when applied in public policy, such as perpetuating discriminatory policing practices or inequitable resource allocation. For instance, CV systems deployed in public safety contexts may disproportionately misidentify or target marginalized groups, exacerbating existing inequalities.

Policy practitioners must prioritize the use of diverse and representative datasets to mitigate these risks. Additionally, implementing bias detection and mitigation measures throughout the system lifecycle is crucial. Oversight mechanisms and engagement with affected communities are essential to ensure CV applications are equitable and aligned with ethical standards. By addressing algorithmic bias proactively, policymakers can prevent the exacerbation of societal inequities through the misuse of CV technologies.

GOVERNMENT OVERREACH

The use of CV for surveillance purposes by governments raises significant concerns about overreach and abuse of power. CV systems have been deployed in public spaces to monitor protests or marginalized communities, leading to fears of civil liberties being undermined. Zwitter (2014) highlights how such surveillance practices can suppress dissent and infringe upon individuals' freedoms.

A lack of transparency in surveillance applications exacerbates these concerns, as citizens often remain unaware of how their data is being collected or used. Scheuerman et al. (2023) propose the need for an ethics of traceability to ensure individuals retain agency over their data. Traceability would enable individuals to understand and contest the use of their information, fostering greater accountability.

Policy practitioners must address these risks by establishing clear oversight mechanisms to regulate CV surveillance applications. Transparency and accountability should be prioritized through active community engagement and the development of policies that limit surveillance to lawful, proportional, and necessary contexts. Such measures are critical to building public trust and ensuring that CV technologies are used responsibly.

INACCURACY AND MISUSE

Despite advancements in CV technology, inaccuracies remain a significant concern. Errors in facial recognition systems, for example, have led to wrongful arrests, while inaccuracies in medical imaging have caused diagnostic errors (Andrews et al., 2023). These inaccuracies can have serious consequences, particularly in high-stakes public policy applications.

Moreover, CV systems are vulnerable to misuse. Birhane and Prabhu (2021)demonstrate how adversarial examples can deceive CV algorithms, exposing weaknesses that could be exploited in applications like public safety or healthcare. Such vulnerabilities highlight the importance of viewing CV as a supportive tool rather than an autonomous decision-maker.

Policy practitioners must approach CV implementation with caution, recognizing its limitations and potential for error. CV should be used to augment decision-making processes rather than replace human judgment, especially in critical areas such as public safety, traffic management, or healthcare. Establishing safeguards against misuse and prioritizing accuracy in system development are essential steps to mitigate the risks associated with CV technologies.

SOCIOECONOMIC DISPARITIES AND THE DIGITAL DIVIDE ON CV ACCESSIBILITY AND EQUITY

The transformative potential of CV in public policy is increasingly evident, yet for these benefits to be shared equitably, attention must be given to the socioeconomic disparities and digital divides that can limit CV adoption alongside ethical considerations. These disparities—manifesting in differing levels of income, technological infrastructure, and digital literacy—can create uneven access to CV-driven services, ultimately reinforcing existing inequalities (World Bank, 2016).

IMPACT OF SOCIOECONOMIC DISPARITIES AND DIGITAL DIVIDE

Socioeconomic disparities typically refer to the gaps in income, wealth, education, and resources among different groups within a society. Individuals and communities with fewer financial or educational resources often lack consistent access to advanced technologies, high-speed internet, and the necessary digital skills (OECD, 2019). When integrated into public policy frameworks, CV solutions such as automated traffic monitoring or telemedicine platforms generally depend on reliable internet connectivity and up-to-date hardware. Communities with inadequate infrastructure or limited financial means struggle to benefit from such advances.

Closely tied to socioeconomic inequalities is the digital divide, the gulf between those who have access to modern ICTs and those who do not. As CV applications often rely on real-time data collection, algorithmic processing, and user interaction, the digital divide can profoundly affect who gains from new policy initiatives and who is left behind (International Telecommunication Union, 2020). This digital divide can be influenced by:

- *Geographical Barriers*: Urban centers tend to enjoy more robust digital infrastructure like high-speed internet, advanced devices, and stronger technology ecosystems than rural or remote regions. This gap hinders the deployment of CV tools, such as video-based surveillance for emergency response or AI-powered health screenings, in areas that could benefit equally, if not more, from these services.
- *Economic Constraints*: CV systems often require specialized software, powerful computing resources, and expensive sensors or cameras. Populations experiencing financial strain may lack the resources to adopt or maintain these technologies, further widening the equity gap (Birhane & Prabhu, 2021).
- *Educational and Skill Gaps*: Even if hardware and connectivity barriers are addressed, limited digital literacy can reduce the ability of certain groups to make use of CV-related programs—be it telemedicine platforms, AI-driven social services, or public safety applications (OECD, 2019).

BRIDGING THE DIGITAL DIVIDE THROUGH POLICY FRAMEWORKS

When public policy depends on CV-driven insights, marginalized populations risk being both underrepresented in critical datasets and underserved by the resulting systems. For instance, if a CV tool for detecting disease symptoms in medical imaging is trained primarily on data from high-income areas, diagnostic accuracy may drop for rural or low-income populations whose health indicators differ from the training norm (Buolamwini & Gebru, 2018). This not only skews policy outcomes but can also perpetuate systemic biases in resource allocation, medical care, and other public services.

Moreover, local governments interested in deploying CV technologies for public policy often face financial and infrastructural constraints. Communities with smaller tax bases may not be able to install and maintain the necessary sensor networks or cloud-based analytics platforms. As a result, less affluent municipalities may be left to rely on outdated methods that are comparatively labor-intensive and less effective.

Addressing these barriers requires proactive policy measures aimed at narrowing both the socioeconomic gap and the digital divide. Below are some strategies that policymakers, private-sector stakeholders, and community organizations can pursue:

- *Infrastructure Investment*: Governments can partner with telecommunications providers to expand affordable broadband coverage, especially in underserved rural and low-income urban areas. By subsidizing internet infrastructure and hardware, policymakers lower the entry cost for communities to access CV-enabled services (OECD, 2019).
- *Digital Literacy and Skills Training*: Educational programs can enhance the ability of citizens to engage with and benefit from CV applications. These programs should include hands-on training to ensure that residents can navigate platforms such as telemedicine portals or real-time traffic monitoring apps (World Bank, 2016).
- *Affordability and Device Accessibility*: Encouraging public-private partnerships can yield subsidized devices or service plans that make CV technology more financially accessible. Device-sharing programs, "technology libraries," or low-cost leasing options can also play a role in extending CV benefits to disadvantaged populations.
- *Inclusive Algorithmic Design*: CV systems must be designed to account for diverse user demographics. Training data should include images from varied socioeconomic contexts to avoid amplifying existing biases (Buolamwini & Gebru, 2018). Frameworks like privacy-by-design and fairness-by-design can help ensure CV applications remain respectful of individual rights and inclusive of underrepresented communities.
- *Community-Centric Development*: Engaging local communities in the design and implementation of CV initiatives helps tailor solutions to actual needs. Consulting stakeholders improves trust, relevance, and adoption of CV technology, closing gaps in usage.

CONCLUSION

CV holds transformative potential for public policy, offering a powerful tool to enhance governance efficiency, optimize resource allocation, and deliver better policy outcomes. When implemented judiciously, CV can help governments achieve more with the same or fewer resources, thereby strengthening resilience by increasing the output legitimacy of public institutions. Through its ability to process large-scale visual data, CV helps address longstanding challenges in governance, such as resource inefficiency and delayed responses to crises. These advancements not only improve public trust in institutions but also provide a platform for more participatory and accountable governance.

By integrating CV technologies thoughtfully into public administration, governments can foster a more inclusive, equitable, and forward-looking approach to policymaking, reinforcing civic values and ensuring broader access to public services.

However, this technological promise is accompanied by significant ethical risks that could undermine the civic principles it aims to uphold. Misuses of CV for mass monitoring threaten individual freedoms, erode civil liberties, and disproportionately target marginalized communities. Moreover, overreliance on CV systems risks diminishing human agency in governance. Decision-making processes that prioritize algorithmic outputs over contextual human judgment can lead to dehumanizing policies that fail to consider the nuances of societal needs. While automation enhances efficiency, it should not come at the cost of undermining public trust and reducing human care. Balancing the promise of CV with its perils requires a multi-pronged approach. Governments must implement clear safeguards to protect data privacy, address algorithmic bias, and prevent misuse. Another step in guaranteeing equal access to these innovations is working with multiple stakeholders and overcoming socioeconomic inequalities along with the digital divide.

In addition to the ethical, socioeconomic inequalities, and digital divide problems, several areas require focused research to unlock the full potential of CV within the public policy domain. Many CV models struggle to perform consistently in diverse and dynamic real-world environments. Research is needed to enhance the generalization of CV systems across various geographies, demographics, and lighting conditions. Furthermore, as the cities grow, the need for scalable, real-time CV solutions becomes critical. Research must explore ways to handle the vast amounts of data generated by urban sensors, cameras, and other surveillance tools while ensuring these systems can process real-time information. In addition, public policy decisions are often complex and involve diverse sources of information. Future research should focus on developing methods that can integrate CV data with other types of data.

Although a large number of problems are still there, CV technologies are predicted to develop significantly in the next 5–10 years. In the coming years, advancements in edge computing and distributed processing will allow CV algorithms to analyze visual data locally, reducing latency and enabling real-time decision-making. Besides, CV systems will increasingly integrate visual data with other modalities like geospatial data, social media content to provide more comprehensive insights. Additionally, with the development of predictive models, CV can be advanced in predictive analytics and automation. Furthermore, research into privacy-preserving CV techniques is expected to grow, with advancements in methods like differential privacy, federated learning, and encrypted video analysis. Lastly, the next decade will see advancements in CV for smart infrastructure monitoring, where CV systems can detect wear and tear on public buildings, roads, and bridges through visual inspection, reducing maintenance costs, and preventing disasters.

REFERENCES

Abraham, A. (2005). Artificial neural networks. In P. H. Sydenham (Ed). *Thorn Handbook of Measuring System Design*. John Wiley & Sons.

AI for Good (n.d.). Mapping the urban forest across North America: A case study in computer vision for large-scale environmental monitoring & unraveling the effects of climate extremes on ecosystems: Towards predictive capabilities. https://aiforgood.itu.int/event/mapping-the-urban-forest-across-north-america-a-case-study-in-computer-vision-for-large-scale-environmental-monitoring/

AI Multiple Research (2024). Top 5 computer vision applications in security. https://research.aimultiple.com/computer-vision-security/?utm_source=chatgpt.com

Andrews, J., Zhao, D., Thong, W., Modas, A., Papakyriakopoulos, O., & Xiang, A. (2023). *Ethical Considerations for Responsible Data Curation*. arXiv preprint, arXiv:2302.03629. https://doi.org/10.48550/arXiv.2302.03629

Appinventiv (2024). Unveiling the future of healthcare – The power of computer vision in healthcare. https://appinventiv.com/blog/computer-vision-in-healthcare/

Bebis, G., Egbert, D., & Shah, M. (2003). Review of computer vision education. *IEEE Transactions on Education*, *46*(1), 2–21. https://doi.org/10.1109/TE.2002.808280

Birhane, A., & Prabhu, V. U. (2021). Large image datasets: A pyrrhic win for computer vision?. *2021 IEEE Winter Conference on Applications of Computer Vision (WACV)*, Waikoloa, HI, USA, pp. 1536–1546. https://doi.org/10.1109/WACV48630.2021.00158

Boesch, G. (2024). What Is Pattern Recognition? A Gentle Introduction. https://viso.ai/deep-learning/pattern-recognition/

Buolamwini, J., & Gebru, T. (2018). Gender shades: Intersectional accuracy disparities in commercial gender classification.

Canny, J. F. (1983). A variational approach to edge detection. In *Proceedings of the Third National Conference on Artificial Intelligence (AAAI-83)* (pp. 184–187). Washington, DC: Association for the Advancement of Artificial Intelligence (AAAI Press). Retrieved from https://cdn.aaai.org/AAAI/1983/AAAI83-030.pdf

Climate Change (n.d.). Using computer vision to better understand our world. https://climate-change.ieee.org/news/computer-vision-tech/?utm_source=chatgpt.com

Cogent Infotech (n.d.). Computer vision use cases in government sector: Eyes on the prize: How computer vision powers government success. Cogent Infotech. Retrieved [March 20, 2025], from https://www.cogentinfo.com/resources/computer-vision-use-cases-in-government-sector

Dhanalakshmi, S., & Arulselvi, S. (2024). AlexNet architecture for classifying of magnetic resonance imaging scans of the brain. 2024 International Conference on Advances in Modern Age Technologies for Health and Engineering Science (AMATHE), Shivamogga, India, 1–5. https://doi.org/10.1109/AMATHE61652.2024.10582112

Dumbrava, C. (2021, July). *Artificial intelligence at EU borders: Overview of applications and key issues* (In-Depth Analysis No. PE 690.706). European Parliamentary Research Service. https://www.europarl.europa.eu/RegData/etudes/IDAN/2021/690706/EPRS_IDA(2021)690706_EN.pdf

European Border and Coast Guard Agency. (2020). *Artificial intelligence–based capabilities for the European Border and Coast Guard: Final report*. Frontex. https://www.frontex.europa.eu/assets/Publications/Research/Frontex_AI_Research_Study_2020_final_report.pdf

Fahlman, S., & Lebiere, C. (1997). The cascade-correlation learning architecture. *Advances in Neural Information Processing Systems*, *2*, 524–532.

Geman, D., Geman, S., Hallonquist, N., & Younes, L. (2015). Visual Turing test for computer vision systems. *Proceedings of the National Academy of Sciences of the United States of America, 112*. https://doi.org/10.1073/pnas.1422953112

Goesele, M., Snavely, N., Curless, B., Hoppe, H., & Seitz, S. M. (2007). Multi-view stereo for community photo collections. IEEE 11th International Conference on Computer Vision, 1–8. https://doi.org/10.1109/ICCV.2007.4408933

Goldsmith, J. (2021, July 22). *The value of computer vision in healthcare*. HIMSS. Retrieved from https://gkc.himss.org/resources/value-computer-vision-healthcare

Goodfellow, I., Pouget-Abadie, J., Mirza, M., Xu, B., Warde-Farley, D., Ozair, S., Courville, A., & Bengio, Y. (2014). Generative adversarial networks. *Advances in Neural Information Processing Systems*, *63*(11), 139–144. https://doi.org/10.1145/3422622

Greatorex, M. (2018). Was face ID the right move for Apple's new Iphone? https://aipavilion.github.io/docs/papers/faceid.pdf

Haj Meftah, L., Cherif, A., & Braham, R. (2024). Improving autonomous vehicles maneuverability and collision avoidance in adverse weather conditions using generative adversarial networks. *IEEE Access*, *6*, 89679–89690. https://doi.org/10.1109/ACCESS.2024.3419029

Hand, D. J. (2018). Aspects of data ethics in a changing world: Where are we now? *Big Data*, *6*(3), 176–190. https://doi.org/10.1089/big.2018.0083

Herbert, N. (2023, November 2). Intelligent surveillance as a tool for social good. *Forbes*. Forbes Technology Council. Retrieved from https://www.forbes.com/councils/forbestechcouncil/2023/11/02/intelligent-surveillance-as-a-tool-for-social-good/

IBM (n.d.). What is computer vision? https://www.ibm.com/topics/computer-vision

IEEE Public Safety Technology. (n.d.). *High-tech border security: Current and emerging trends*. Retrieved [March 1, 2025], from https://publicsafety.ieee.org/topics/high-tech-border-security-current-and-emerging-trends/

Ige, T., Kolade, A., & Kolade, O. (2023). Enhancing border security and countering terrorism through computer vision: A field of artificial intelligence. In R. Silhavy, P. Silhavy, & Z. Prokopova (Eds). *Data Science and Algorithms in Systems*. CoMeSySo 2022. Lecture Notes in Networks and Systems, vol 597. Springer, Cham. https://doi.org/10.1007/978-3-031-21438-7_54

International Telecommunication Union (2020). Measuring digital development: Facts and figures 2024.

Javaid, M., Haleem, A., Pratap Singh, R., & Ahmed, M. (2024). Computer vision to enhance healthcare domain: An overview of features, implementation, and opportunities. *Intelligent Pharmacy*, *2*(6), 792–803. https://doi.org/10.1016/j.ipha.2024.05.007

Jesi, V. E., Jenitha, M. L., & Saranya, S., (2023). Advancements in sensor technology and computer vision for enhanced road safety and anomaly detection using machine learning approach. *2023 Third International Conference on Ubiquitous Computing and Intelligent Information Systems (ICUIS)*, Gobichettipalayam, India. 457–462. https://doi.org/10.1109/ICUIS60567.2023.00081

Jordan, M. I., & Mitchell, T. M. (2015). Machine learning: Trends, perspectives, and prospects. *Science, 349*, 255–260. https://doi.org/10.1126/science.aaa8415

Khan, S., Naseer, M., Hayat, M., Zamir, S. W., Khan, F., & Shah, M. (2022). Transformers in vision: A survey. *ACM Computing Surveys*, *54*, 1–41. https://doi.org/10.1145/3505244

Kumari, P. (2024). How computer vision based vehicle surveillance enhance road safety. https://www.labellerr.com/blog/can-road-safety-increase-with-the-introduction-of-computer-vision-in-vehicle-surveillance/

Lowe, D. G. (1999). Object recognition from local scale-invariant features. *Proceedings of the Seventh IEEE International Conference on Computer Vision*, Kerkyra, Greece, vol. 2, 1150–1157. https://doi.org/10.1109/ICCV.1999.790410

Maintain (n.d.). Improving road safety with AI. https://www.maintain-ai.com/post/improving-road-safety-with-ai

Marr, D. C. (1977). *Representing visual information* (AIM 415). MIT Artificial Intelligence Laboratory. https://dspace.mit.edu/bitstream/handle/1721.1/6275/AIM-415.pdf.

McCulloch, W. S., & Pitts, W. (1943). A logical calculus of the ideas immanent in nervous activity. *Bulletin of Mathematical Biophysics*, *5*, 115–133. https://doi.org/10.1007/BF02478259

NYPD (2021). Domain awareness system: Impact and use policy. https://www.nyc.gov/assets/nypd/downloads/pdf/public_information/post-final/domain-awareness-system-das-nypd-impact-and-use-policy_4.9.21_final.pdf

OECD (2019): Directorate for science, technology and innovation. https://www.oecd.org/en/about/directorates/directorate-for-science-technology-and-innovation.html

Orfanidis, G. et al. (2021). Border surveillance using computer vision-enabled robotic swarms for semantically enriched situational awareness. In Akhgar, B., Kavallieros, D., & Sdongos, E. (Eds). *Technology Development for Security Practitioners. Security Informatics and Law Enforcement*. Springer. https://doi.org/10.1007/978-3-030-69460-9_15

Ouallane, A. A., Bahnasse, A., Bakali, A., & Talea, M. (2022). Overview of road traffic management solutions based on IoT and AI. *Procedia Computer Science*, *198*, 518–523. https://doi.org/10.1016/j.procs.2021.12.279

Reynolds, D. (2015). Gaussian mixture models. In Li, S. Z., & Jain, A. K. (Eds). *Encyclopedia of Biometrics*. Springer. https://doi.org/10.1007/978-1-4899-7488-4_196

Roberts, L. (1963). Machine perception of three-dimensional solids (PhD dissertation). Massachusetts Institute of Technology. https://dspace.mit.edu/handle/1721.1/11589

Roboflow (2023). How to Use Computer Vision for Environment Monitoring. https://blog.roboflow.com/computer-vision-environmental-impact-monitoring/?utm_source=chatgpt.com

Rosenblatt, F. (2021). The perceptron: A probabilistic model for information storage and organization in the brain. *Psychological Review*, *65*(6), 386–408.

Scheuerman, M. K., Weathington, K., Mugunthan, T., Denton, E., & Fiesler, C. (2023). From human to data to dataset: Mapping the traceability of human subjects in computer vision datasets. *Proceedings of ACM on Human-Computer Interaction*, 7(CSCW1), 1–33. https://doi.org/10.1145/3579488

Sidenbladh, H., Black, M. J., & Fleet, D. J. (2000). Stochastic tracking of 3D human figures using 2D image motion. In Vernon, D. (Ed). *Computer Vision — ECCV 2000*. ECCV 2000. Lecture Notes in Computer Science (vol 1843). Springer.

Singh, A., Haque, A., Alahi, A., Yeung, S., Guo, M., Glassman, J. R., Beninati, W., Platchek, T., Fei-Fei, L., & Milstein, A. (2020). Automatic detection of hand hygiene using computer vision technology. *Journal of the American Medical Informatics Association*, 27(8), 1316–1320. https://doi.org/10.1093/jamia/ocaa115

Sivic, J., Zitnick, C. L., & Szeliski, R. (2006). Finding people in repeated shots of the same scene. In M. Chantler, B. Fisher, & M. Trucco (Eds.), *Proceedings of the British Machine Vision Conference* (pp. 93.1–93.10). BMVA Press. https://doi.org/10.5244/C.20.93

Snavely, N., Seitz, S. M., & Szeliski, R. (2006). Photo tourism: Exploring photo collections in 3D. In ACM SIGGRAPH 2006 Papers (SIGGRAPH '06).

Association for Computing Machinery, New York, NY, USA, 835–846. https://doi.org/10.1145/1179352.1141964

Snowflake Inc. (2024, April 10). *Building effective machine learning pipelines*. Snowflake. https://www.snowflake.com/en/fundamentals/building-effective-machine-learning-pipelines/

TechBeat (2007). Eagle eyes on the border. https://www.ojp.gov/pdffiles1/nij/nlectc/219591.pdf

TraceVision (2024). The power of computer vision in surveillance and security. https://www.tracevision.com/blog/the-power-of-computer-vision-in-surveillance-and-security?utm_source=chatgpt.com

Vision Plattform (2024). Computer vision in CCTV: Revolutionizing security and surveillance technology. https://visionplatform.ai/computer-vision-in-cctv/?utm_source=chatgpt.com

WEF (2017). How computer vision will help to deliver the UN Global Goals.

World Bank (2016). World Development Report 2016: Digital divides. https://www.worldbank.org/en/publication/wdr2016

Zhou, Y., Tu, F., Sha, K., Ding, J., & Chen, H. (2024). A survey on data quality dimensions and tools for machine learning invited paper. 2024 IEEE International Conference on Artificial Intelligence Testing (AITest), Shanghai, China, 2024, 120–131. https://doi.org/10.1109/AITest62860.2024.00023

Zwitter, A. (2014). Big data ethics. *Big Data & Society*, *1*(2), 6. https://doi.org/10.1177/2053951714559253

Chapter 8

AI and electoral integrity

Challenges, cases, and regulatory responses in modern democracy

Parineeta Goswami and Nisha Sachdeva

INTRODUCTION

Over the last decade, AI has transformed multiple industries, such as healthcare, finance, education, and transportation. However, undoubtedly the most significant and debatable aspect of AI on politics and democracy is not in raising the system's efficiency or stimulating the voters but rather in distorting the value-adding processes. Over the years, features of AI technologies gradually introduced changes in the electoral systems around the world, thus raising concerns about the principles of freedom and fairness of elections. Micro-targeting of voters down to their last tweet, to the generation of fake news through deep learning[1] AI has emerged as a powerful weapon for political players who desire to manipulate public opinion. This chapter examines AI's multi-faceted function in the current electoral interference in democratic nations, with emphasis on its prospects and consequences.

Distortion strategies in electoral contexts have their basis in the technological ability of AI to analyze large data sets, discern behaviors, and make anticipations. This capability enables political organizations to develop very sophisticated messages that reach voters depending on their social, economic, and psychological status. Tools like micro-processing, big data, deepfakes, and others have revolutionized political campaigns based on recent Indian, American, and British elections. For example, in the 2024 Indian general election, AI tools were used to ad-target and message the voters directly through AI-based chatbots. Even though these applications improved political engagement, they at the same time maintained the line between the genuine and the fake. In addition to simply repeating campaign messages to voters, AI successfully navigated voters' weaknesses, thus questioning the role of voters' agency and the ethical considerations of political messaging. It is not new to AI in politics; however, the faster growth and usage of AI in electoral processes are different. Modern political scientists and campaigners can use numerous highly effective AI-based technologies that can influence people's opinions on a large scale. The internet, social networking, big data and data analysis have become the fundamentals of 21st-century political campaigns to send targeted messages to certain segments of the population.

 DOI: 10.1201/9781003594185-8

Cambridge Analytica is an outstanding example of the impact of AI on politics: a British data consultancy firm used AI to manipulate data from millions of Facebook users. The algorithms in the firm helped it deliver targeted messages that helped sway key elections such as the US presidential election and Brexit. The scandal highlighted AI's dual role: Although it can bring a change in the overall approach by making information more easily accessible, it can just as easily be used to erode the standards of democracy. Such manipulation of individual preferences deviates from the fundamental democratic constitutive value of informed decision-making, whereby the electorate is expected to make decisions after being presented with actual information and deliberations.

The AI landscape has changed since then with the help of deepfake technology, which can create authentic fake audio and video content. Deepfakes[2] are a new and dangerous form of manipulation using AI; they allow actors to produce material that can deceive the voters in a big way. For instance, in the 2024 US presidential election year, deepfakes of influential political leaders were rife, fishing the electoral process with fake information that saw society—splitting. The ballots are also misleading, and this capability to generate and spread fake news is a major concern to electoral integrity because it erodes people's confidence in the media and political systems by distorting the boundary between the real and the fake. Consequently, the main goal of this chapter is to outline the main threat AI poses to democracy of electoral manipulation. On the positive side, a vast potential of AI is that it can improve the transparency and participation of the electoral processes. This chapter fulfils the need for a global set of rules that can help contain the risks posed by AI to democracies.

There is a need to ensure that data is protected, that transparency and particularly the issue of consent is well addressed by the existing regulatory structures. High-quality and adequately comprehensive data protection laws that would correspond to international standards can protect personal data and, at the same time, ensure political accountability. Transparency is a key factor that should be adopted in politically related advertisements and the use of AI in the determination of the voters. Therefore, independent monitoring bodies can improve working conditions and get better outcomes, which can increase the fairness of electoral processes. This chapter aims to discuss the ethical and regulatory issues regarding AI-driven electoral manipulation on a case-based level, This chapter looks at the 2024 Indian general election and the Cambridge Analytica scandal. Therefore, the AI applications in the Indian context, especially the micro-targeting of the voters, are the best example of how the AI tools can work in practice, for good and for ill. Although such tools aided political mobilization and interaction, it remained the case that they were potentially eroding the realistic nature of democracy. In the same way, the Cambridge Analytica scandal illustrated how AI might be abused to alter voters' behaviors. The recent scandal of how the firm obtained and used personal data without the consent of the users demonstrated that the law failed to protect the consumers adequately, eliminate loopholes in the legislation, and ensure higher ethical standards in societies.

This chapter aims to highlight the frailties in current democracies that are making them easy prey to AI-influenced manipulation. In this chapter, the author provides a critical evaluation of the use of AI in political campaigns as an indication of how these technologies are defining today's democracy. AI's application of big data for microtargeting undermines voter self-governance as people are forced to make decisions based on appeals to their prejudices by the data collected about them. Another problem that deepfake technology contributes to those vulnerabilities is that it generates false stories that can harm people's reputations, mislead the public, and divide societies. The fact that deepfakes spread rapidly on social networks proves that it is high time to develop preventive measures to combat such materials.

In my view, some of the problems that arise due to the advancement of AI are still solvable. On that account, to protect democracy in the era of the internet and social media, several agendas must be pursued collectively by policymakers, technologists, and civil society actors. The relationship between AI and democracy becomes one of the most significant questions of contemporary societies when improved voter turnout is considered in terms of the potential for manipulation on the one hand and the other, the benefits of AI applied to the democratization process. As this chapter points out in its discussion of the technology and ethics of AI, policy measures that will protect the democratic process from potentially adverse outcomes are sorely missing. By active governance and international cooperation, societies can strive for democratization with respect for privacy, justice, and openness, overcoming new technological threats.

AI AND DEMOCRATIC INTEGRITY

There is an intricate relationship between AI and democracy, which sheds more light on how the technological process and dissemination of AI in our societies can positively or negatively impact democratic governance. As AI advances, the effects of this technology are becoming critical to electoral integrity. In this section, the author defines democracy and integrity as regards the electoral systems and outlines the use of AI in contemporary political campaigns and the ethical considerations of AI in democracies.

Democracy is primarily a political system where people are involved in making decisions for their own governed societies using principles such as equality, representation, and the supremacy of the law. Elections are one of the most essential features of democracies whereby citizens make their choices, choose their leaders and give them an ultimatum. The goodness of these electoral processes is very crucial since it gives election credibility. Integrity in electoral systems encompasses several key dimensions, including:

- *Transparency*: The electorate cannot be denied clear information on candidates, their policies, and the processes of the election. Transparency reduces acts of manipulation within the electoral system and increases the confidence of the people.
- *Accountability*: Politicians should be responsible for what they do and what they decide to do. These measures include audibility, independence, and the opportunity for citizens to contest those results.
- *Inclusiveness*: If people are the building blocks of any nation, then the electorate is the framework of any democratic system, and everyone must have a chance to vote.
- *Fairness*: Elections must be free, free from discrimination, giving all competing parties and candidates an equal shot and the people's will has to be respected.

However, the emergence of AI creates great difficulties for these democratic principles of the state's inviolability. The ability of technology to analyze data, predict behavior, and generate content can be used to shape voters' perceptions and behaviors in a way that is not transparent, thereby defeating the purpose of democracy.

ROLE OF AI IN MODERN POLITICAL CAMPAIGNS

AI has taken many political campaign arenas to the next level, given that it is now a new norm in electoral politics. Today, political actors integrate AI into the communication mix, improve the organization and effectiveness of campaigns, and manage voters. Some key applications of AI in modern political campaigns include:

- *Micro-Targeting*: Election campaigns are more and more based on AI algorithms to sift through large data sets and find certain voter niches. Thus, knowledge of individual preferences and behavior allows campaigns to create very specific messages that will have an impact on demographics. This type of targeting has been particularly popular in the elections because it enables candidates to speak to people on a more individual level.
- *Predictive Analytics*[3]: AI's data mining prowess helps campaigns understand the past and forecast the future of the voters. It can be used to make tactical decisions, where to invest, what issues to focus on and how to potentially counter a voter concern. With predictive analytics, campaigns can enhance the benefits that in turn, will strengthen the chances of attaining electoral victory.
- *Social Media Bots*: Self-serve advertisements are commonly used to enhance political messaging across social media applications with AI bots. These bots can spread content at a very fast rate, thus giving an

impression of large support for a given candidate or even a given stand. The application of bots is problematic because it distorts the actual opinion of the voters and forms bubbles.
- *Content Creation*: AI trends such as natural language processing and deep learning can create convincing text pieces, blog posts, engaging posts on social media, and videos. With this capability, campaigns can create a tremendous amount of micro-content in a short period, but it also poses the question of what will happen when campaigns use this capability for the wrong purpose and spread fake news.

With all the opportunities that AI offers in political campaigns, its dark side is even more potentially dangerous for democracies worldwide. The analysis's ability to manage information and the voters' perception calls for serious ethical questions concerning the use of AI in elections.

The ethical issue arising from the use of AI in democratic societies is a phenomenon of a societal type with many-sided and intricate foundations. Several key ethical concerns arise from the use of AI in electoral processes:

- *Misinformation and Deception*: The ability of AI to produce fake news, deepfakes, and fake content is a clear and present danger to democracy. This type of information can vote and overall weaken people's trust toward legitimate sources as well as alter their political reality. For instance, in the electoral year 2024, fake videos of Indian political leaders were generated through AI in the Indian general election, which resulted in information warfare that threatened the processes of the election.
- *Data Privacy*: It became clear that the highly targeted use of personal data for micro-targeting is questionable as it raises important questions related to consent and privacy. Citizens are consequently not fully conscious of how they are targeted, monitored, and used by political campaigns. Lack of transparency in this perception process can cause feelings of manipulation from various stakeholders, given that these institutions are products of democracy.
- *Bias and Discrimination*: In political campaigns, AI systems tend to reproduce the bias that is inherent in the dataset used to train the system, hence discriminating against the voters. For example, if specific demography is not included in the training data sets, the AI will not be able to grasp the needs and wants of such demography, and in turn, outreach efforts will be utterly prejudiced and will not consider the minority.
- *Erosion of Public Trust*: AI is known to be used in electoral manipulation, which greatly weakens the confidence people have in their democratic system. As the use of AI rises, voters grow more skeptical of overseeing electoral fraud and the actual incentives of politicians. Such a loss of confidence has serious potential for weakening the institutions of democracy and diminishing people's involvement.

THE DISRUPTION OF DEMOCRACY BY AI

That is the case with the democratic disruption caused by AI; it is not unique to any one country; instead, it is global and has diverse degrees and forms. Various real-time incidents illustrate how AI has influenced or disrupted democratic processes across the world:

- *Cambridge Analytica Scandal*: It is important to mention the case of the firm Cambridge Analytica, which shows the potential of AI in political campaign abuse. The company collected information from millions of Facebook users without their knowledge or permission, then used that information to influence political advertisements in high-stakes elections, including the US presidential election in 2016 and Brexit in Great Britain. This case brought into sharp focus issues to do with data privacy and consent, especially where AI is concerned and the corrupting influence of personal data when used to manipulate democracy.
- *AI in the 2024 US Presidential Election*: The US presidential elections held in the year 2024 saw a rise in the use of AI in creating deepfake news to fill the campaign space. These deep fakes mislead the candidates and twist their stand, hence complicating the electoral debate. The growth of AI-generated content on social networks demonstrated that the existing political democracies had some weaknesses when people were unable to differentiate between real information and fake news.
- *AI in the 2024 Indian General Election*: The recent 2024 general election in India provides examples of both the positive application of AI to advance democratic processes and the negative way AI is used to subvert them. While the application of the analyzed technologies involved in AI allowed reaching the desired electorate and mobilizing voters, it also promoted the distribution of fake news. The spread of fake videos and manipulated content brought the issues of electoral integrity and the rise of new technology forward.

These cases explain the necessity of the requirement of additional suits of legislation to tackle the problems of practical and ethical uses of AI in democracy. As advanced technologies remain a feature in societies, the world must come to terms with the challenges, hazards, and opportunities AI poses to democracy and its political process (Table 8.1).

AI and Democracy: Complicating factors affecting the integrity of elections. On the one hand, AI can improve political communication and participation; on the other hand, AI's improper application eliminates the foundations of political systems based on open and fair cooperation. In this chapter, it has been demonstrated that while AI is an intricate factor of contemporary political campaigns, notable ethical issues arise when employing this technology in political processes. In future, policymakers, technologists, and civil society should come together to fashion out the legal frameworks within which AI can be used to enhance electoral processes without compromising the democratic processes.

Table 8.1 Comparative analysis of AI's role in elections: India, the United States, and the United Kingdom

Aspect	*India*	*United States (US)*	*United Kingdom (UK)*
AI in Election Security	AI technology serves as a system to find fake news as well as prevent cyber-attacks against voting systems and stop misinformation.	Media platforms utilize AI systems to discover information disturbances that endanger electoral integrity alongside cybersecurity threats.	The monitoring system supported by AI tools helps identify disinformation along with detecting online threats targeting the electoral system.
AI Usage in Elections	Increasing use of AI for data analytics, voter profiling, and social media targeting.	Extensive use of AI for voter data analysis, micro-targeting, and influence via social media.	AI applications in social media campaigns alongside voter analysis exist in France but reach fewer extents than seen in the United States.
Voter Profiling	AI tools for profiling voters based on demographics, behavior, and voting history.	AI-driven data analysis to segment voters and predict voting behavior.	AI technologies should be used for voter segmentation through ethical practices that protect privacy.
Social media and Influence	AI sorting procedures for political advertising campaign delivery operate primarily through Facebook and WhatsApp platforms.	Social media manipulation through AI, such as deepfakes and bots influencing voter behavior.	A system using AI for targeted marketing should exist under more strict regulations.
Data Privacy and Ethics	Minimal regulation; growing concerns over privacy violations due to AI-driven profiling.	Concerns about privacy and AI usage for political influence (e.g., Cambridge Analytica scandal).	The General Data Protection Regulation (GDPR) enhances data privacy standards through better regulations.
Challenges	Misinformation, lack of regulation, and the digital divide in rural areas.	Concerns over privacy breaches, bias in AI algorithms, and foreign interference.	Balancing AI innovation with ethical practices and the need for stricter regulations.

SOCIOECONOMIC DISPARITIES AND AI-DRIVEN ELECTION MANIPULATION

The treatment from AI-driven election manipulation operates differently for each voter population. The three groups who lack economic stability together with low education status and marginalized backgrounds demonstrate high susceptibility to misinformation as well as targeted political advertisements and digital access barriers.

Misinformation and the vulnerability of low-income voters

Low-income voters, alongside undereducated populations, are most severely affected by AI-generated misinformation because they mainly obtain news from social media platforms, including WhatsApp. Electronic content detection and fact-checking services remain unavailable to some communities, preventing them from distinguishing authentic AI-created false information thus exposing them to electoral manipulation.[4]

AI-Powered political ads and minority manipulation

AI-driven micro-targeting allows political campaigns to tailor different messages to different voter groups. This has been used to exploit religious, ethnic, or regional divides, influencing voting behavior through fear-based narratives. For example, targeted misinformation campaigns have manipulated religious minorities in India, while in the United States, AI-powered ads have been used to discourage African American voter participation.

Digital divide and political awareness

Wealthier citizens who live in cities possess digital literacy tools along with ways to check facts, whereas poor residents of rural areas do not have access to these capabilities. The digital divide allows the advantaged population to counter AI propaganda, whereas the less fortunate are easily swayed by these methods, thus worsening their ability to both know and decide politically.

THE 2024 INDIAN GENERAL ELECTION

The 2024 Indian general election was marked by a profound intertwining of technology and political campaigning, fundamentally transforming the landscape of political discourse in the country. The rapid rise of AI, the omnipresence of social media, and the expansive reach of the internet allowed political actors to harness digital tools not only to engage with voters but also to shape narratives and manipulate perceptions. This section explores the background and context of the election, delves into the mechanisms of micro-targeting and voter manipulation, examines the AI-driven campaign tools employed, discusses the prevalence of misinformation and deepfakes, and analyses the overall impact on public perception and voter behavior.

The backdrop of the 2024 Indian general election was characterized by a complex socio-political environment, including economic challenges, social unrest, and the ever-increasing influence of technology in daily life. As the ruling government completed a decade in power, the opposition parties aimed to capitalize on public dissatisfaction regarding various issues, including economic performance, unemployment, and agricultural distress. Against this backdrop, the stakes were high for all political actors, who recognized the necessity of innovative strategies to connect with a diverse electorate.[5]

The election unfolded in a digital-first environment, where political discourse increasingly occurred on social media platforms. With India being one of the largest markets for social media globally, platforms like Facebook, Twitter, and Instagram have become critical battlegrounds for political parties. The emergence of AI technologies added another layer of complexity, enabling parties to analyze voter behavior, craft tailored messages, and leverage data-driven strategies to sway public opinion.[6]

That is why one of the most remarkable characteristics of the elections held in 2024 is the intensive use of social media monitoring and specific advertising options. To this end, political parties and candidates used machine learning to process a large amount of data originating from different sources, such as social network activity, demographic data, as well as consumer behavior. This analysis enabled political parties to vote segment; parties could target voters who are most likely to vote for them with political messages.

In a broader sense, micro-targeting[7] is founded on the assumption that voters are much more likely to attend to messages that they find of personal relevance. Through the development of the types of content mentioned above, the political parties could extend the effects of the campaigns and address the voters better. For instance, a party will come up with different ad campaigns to speak to the economic challenges faced by urban people while at the same time talking about the farmer's policies in rural areas. And it not only allowed direct voter turnout to be at its highest but also avoided any possible negative backlash of the campaign by making sure messages were targeted and based on voters' issues.

In the 2024 election, AI was not limited to micro-targeting but was also used in several other sophisticated campaign technologies. Of these, AI-implemented chatbots have shown themselves to be fundamental necessities in e-campaigning. These virtual assistants offered live interaction with voters to answer questions, share information about the candidates and policies and use another interactivity. Chatbots help political parties be constantly active in voters' daily lives and provide them with support and engagement.

Furthermore, AI extended to target placement for advertising where parties can also efficiently use their resources. Current AI could have the capability of assessing the effectiveness of different ads and then enable campaigns to change their approach in relation to the data received. Implementing such a study will demystify which materials have value to groups, thus making it possible for political parties to achieve high magnitudes of impact. The part of the turn-around strategy which again saw the use of predictive analytics was the targeting of the swing voters in the 2024 elections. Social, economic, and behavioral sciences could be used to train AI, algorithms that could identify people who looked confused or those that were easy to influence. Political parties adapted their communication approaches, therefore, directing their campaign strategies according to the anticipated outcomes of their strategies. Out of these important electoral information sources, this focus on critical voter segments played a tremendous impact on the pot of changing election potential, thereby proving that AI can change the nature of electoral processes.

AI-targeted tools have opened new ways for engagement and outreach; at the same time, they have provoked deep concerns over the misrepresentation and management of public opinion. The process of dissemination of fake news is quicker during the election moment, as AI technology facilitates the delivery of misleading stories. One case includes the memes that used clips with Bollywood stars, including Aamir Khan and Ranveer Singh, pretending to insult Prime Minister Narendra Modi and call people to vote against the incumbent government. These short clips appeared as if the actors were discussing various problems faced by the nation under the ten-year rule of the Modi government, particularly on the economic aspect. The appearance of these deepfakes shows that AI-generated content threatens the electoral discussion and lies about candidates. Though the Election Commission of India tried to curb such practices, the extensive engagement of AI in the act led to a problem where it became hard for people to differentiate between news and fake news. Popular and political actors used AI bots to expand these narratives, making it even harder to navigate the electoral process and impacting the democratic tenets of accountability and transparency.

Targeted messaging AI technologies that brought about change through converging with social media and the spread of misinformation affected the general views and voters' actions during the 2024 India General Election. With the relative autonomy from political messages, the voters' opinions were more and more dependent on the frames constructed by the political actors.

Due to the AI-driven micro-targeting techniques, parties could especially address certain issues that would allow voters to feel part of something. But this also led to a new form of polarization because people only engaged with posts that only made sense in their narrow frame of reference. This phenomenon produced echo chambers suppressing the view of other opinions and deepening the rift in society. However, these moral issues degenerated the trust of the citizens in the political system due to the appearance of fake news and deepfakes. With such cases of a clash of information, the voters were left with no option but to doubt the content they received. Such skepticism has a virtualizing effect on the electoral process since the average voter does not know what information to believe and can doubt the very effectiveness of the upcoming elections.

The Indian general election of 2024 is one of the best examples of how deep AI has penetrated the political campaign and voters' manipulation, and the election process. The usage of micro-targeting, the AI-based campaign tools and the spread of fake news revealed both the possibilities and threats coming with new technologies. Considering these changes, stakeholders must not only analyze how AI affects democratic processes and values positively or negatively but also act in a way that guarantees that democratic processes gain the highest level of credibility attestations in a world driven by technological innovation.

THE CAMBRIDGE ANALYTICA SCANDAL

Technology and politics are becoming inseparable today, and problems of an ethical nature have emerged as the most frequently discussed issues in the sphere. Ever since the primary mischief was done in the 2010s, the case of Cambridge Analytica has been a vivid example of how personal identity data can be used to psychologically profile the public in political advertisements. This scandal not only involved major and dangerous violations of privacy but also raised the world's discussions on the permissiveness of data in electoral systems. This part discusses the scrutiny of the data collection methodology used by Cambridge Analytica, the company's involvement in critical political elections, the ethical issue that arose and the legal consequences that were acted on.[8]

The scandal involved the US-British political research firm Cambridge Analytica and the use of an app called 'This Is Your Digital Life' launched by psychologist Aleksandr Kogan in 2013. This app used the cover of a personality quiz, and people were encouraged to engage in the process. However, the app had a far more significant capability: it could collect wide-ranging personal data not just from users of the application but also from their friends on Facebook. This data collection method relied on Facebook's Open Graph, through which CA was able to get information from as many as eighty million Facebook profiles, many of which were of people who never knew that Cambridge Analytica was collecting data about them.[9]

The psychological profiling that was generated from this data collection formed the core of Cambridge Analytica's business. This firm began to assemble extensive psychological portraits of users that would allow them to 'address' them in the political way most likely to get a positive response. Through the possibility of psychological targeting, political campaigns could deliver content that was particularly intense for each voter's fears and desires. The subtlety of this approach established a worrying tone for the application of data in politics which leads to questions regarding moral rights when using the ability to influence the actions of the voters by using such techniques as advertising.[10]

Cambridge Analytica got involved in the political campaigns, most probably to the apex in the 2016 US presidential election. The firm assumed an important role in endorsing the campaigns of Ted Cruz and Donald Trump, relying on the data accumulated to advance appealing messaging tactics toward the floating voters. The Trump campaign was possible due to one digital tool, which allowed influencing voters depending on their psychological traits—micro-targeting.

In the United Kingdom, Cambridge Analytica's involvement in the Brexit referendum also proved its further political manipulation. Even as studies established that the direct engagement of the firm in such an important political event was less pronounced than in the US election campaigns, the affiliation with such monumental political processes exhibited how psychological persuasion and control functioned. The story it told was one of a new form of an overtly data-fueled political campaign that could swing elections in its favor, raising questions around the world about the future of democracy.[11]

The scandal process peaked in March 2018 when the former Cambridge Analytica employee, Christopher Wylie, revealed in The Guardian and The New York Times the firm's misuse of the data. His revelations sparked international concern, numerous people asked themselves how it is ethical to use data from personal accounts in political campaigns without the people's permission. The scandal first unveiled the security issues innate in social media and secondly initiated extensive debates about the moral obligation of companies which deal with individuals' data.

Cambridge Analytica's acts of privacy violation were heinous in several ways. The activities performed by the firm led the public to ask pertinent questions about the power that people have over their data, as well as, asking the organizations that gather, manage, and analyze the data what is expected of them. Since many people who are active on social media, such as Facebook, continue to ignore how their data is being processed, the scandal pointed to the fact that data practices in the political sphere deserve clearer standards.[12] After the data leak by the Cambridge Analytica outlet, Facebook received much criticism and considerable legal repercussions. This company released public statements of regret, and its head and creator, Mark Zuckerberg, was called to appear before the US Congress, where he was interrogated on data privacy and user permission. The FTC finally set a record fine of $5 billion for Facebook's violation of user privacy—the largest fine in the FTC's history.

Further, the UK Information Commissioner's Office (ICO) fined Facebook £500,000 for creating potential risks for its users and not properly protecting their data. These legal consequences exposed the importance of better regulation on the protection of personal information as well as the acceptable application of AI in political processes.

The experience of Cambridge Analytica elicited a discussion on the necessity of international data protection laws. Members in Congress are starting to look for regulations that will help protect users' privacy and provide information about how their data is used. It also led initiatives such as GDPR in Europe's Union whose main intention was to provide individuals with easy ways and means to control their information as well as see that those organizations that violated the privacy of their information received maximum penalties.

Eventually, in May 2018, the company formally closed through Chapter 7 bankruptcy, but the problem it unveiled did not cease. It brought up long-term questions about how personal data are understood and used in the digital climate and still resonates in the current discussions about privacy and AI, technology and democracy. The marred election influenced by Cambridge Analytica stands as a good example of the misuse of data in political processes. It is important to consider that such a great combination of technology, psychology, and politics gives rise to unprecedented circumstances that need to be considered for their ethical and legal implications. Since societies remain in the process of globalization, it is necessary to provide timely protection for personal data and protect citizens' rights and democracy. The practical implication of the present scandal is that it continues to demonstrate the general principles of transparency, accountability, and ethical responsibility in the growing world of technology and politics.

THE 2024 US PRESIDENTIAL ELECTION

The 2024 US presidential election has provided insight into how technology will influence politics, especially given the existence of AI and deepfake technology. With advancements in AI, tools have been applied to the manufacturing of realistic but fake videos of political leaders. This level of manipulation of media has not only contributed greatly to raising questions concerning the credibility of electoral but has also raised massive concern about the issue of fake news affecting the public. Deepfake technology refers to the use of AI to create videos that can be easily passed off as original content featuring people when in fact, they were never told or did those things. This innovation has shown brilliant technological progress yet has been utilized as an instrument for achieving distinctly antagonistic goals, mostly in the sphere of politics. In the 2024 election, there were also deep-fake videos that were aimed at the candidates and aimed at changing the ways that voters saw them.[13]

Such videos are produced using clips of celebrities and politicians and, by applying machine learning algorithms, replacing their words and movements. The outcome is often so realistic to a point that a common observer might find it hard to tell the difference between what is real and what is acted out. This poses a great danger to democracy given the fact that a voter may be influenced by information that is fed to him/her by the elite, which is falsehood. The most famous case is the deepfake video of the current President of the United States, Joe Biden, who made provocative statements regarding policy and power. This video went viral within a short time and received many followers on social media before being dismissed by fact-checkers. But by the time the truth was brought out, many people had already endorsed the porn video as being original, and this resulted in chaos among the masses.

Not only Biden but also other politicians like Vice President Kamala Harris and Florida Governor Ron DeSantis were on the receiving end of deepfake material. They complained that videos found on different social media platforms portrayed them in a wrong light that did not depict their real stands. These videos were shared at a very high rate, and the use of AI to sort and recommend content based on the engagement with the material that evokes strong emotions led to an unpredictable information space before the election.[14] This rise in deepfakes is part of a broader phenomenon of lying with the help of AI when it becomes ever more difficult to distinguish between truth and falsehood. When inexperienced voters come across such manipulated content, they develop a culture of distrusting all news feeds they come across, thus exacerbating the division of the voters and the overall demoralization of the democratic system.

It is impossible to overemphasize the impact that deepfake technology poses on the behavior of voters. Fake news greatly influences people's attitudes toward the candidates and their programs. When deepfakes are used more and more, they undermine the ability of voters to interact with information and create an atmosphere of mistrust and chaos. The polarization effect is attributed to the fact that with the spread of fake news and fake information, people will tend to stick to the kind of information they hold rather than change their belief system. It makes concentric circles of closed systems in which fake news can spread, thereby deepening polarization. People may be convinced that the adversary is a criminal or that fake news regarding the competitor is true, and therefore, a highly polarized political territory can ensue.

Lastly, the psychological aspect of deepfakes, which is generally intended to generate anger or fear, can greatly increase the interaction with social network users. When people spread enthralling content without confirmation, the vicious cycle of false information is created, and voters' attitudes and behaviors are shifted in a very unpredictable way. The combined outcome is a democratization process which in its final stages, is becoming open to manipulation: thus, the legitimacy of the electoral process and the result it produces must be questioned. The development of deep fake technology has made people come up with ways of regulating the use of fake news and coming up with technological ways of discouraging fake news in electoral processes. It has become increasingly clear for policymakers and advocacy groups that there is a need for frameworks to deal with the problem of AI misinformation.

Among the significant responses is the work carried out to enact bills that will help to implement necessary prohibitions referring to the ill-considered use of deepfakes in political campaigns. Some proposals involve calling for the identification of AI-created content and insisting that designers put a warning on doctored videos. It would also alert viewers that they are using possibly fake material, which would make them inevitably check such information with suspicion. Not only have attempts on the legislative level been made, but technological approaches to improving the identification of deepfakes have also been sought. Scholars and technology firms are working on algorithms that would help detect fake news in the context of photographs and videos. These tools use machine learning algorithms to scan through videos and identify discrepancies as a method of determining deepfakes within hours instead of days.

Social media have also signaled efforts to curb misinformation. Many sites are already coming up with more rigid measures of moderating content and using AI techniques to recognize undesirable posts like deepfakes. For this reason, stakeholders in technology firms, government and NGOs should combine efforts in formulating a multi-stakeholder strategy. The 2024 U.S. presidential election is, therefore, an essential crossroad in analyzing the effects of AI-enabled technologies on democracy. Due to the new characteristics that deep-fakes are developing, which present a major risk, stakeholders at all levels must work together. The strategies that will emerge from this election will be useful in containing future misuse of falsehoods and protecting the electorate franchise in a world that is fast moving to the internet as the major source of information.

The synergy between deepfakes and political campaigning that played out as evidenced in the 2024 US presidential election simulation brings out an intrinsic relation between democracy and change. The technical advances in AI-driven tools suggest that political processes can be equally distorted by misinformation. The main case studies of deep fakes are a perfect example of the weak points in today's information environment. Tackling these issues will call for a synergy of stepped-up regulation, and deployment of technology, as well as raising awareness. It is necessary to prevent voters from being deceived to prevent such results which undermine the electorate's trust in democratic institutions. From the upcoming 2024 election, future arguments regarding the ethical application and deployment of technology in elections and the implementation of strict measures against manipulation will take cues.

REGULATORY FRAMEWORK FOR AI IN ELECTIONS

The expansion of AI technology within electoral processes creates serious doubts about information manipulation as well as unconstitutional utilization of data while affecting voter participation. The benefits AI provides to political participation need strong regulations since it concurrently threatens electoral integrity. Modern political tools using AI continually evolve between authentic political dialogue and deceptive information distribution through micro-targeting algorithms and deepfake methods alongside automated deceitful propaganda. Political entities take advantage of unregulated AI technologies because there is no sufficient oversight, thus damaging both fair electoral practices and transparency. AI can persistently be used for deceptive, manipulative political advertising since laws do not exist to curb such practice, in addition to hiding voter profiling methods that raise severe doubts about election honesty.

Major nations tried to control AI usage during electoral races yet achieved only limited success because their regulatory approaches were unclear and different from one another. Political advertisements in the United States must be transparent according to rules from the Federal Election Commission, although the body lacks adequate enforcement tools to stop AI-created misinformation. The European Union's General Data Protection Regulation (GDPR) offers clear data protections to personal voter information through restrictions of unauthorized usage yet does not successfully address AI's novel manipulation during elections. The Enforcement Commission of India has cautioned against deepfake content, yet it lacks proper legal frameworks to charge political actors responsible for AI-based electoral manipulations with any legal consequences. Democratic processes face insufficient protection from the existing laws that address AI development, even though these regulations are deemed important for their purpose.

The regulations must strengthen to achieve fair and transparent voting while dealing with two key elements: AI transparency and control of AI-targeted advertising features alongside strategies to stop manipulated information from AI systems. Political parties and candidates need to show public information about their campaign AI usage including political advertisement strategies, while AI-created content demands mandatory warnings to stop voter manipulation. The protection of personal data requires strict laws which should limit AI-based voter profiling because political entities should not be able to use personal information to manipulate voters. Regulatory bodies need to create AI detection technology that checks for deepfake content as it emerges so it can be flagged until fact-checkers from validated partnerships review and counter the rise of AI-manipulated misinformation.

AI election governance requires enhanced international partnerships among countries to govern its use. AI regulation must receive global coordination for ensuring standard ethical guidelines since digital political influence operates between borders. Governments need to form AI supervision boards which will control the political campaign utilization of AI platforms while maintaining ethical boundaries in their operation. AI advancement will increase its impact on democracy, which requires governments to work proactively with regulatory bodies. Security measures need to be implemented by law to protect democratic systems because otherwise, electoral manipulation through AI will result in lost trust between voters and democratic systems. Worldwide collaborative work is vital to produce sound AI governance in politics because it will protect elections through transparent systems which adhere to ethical AI standards and maintain voter protection.

FUTURE RESEARCH DIRECTIONS AND POLICY RECOMMENDATIONS

Future research in the field of democratic processes with AI needs to concentrate on creating methods to address the disruptive effects AI has on elections. New research must center on the following topics:

1. *Longitudinal Studies on AI's Impact on Electoral Integrity*: Research examining the duration of AI influences on electoral integrity consists mostly of separate studies that study individual incidents instead of broader trends. Research studying how AI-based misinformation transforms over successive election periods needs to be carried out through extended timeframes. Time-based analysis of AI-propaganda demonstrates patterns which enable policymakers to maintain developing rules that match advancing technological progress.
2. *Cross-National Comparisons of AI Regulations in Elections*: AI regulation in political campaigns follows separate paths in different nations. AI regulation assessment between India and the United States, and European Union electoral systems enables identification of optimal strategies to monitor AI political manipulation. Future investigations need to assess existing legal structures which should display their successful methods alongside pointing out ways to improve them.
3. *Strategies for Enhancing Digital Literacy to Combat Misinformation*: Misinformation generated by AI technologies, such as deepfakes and micro-targeted disinformation, pose a threat to democratic processes. Future research should disclose which strategies offer the best results when teaching voters to recognize and oppose propaganda produced by AI systems. Knowledge about media literacy systems across nations enables policymakers to create extensive educational programs which establish political content scrutiny abilities within citizens.

By tackling these issues, future research can help to build more resilient democratic processes, ensuring that AI is used for political engagement rather than election fraud.

CONCLUDING REMARKS

The integration of AI into democratic processes presents both significant opportunities and complex challenges. Key issues revolve around its impact on elections, voter engagement, data privacy, and the regulatory frameworks required to govern these dynamics.

The Cambridge Analytica scandal underscores how data privacy breaches and psychological targeting can undermine electoral integrity. This incident revealed the urgent need for robust data protection and transparency in how personal data is collected and utilized. Cambridge Analytica's manipulation of user data raised ethical concerns, prompting global discussions on the consequences of data misuse in shaping political narratives. The fallout emphasized the need for regulations safeguarding voter privacy and ensuring informed consent, empowering individuals to understand how their data is being used.

The 2024 US presidential election highlighted AI-driven challenges, particularly deepfakes and misinformation. The creation of hyper realistic yet fictitious videos of political figures eroded public trust and added complexity to an already polarized political environment. Incidents involving deepfakes, such as misleading portrayals of candidates, demonstrated the necessity of regulatory measures to combat misinformation and protect electoral integrity. The ease of creating and spreading deceptive content exposed vulnerabilities in democratic systems, demanding collective responses through technological solutions and enhanced oversight AI's influence on democratic systems extends globally, reshaping political landscapes across nations, particularly in emerging democracies. Challenges like AI-driven misinformation, data privacy violations, and algorithmic biases[15] highlight the need for a comparative global perspective. Lessons from both advanced and emerging democracies emphasize the importance of adaptive regulatory frameworks that address diverse electoral contexts.

Effective regulations must prioritize data privacy and ethical standards for AI use. Comprehensive data protection laws aligning with international standards can safeguard personal information while promoting accountability among political actors. Transparency in political advertising and AI-driven campaigns is critical for fostering trust and ensuring voters are informed about the methods influencing their decisions. Establishing independent monitoring bodies can enhance oversight and compliance, promoting fairness in electoral processes.

Ethical standards for AI use in elections should prioritize accountability, fairness, and informed consent. Developers and users of AI tools must actively mitigate biases and discrimination in algorithms, ensuring that AI systems are transparent and open to independent scrutiny. Public engagement and voter education are vital for equipping citizens to navigate the complexities of AI in elections. While AI holds transformative potential for enhancing democratic engagement, technology alone cannot ensure electoral integrity. Collaboration among civil society, political actors, regulatory bodies, and technology developers is essential for addressing the multifaceted challenges posed by AI. By prioritizing data privacy, promoting transparency, and establishing robust regulations, societies can harness AI's benefits while safeguarding democratic principles.

In conclusion, the balance between the benefits of AI and the ethical considerations it raises is critical to the future of democracy. The lessons from past incidents like Cambridge Analytica and challenges during recent elections underscore the importance of proactive governance. By embracing adaptive regulations and fostering collaboration, societies can work toward a democratic future that upholds privacy, fairness, and transparency while addressing evolving technological challenges.

NOTES

1. Deep learning is a subset of machine learning that uses multilayered neural networks, called deep neural networks, to simulate the complex decision-making power of the human brain. Some form of deep learning powers most of the AI applications in our lives today.
2. Deepfakes are AI-generated fake videos that look highly realistic, often used in political propaganda to manipulate public perception by making it appear as if politicians said or did things they never actually did.
3. AI tools analyze past voter behavior and predictive election trends, similar to how online shopping websites make suggestions based on your browsing history.
4. Available at: https://www.researchgate.net/publication/376600105_THE_ROLE_OF_AI-DRIVEN_TOOLS_IN_SHAPING_THE_DEMOCRATIC_PROCESS_A_STUDY_OF_INDIAN_ELECTIONS_AND_SOCIAL_MEDIA_DYNAMICS
5. Available at: https://www.hindustantimes.com/ht-insight/future-tech/how-ai-social-media-and-internet-shape-elections-2024-101715321970067.html
6. Available at: https://www.hindustantimes.com/india-news/deepfakes-of-aamir-khan-and-ranveer-singh-raise-worries-over-ai-misuse-in-lok-sabha-election-2024-101713762883265.html
7. AI helps political campaigns deliver specific messages to select groups of voters based on their interests and demographics, like how Facebook shows ads based on user preferences.
8. Available at: https://www.businessinsider.in/tech/news/the-cambridge-analytica-whistleblower-explains-how-the-firm-used-facebook-data-to-sway-elections/articleshow/71461113.cms
9. Available at: https://www.cnbc.com/2018/04/10/facebook-cambridge-analytica-a-timeline-of-the-data-hijacking-scandal.html
10. Available at: https://www.theguardian.com/news/2018/mar/26/the-cambridge-analytica-files-the-story-so-far
    Available at: https://www.bbc.com/news/world-us-canada-48972327
11. Available at: https://www.bbc.com/news/world-us-canada-48972327
12. Available at: https://edition.cnn.com/2018/05/18/politics/cambridge-analytica-bankruptcy/index.html
13. Available at: https://www.aljazeera.com/news/2024/6/18/white-house-says-joe-biden-is-a-victim-of-cheap-fakes-what-are-they
14. Available at: https://qz.com/elon-musk-ai-deepfake-video-kamala-harris-trump-biden-1851607652
15. Algorithm bias occurs when AI unintentionally favors one political candidate or ideology over another due to how the system was designed or trained on biased data.

Chapter 9

AI solutions for election integrity

Combating misinformation in developing democracies

Nicholas Sesugh Iwokwagh and Paul Uko Obagwu

INTRODUCTION

Instructively, Anderson (2019) states that the use of AI in politics has been around since late 2010. He notes that the adoption of technological innovations in the areas associated with democracies and the election process has grown with recent advancement in AI technology. Corroborating Anderson, Akinyetun (2022) says that the development is the result of the advent of AI tools like Chat GPT, Claude, Bard, Google AI and automation, voice recognition, and dynamic AI applications, including explainable AI (XAI), AI-driven automation, AI in natural language processing (NLP), and many more. These tools present an array of options that could transform political realms of the nations.

While there have been concerns about the use of AI in politics and its impact on the democratic process, there also is a consensus that AI has great potential to improve democratic values, institutions, and processes, including elections in various ways particularly in those nations adjudged to be democratically strained (Taylor & Francis, 2022). Democratically strained nations have faced challenges in establishing a credible and trustworthy electoral framework. Yet, the credibility of elections is crucial for the stability of these nations. Fortunately, AI tools have emerged to enhance transparency, efficiency, and credibility, the desirable qualities of the electoral processes that are seriously lacking in those societies. The belief is that the application of AI in political activities, especially in electioneering and voting has the potential to benefit citizens of these nations by helping them to understand governance better and to enhance participation in democratic activities (Geissel, 2012). Besides, application of AI can assist not just the citizens but also the politicians in comprehending the needs of the citizens better and representing them more effectively. The resultant synergy between politicians and citizens could revolutionize elections and significantly enhance the policy-making process, making it more precise and efficient (Bermeo, 2016).

No doubt, electioneering processes in most strained democracies in the world have been tumultuous, mostly fraudulent, rancorous, and violent. Akinyetun (2022) posits that the development has affected the circle of

DOI: 10.1201/9781003594185-9

elections in those societies consequent to which there has been an avalanche of election petitions with many ending up at the Apex Court several months after the elections have been concluded and the declared winners sworn in. This also has constituted an impediment, preventing those nations from faring well.

This, consequently, has reinforced the need for an innovative panacea to tackle the complex challenges plaguing electoral processes in democratically weak nations. The call is based on the conviction that technology can make for a more efficient and transparent management of elections by minimizing pernicious human interference in the electoral process. The infusion of AI, which is a crucial innovative measure, into the electoral process according to Geissel (2012), holds great promise for enhancing transparency and efficiency.

While the use of technology to tackle election issues in these societies may come with its corresponding challenges especially with infrastructural deficits and other developmental problems, Merkel (2004) asserts that if the human element, which represents the core of the electoral challenges in those societies is ridden out, it is certain that infrastructural deficits and other developmental problems can easily be addressed thereby paving way for seamless adoption of AI to foster a climate for inclusive and open participation. This, as a result, will lead to a democratized electoral innovative ecosystem where barriers to right and credible information are lowered, enabling a broader diversity of stakeholders to make informed contributions based on their unique perspectives, experiences, and ideas as well as creating a culture of cooperation, information exchange, and collective resolution of issues, to help shape the future of electoral integrity (Tar, 2010).

The ultimate objective of the use of AI technology against misinformation is to establish elections that are free and fair. By harnessing the power of AI, researchers have argued that targeted strategies to detect and counter election misinformation can be achieved toward safeguarding the health of democratic institutions in the most affected nations (Anderson, 2019; Bermeo, 2016; Salih, 2021; Taylor & Francis, 2022). The application of AI to forestall election misinformation aims at ensuring more efficient, transparent, and inclusive democracy, improving and eventually enhancing democratic processes in the underdeveloped nations.

Against this background, this chapter examines the landscape by which an AI-driven approach can be deployed to forestall election misinformation. It also explores the prospects, pitfalls, and future directions of AI-driven solutions in combating election misinformation in strained democratic societies.

AI: A BRIEF HISTORICAL PERSPECTIVE

The history of AI is generally believed to be unclear and difficult to place categorically. However, Haenlein and Kaplan (2019) opine that the advent of AI can be traced to 1942 when American Science fiction writer, Isaac Asimore released a short novel, *Runaround*. Russell and Norvig (2010), however, state that the history of AI began in antiquity, with myths, stories, and rumors of AI being endowed with intelligence or consciousness by master craftsmen. Here, it was believed that the study of logic and formal reasoning from antiquity to the present led directly to the invention of the programmable digital computer in the 1940s, a machine based on the abstract essence of mathematical reasoning. Russell and Norvig (2010) note that this device and the idea behind it inspired a handful of scientists to seriously discuss the possibility of building an electronic brain.

Following this, Tai (2010) explains that the field of AI research was founded at a workshop held on a campus of Dartmouth College during the summer of 1956. Participants at the workshop thus became the leaders of AI research for decades. They believed that machines, as intelligent as humans, could be developed. Based on the conviction, Ukwela (2021) says that the US Government thus provided the funds to make the development of machines with human intelligence a reality. Arising from the initial success of the invention, the British and Japanese Governments joined in the massive funding of the invention of AI machine.

In the early 2000s, Cave and Dihal (2015) reported that machine learning was successfully applied to a wide range of problems in academia and industry. The success was attributed to the availability of powerful computer hardware, the collection of immense data sets, and the application of solid mathematical methods. Subsequently, in 2012, Cave and Dehal observed that deep learning proved to be a breakthrough technology, eclipsing all other methods.

It was reasoned that a close relationship between Claud Shannon's Information theory, and Allan Turing's theory of computation suggested that it might be possible to construct an electronic brain. Thus, around the 1940s and 1950s, scientists from the fields of mathematics, psychology, engineering, economics, and political science explored several search directions that consequently led to research in AI (Broussard, 2019). According to Broussard, Turing was among the first scientists to seriously investigate the theoretical possibility of machine intelligence.

Carlson (2015) states that in 1950, Turing published a landmark paper *computing machinery and intelligence* in which he opined that there was possibility of creating machines that think. Turing believed that if machine could carry on a conversation over a teleprinter, that was indistinguishable with a human being, it was reasonable to say that the machine was thinking. The Turing proposal became the first serious attempt in the philosophy of AI.

The breakthrough made by the researchers, who are regarded as AI pioneers, impacted generations of researchers, and consequently advanced the science of AI. Subsequently, McCarthy, Minsky, Newell, and Simon, invented the name AI at a meeting in Dartmouth, marking the birth of AI field (Aleksandra, 2018). The field of AI research was thus founded as academic discipline in 1956.

DISCOURSE ON CONCEPTS

Concept of AI

AI is a branch of computer science that deals with the development of computer programs that perform tasks that would normally need human intelligence. Furthermore, AI refers to the simulation of human intelligence in machines, which enables them to perform. tasks that typically require human kind of intelligence (Kaplan & Haelein, 2019). As noted by (Haenlein & Kaplan, 2019), AI is a system's ability to effectively receive external data, learn from it, and apply what it has learned to achieve the desired goals and objectives, and adjust its behavior accordingly.

AI systems are engineered to always perform appropriately or do the right thing with precision and think rationally. According to Aleksandra (2018), there are two distinct characteristics of AI systems; first, the machines think like people; and second, the machines reason rationally. By implication, AI refers to machines that not only think like people, but also reason rationally, and act rationally like humans.

Humans are creatures that are capable of thinking and acting rationally. Thus, artificial machines are programmed to receive data derived from human behaviors to act like humans. They are modem technologies aimed at assisting humans in developing effective and efficient communication mechanisms through advancements in communication systems in the modern world. The emergence of AI in modern communication has provided a standard platform where individuals can communicate effectively with one another without misunderstanding.

Concept of strained democracy

The state of democracy in the world is faced with pessimism arising from recurring relapse of vital democratic principles. Nomenclature notwithstanding, these terms refer to a varying state of deterioration in the democratic process and the democratization of democratic values. The consequences of the version of democracy that is described in the foregoing terms is what is referred to as strained democracy (Akinyetun, 2022). The terms describe a form of relapse in most of the cardinal principles and indicators of a democratic system (Akinyetun, 2022).

Lucidly stated, a strained democracy is a democratic system that contends with significant challenges, threats, erosion that potentially undermine its legitimacy, effectiveness, or survival (Tar, 2010). Furthermore, a strained democracy can be understood as a democratic setting in which the values and principles that define democracy are nearly totally disregarded by the leaders, leading to manifest and pervasive threats and abuse of the rule of law. It is a setting in which democratic institutions are vulnerable to setbacks leading to the erosion of rights and manipulation of electoral processes. In such a society, democratic health is frail and feeble (Merkel, 2004).

In more pragmatic terms, Taylor and Francis (2022) summarize the concept of a strained democratic system as one which is defined or characterized with rising polarization and partisan divisions, distrust in institutions, increasing authoritarian tendencies, decreased civic engagements, electoral interference, inequitable representation, misinformation, disinformation, and propaganda. Therefore, Bermeo (2016) says a strained democratic system often results in human rights violations, decrease in legitimacy, increase in conflicts, democratic backsliding, and loss of international credibility.

IMPORT OF AI IN THE ELECTORAL PROCESS

A democratized electoral innovative ecosystem empowers individuals and communities to develop context-specific solutions that address their unique challenges in exercising their democratic rights and holding free and fair elections (Geissel, 2012). Establishing confidence in the electoral process in the minds of the citizens will foster a culture of civic democratic ownership, inspiring grassroots initiatives and bottom-up approaches that promote transparency, accountability, and adherence to the principles of inclusive governance. This can strengthen the resilience of democratic institutions and reduce political tensions and conflicts in the stressed democratic societies (Figueiredo & Moraes Filho, 2019).

On their part, Kehinde et al. (2024) opine that application of AI approaches to election misinformation would go a long way to enhancing the adaptability and responsiveness to solutions ensuring they are better equipped to navigate the complex and rapidly evolving political atmosphere in those nations. Combating election misinformation is integral to upholding the fundamental democratic principles of equal representation and citizens participation. Dismantling the scourge of misinformation can foster inclusive participation and censure that every citizen, regardless of their backgrounds or circumstances, has a voice in shaping the processes that govern their lives and determine the future of their nation.

AI can act as a powerful catalyst for a stable and sustainably entrenched democratic governance through its ability to process vast amounts of data in real time, automate complex tasks, uncover insights, and augment human capabilities. This implies that AI applications have the potential to revolutionize elections and electoral processes in the strained democratic societies.

By leveraging AI technologies, barriers to entry can be lowered enabling individuals and communities to participate in the electoral process effectively. For instance, machine learning algorithms can identify patterns and trends in voter behavior, election data, and logistical challenges, thereby facilitating the discovery of novel solutions tailored to local contexts. NLP can break down language barriers, fostering cross-cultural collaboration and knowledge sharing among diverse stakeholders involved in the electoral process. Computer vision and image recognition can enhance voter verification, ballot security, transmission of results, strengthening the integrity and transparency of the entire election circle (Kehinde et al., 2024).

COMBATING ELECTION MISINFORMATION: THE AI APPROACH AND RATIONALE

Although the point has already been made that a democratized electoral innovative ecosystem empowers individuals, communities, and civil society organizations to develop context-specific solutions that address their unique challenges in exercising their democratic rights and holding free and fair elections (Geissel, 2012), it is pertinent to reiterate it because of its importance to the sustenance of a credible electoral process. This is because innovations help to rejoin the electoral process and ensure that elections are widely accepted and acceptable both to the electorate and to the teeming populace. Such innovations also increase public trust and participation in the democratic process.

In the same vein, curbing electoral misinformation in a democratic setting can foster a culture of civic engagement, inspire grassroots initiatives, and engender bottom-up approaches that promote transparency, accountability, and adherence to the principles of inclusive governance (Carrilho, 2023). This suggests that a transparent electoral process void of misinformation or disinformation or manipulation can potentially strengthen democratic institutions and reduce political tensions and conflicts. Fair, objective, and accurate information in the electoral process can further enhance the adaptability and responsiveness of solutions to issues that characterize weak democracies. Arguably, credible election information equips citizens to navigate the complex political atmosphere in the communities.

Expressing this view, Diamond (2008) says when the people are satisfied with, and confident in the electoral information, it not only strengthens democratic principles, of equal representation and citizen participation, but also breaks down barriers and ensures that everyone, regardless of their circumstances, has a voice in shaping the processes that govern their lives. With this conviction, AI has been perceived as a powerful catalyst for combating electoral misinformation in societies fraught with electoral challenges. Within the context of its ability to process vast amounts of data, automate complex tasks, uncover insights, and augment human capabilities, AI holds enormous potential to reduce the challenges, and address the contentious issues that arise from electoral misinformation as well as contribute to the strengthening of democratic governance.

According to Carrilho (2023), AI can play a pivotal role in information and knowledge sharing by providing platforms and tools that enable diverse stakeholders to connect, exchange ideas, and collaborate on solutions to issues that tend to undermine the electoral processes and democratic governance. To

Cave and Dihal (2015), effective AI-powered information management systems and collaborative platforms can serve as central repositories for democratic best practices. Further, AI can be deployed to support data-driven and evidence-based information about elections and enable the people to make informed choices that will consequently enhance the integrity and credibility of electoral processes.

Elections stand as one of the pillars of a well-functioning democracy, playing a pivotal role in shaping such a nation's political landscape and determining its destiny. Beyond the mere act of casting votes, elections are integral to the core principles of democracy, exerting profound influence on the effectiveness and the integrity of a nation (Bermeo, 2016). In other words, the significance of elections extends beyond the ballot box. It encompasses broader ideals of democratic governance, the rule of law, social inclusivity, economic progress, and the safeguarding of human rights. In essence, active participation in elections by the citizen serves as mechanism for combating marginalization, prejudice, and inequality while concurrently upholding essential human rights such as freedoms of expression and of the right to peaceful assembly and association (Salih, 2021).

Additionally, elections serve as the cornerstone for selecting and appointing leaders within democratic societies. In representative democracies, transparent and equitable elections are sacrosanct to the functioning of democratic governance. The electoral processes empower the people to choose their leaders and representatives while simultaneously holding them accountable for their actions. In view of this, flawed electoral systems where the people are misled and misinformed can potentially engender political authoritarianism and crises (Tar, 2010).

Sadly, Geissel (2012) regrets that the mechanisms governing elections and the principles and procedures that underpin them in most developing democracies, frequently deviate from established standards, resulting in practices such as violence, misinformation, and election nullifications within such societies. Voters would benefit from AI-driven tools that help them make informed decisions by presenting balanced views on candidates and issues. AI would assist in identifying and mitigating misinformation and disinformation, ensuring that voters receive truthful and clear information. Based on this, Taylor and Francis (2022) say that if AI is used responsibly and transparently, it would support the democratic process without compromising its integrity.

AI tools for combating election misinformation

As misinformation continues to pose a significant threat to the integrity of information ecosystems and public trust, AI offers innovative solutions to identify and address the threats. AI does this by providing powerful tools to detect and mitigate the spread of false or misleading information (Santos,

2023). This segment examines some AI tools that can be harnessed to proffer solutions to election misinformation.

FACT-CHECKING

One of the primary ways AI can help to combat misinformation is through automated fact-checking. AI fact-checking tools analyze text content and compare it with trusted sources to determine its credibility. According to Shin et al. (2022), these tools can scan entire articles or specific facts and provide a verdict on their accuracy. Furthermore, Shin et al. (2022) state that there are some kinds of AI fact-checking tools that use a traffic light system, with green indicating confirmed information, red indicating false or refuted information, and gray indicating inconclusive results.

As stated by Moller (2018), the benefits of AI fact-checking involve improving accuracy by ensuring that the information people consume is reliable and trustworthy. The efficient verification tools analyze volumes of data quickly and forestall misinformation by preventing the spread of false information. Furthermore, AI algorithms can quickly cross-reference content with reliable sources and flag potential misinformation for human verification. This enables timely responses to misinformation, preventing its spread and allowing corrective action. Another important aspect of AI's role in combating misinformation is its ability to classify and categorize content based on its credibility. It can analyze the source of information, its historical accuracy, and its alignment with established fact(s) to assign credibility score.

CONTENT VERIFICATION

Content verification is the process of using AI to check the authenticity and originality of content. Clear labelling approaches can be deployed as content verification methods to detect or identify election misinformation and disinformation in AI generated election material(s). Watermarking methods and digital signatures are common examples of content verification approaches that could be used to fish out election misinformation in AI-generated election content.

MISINFORMATION CAMPAIGN DETECTION

Misinformation detection according to Bozdag (2013) refers to the process of identifying and verifying the accuracy of information to prevent the spread of false or misleading information. The methods used in detecting these types of misinformation include source evaluation, text analysis, image and ideas verification, audio verification, network analysis, machine learning algorithms, and NLP.

SOCIAL MEDIA MONITORING

Social media monitoring is another crucial area in which AI can be instrumental to curbing election misinformation. This is crucial as it has the capacity for real-time checking to identify and address misinformation as it spreads. In addition, Shimasaan and Bukohwo (2015) state that the vast user base of social media platforms makes monitoring crucial in the fight against misinformation. Beyond this, AI can also monitor influential users' accounts and check possible misinformation by these influences. Some of the special strategies used in monitoring social media include tracking hashtag and keywords, setting up alerts per misinformation related topics, identifying influential users, monitoring content sharing and propagation, and using machine learning algorithms to detect patterns of information to establish a possible suspicious misinformation (Nsude et al., 2021). In addition, AI can play a key role in monitoring social media platforms for misinformation by analyzing user-generated content and detecting trends and narratives that may indicate the presence of false or misleading information. More still, these systems can track how information spreads, identify key influencers propagating it, and help platforms take targeted action to limit the reach of false content (Singh, 2018).

CHATBOTS AND VIRTUAL ASSISTANTS

Chatbot is a computer program that has been designed to simulate conversation with a user. It is typically used for task-oriented interactions like answering FAQs or processing orders. Virtual Assistant on the other hand is a more advanced AI program that is capable of handling complex tasks, managing schedules, setting reminders, and interacting with smart devices (Stevenson, 2024). Virtual assistants often act as personal helpers across various platforms. Both chatbots and virtual assistants use NLP to understand user input, but virtual assistants generally have more sophisticated capabilities and can learn from user interactions to personalize responses (Nsude et al., 2021).

Chatbots and Virtual Assistants can play an important role in combating election misinformation. According to Tai (2020), chatbots can be trained to recognize patterns and anomalies in language that may indicate misinformation. This enables them to swiftly flag suspicious content for human review. Furthermore, chatbots can be programmed to offer accurate and unbiased information about candidates, voting procedures, and election dates. This helps to counter misinformation and promotes informed decision-making. In addition, Chatbots can be used to provide personalized information that can help build trust and increase the likelihood that voters will seek out credible sources of information. Finally, Chatbots can be integrated with fact-checking organizations to verify the accuracy of information in real-time.

MACHINE LEARNING LIBRARY

Machine learning libraries are a compilation of functions and routines readily available for use. It refers to a collection of pre-written code functions and tools that developers use to build and implement machine learning models without writing complex algorithms from the scratch.

Some of the ways by which machine learning library can help curtail election misinformation according to Tai (2020) include: anomaly detection, NLP, image and video analysis. Machine learning models can be trained to identify unusual patterns in data, which can indicate the presence of misinformation. Also, NLP algorithms can analyze text and speech to detect false or misleading election information. Finally, machine learning models can be trained to detect manipulated images or videos (Moller, 2018). In the area of information manipulation, AI systems have the capacity to identify and counter manipulated media such as deep fakes. With its advanced algorithms, AI can effectively analyze visual and audio data to detect signs of manipulation, such as anomalies in facial expressions, voice patterns, or editing techniques. By flagging potential deep fakes, Broussard (2019) says AI can help to maintain the authenticity of information and prevent the spread of false narratives.

AI STRATEGIES IN COMBATING ELECTION MISINFORMATION: CASE STUDIES FROM NIGERIA, KENYA, AND THE PHILIPPINES

Nigeria is one of the nations that can be classified as democratically strained. A number of indices that characterize a strained democratic nation as identified earlier in the conceptual clarification are also pervasive in Nigeria. Prior to the 2023 Nigerian general elections, there were clamors for a novel means that could help strengthen the credibility of the elections. This came at a time when trust in the electoral system had virtually eroded. False and misleading claims spread rapidly, and undermined voters' ability to make informed decisions (Carrilho, 2023).

Thus, the 2023 general election offered the opportunity via which Nigerian fact checkers used new AI tools developed by *Full Fact* with support from *Google.org* to fight election misinformation (Bahri et al., 2024). The Nigerian fact checking organization formed as a non-governmental organization along with the media houses came together to form the *Nigerian Fact Checkers Coalition*. The group was reported to have encountered and debunked common election disinformation trends and fact-checked false claims that were attributed to politicians and past presidents. Examples of false information which the group debunked included false claims about the size of the rally, misleading statements about the achievements attributed to candidates, and fake giveaways and scams.

A total of 23 Nigerian fact checkers were onboarded to the AI tool. The tool was reported to have presented over 40,000 fact checkable claims to users from over 80 media houses. The facts were filtered by sophisticated tools using keywords, claim types, and speakers. Full Fact AI tools were said to have saved users time, money, and effort in identifying the most important bad information to address. According to Kehinde et al. (2024), the tools helped fact checkers find the most important statements to fact-check each day. These AI tools monitored online media and social media. The fact-checkers were informed when something they knew was false was repeated. This enabled them to act quickly by inserting accurate information to the public debate, thus squashing false information.

Also, the tools provided an accurate record of what was said, and which claims were fact checkable.

LESSONS FROM KENYA

As established earlier in this chapter, combating election misinformation is a crucial task in the overall effort toward ensuring election integrity for sustainable democratic governance especially in the democratically volatile nations. Kenya, a stressed democratic nation in East Africa, has taken a stride in the attempt to curb election misinformation and disinformation. Lessons from Kenya are of valuable contribution and significance to this chapter.

As reported by Taylor and Francis (2022), Kenya experienced a considerable upsurge in political disinformation. The surge was a significant reminder of the contentious challenges which most democratically strained nations across the world-encounter while trying to protect election information. According to Salih (2021) disinformation campaigns in Kenya's case were driven primarily by domestic sector, which included politicians as well as their crowds of supporters. Thus, the 2022 general elections in Kenya witnessed an astonishing rise in misinformation and disinformation with the social media becoming a major platform to perpetrate electoral aberrations.

Kenya's 2022 general election was marred by onslaught of hate speech online, putting supporters of the two major candidates against each other. As vividly captured by Githongo, over 550, 000 toxic posts were identified by MAPEMA Consortium on *Facebook* alone during the election. MAPEMA Consortium, a pioneering initiative formed by Code for Africa (CFA), AIfluence, and Shujaaz Inc. utilized AI and ML technologies to combat the rise of misinformation and toxic online posts (Stevenson, 2024).

These AI-driven approaches successfully detected and countered cases of misinformation and other polarizing content online. Furthermore, MAPEMA used an array of AI tools to monitor social media, utilized machine readable database called *Hatlex, Crowd Tangle*, as well as *Meltwater* to monitor conversations and identify networks involved in elections misinformation campaigns. Furthermore, the team utilized its inbuilt media monitoring solution

CivicSignal and proprietary AI-based solution from Prime AI to track digital media, analyze trends, and generate real-time reports for key stakeholders and decision makers (Shin et al., 2022).

Consequently, Carrilho (2023) reports that over 550 toxic *Facebook* posts were identified, while 800 cases of hate speech content and misinformation were successfully flagged. The team deployed extra skill sets in digital forensics as well as data analytics to monitor social media platforms and digital media for cases of hate speech, incitement, misinformation, and communicated the results accordingly for appropriate speedy countermeasures. Furthermore, the team developed messaging from the insights gained and integrated into comical and animated content targeting the youthful audiences through its network of 7.5 million youth ambassadors in Kenya. The ambassadors propagated messages of peace to millions of citizens of Kenya.

It should be noted that, addressing hate speech, incitement, misinformation, and disinformation requires an active collaborative approach involving multiple stakeholders as the case of Kenya has shown. The successes recorded in the use of AI-driven approaches to curbing election misinformation in Kenya can be attributed to the combined efforts of key individuals and organizations supported actively by the UN agencies and state actors (Shin et al., 2022). Instructively, these challenges, however, persisted into the post-election periods, which necessitates continuing active vigilance and monitoring.

A CASE STUDY OF THE PHILIPPINES

Since the 2016 Philippines elections, and social media platforms like *Facebook* and *Twitter* have been central to campaigns, but this also marked the beginning of widespread misinformation where voters found themselves caught between legitimate political discourse and cleverly disguised disinformation campaigns (Odedinran, 2021).

Combating election misinformation with AI-driven approaches received crucial attention by the Philippines nation especially during the nation's 2016 elections. The use of AI approach was conceived and spearheaded by the Philippines national electoral body—Commission on Election (COMELEC). Carrilho (2023) reports that the COMELEC formed a Task Force known as Katotohanan, Katapatun at Kertarungan (KKK) which was saddled with the responsibility of monitoring and regulating misinformation and disinformation on social media and the Internet. The task force aimed to protect the integrity of the electoral process and prevent the spread of false information that could undermine democracy in the nation (Bermeo, 2016).

According to Akinyetun (2022), the COMELEC deployed key AI strategies to accomplish the objectives. Among the key strategies deployed by the Philippines COMELEC to counter election misinformation as noted by Akinyetun were fact-checking initiatives, civic education, and collaboration.

Using the fact-checking initiatives, a non-profit organization known as *Interviews* was said to have implemented the Philippines Fact-Checker Incubator (PFCI) to support media organizations in fact-checking and debunking false information. Also, the COMELEC rightly assessed and unequivocally realized that educating citizens to foster critical thinking and media literacy was fundamental to a holistic objective of successfully combating election misinformation. With the realization of the essential combating strategy, an organization called *Politize* readily offered free and unbiased digital content laden with civic education campaigns (Akinyetun, 2022).

On the collaboration strategy, partnerships between government, civil society, and tech companies were considered vital in addressing the fundamental issues behind misinformation and disinformation. This was on the belief that grassroots initiatives and community engagement were critical in building a strong force against the scourge of misinformation. Part of the functions of the Task Force, KKK established by COMELEC according to Odedinran (2021) was to work closely with the nation's technology providers, the National Telecommunication Commission (NTC), the Cybercrime Investigation, and Coordinating Centre (CICC), using AI approaches to monitor, report, take down, or block offending content from candidates or political groups.

A good lesson to learn from the Philippines efforts at combating election misinformation is the directive by her electoral commission COMELEC, to all political parties and the candidates to register their social media accounts to ensure effective monitoring of the accounts. In addition, supporters and influencers that support candidates are expected to register their social media accounts. Carrilho (2023) reports that by October 2024, COMELEC had registered social media accounts from 62 aspirants for the different positions in the 2025 elections, with the deadline for registration set for December 13, 2024. This is a commendable and a strong pragmatic step in the right direction to counter, combat, and contain election misinformation toward enthronement of sustainable democratic integrity.

PITFALLS TO USING AI-DRIVEN APPROACHES FOR COMBATING ELECTION MISINFORMATION

Algorithmic bias

Algorithms are a set of step-by-step instructions that computers follow to perform a task. Utilizing AI algorithms in the electoral process as transformative as it may be, is still fraught with challenges. This is because AI-driven systems can be vulnerable to biases, either inherent in the data or introduced during the development process. These biases can lead to the propagation of skewed or false information and potentially mislead voters with the resultant erosion of trust in the electoral process (Bozdag, 2013). If voters lose confidence in the information they receive and in the fairness of elections, it could threaten the legitimacy of the democratic process, and the consequences of this could be severe.

Algorithms are popular and effective tools utilized by different organizations, but their popularity comes at the expense of systemic discrimination, limited transparency, and vague accountability (Moller, 2018). They can create unfair outcomes such as privileging one group of users arbitrary over others. The unfair outcomes are due to skewed or limited input data, unfair algorithms, or exclusionary practices during AI development. On that note, de Figueiredo and de Moraes Filho (2019) state that algorithmic biases can manifest in several ways, and with varying degree of consequences for the intended objective(s).

A growing concern about the global rise against misinformation using AI approaches could be summed in the following posers: What happens if the data fed to AI are biased? What happens if the chatbot spreads misinformation? Instructively, Stevenson (2024) discloses that, many seem unaware that AI is as biased as humans. He maintains that bias can originate from different venues, including the design and unintended use of the algorithm or algorithmic decisions about the way data are coded, framed, filtered, or analyzed to train machine learning. Algorithm bias, for instance, has been seen in content recommendations, and search engine results. Algorithmic recommendation processes have been criticized for their tendency to intensify and reproduce bias, distortion of facts, information asymmetry, and process opacity. This can give rise to perpetuating unjust and discriminatory patterns, algorithmic amplification of dishonesty, and biased realties (Kaplan & Haelein, 2019). These algorithmic-induced biases can exert negative impact on a range of social interactions, including the fight against misinformation.

This, no doubt, can be counter-productive to the overall objective of combating election misinformation. To avert the negative impact, the institutions using AI are expected to apply specific approaches to ensure that the bias is overcome. These approaches according to Shimasaan and Bukohwo (2015) include, choosing the right or correct learning models, using the right training data set; performing data processing meaningfully; monitoring real-world performance across the AI life's cycle; and avoiding infrastructural issues.

This is necessary because algorithm bias can produce false information and conclusions about certain election matters—which can lead to disinformation. Biased information can distort people's understanding and decisions by making them prone to taking irrational or inaccurate decisions about the elections based on the information at their disposal. For example, if algorithm incorrectly assesses our vets' information based on biased data, it could lead to certain people receiving false information, and this, could produce wrong conclusions and decisions (Odedinran, 2021). It is therefore important to apply appropriate methods and techniques to process, analyze, and interpret data.

Also, there is need to continuously monitor and update algorithms to prevent biases and ensure fairness. In addition, there is a need to develop more robust fairness metrics that can better capture algorithmic biases while research techniques to improve transparency and explainability in AI decision-making processes could be carried out. This will also require developing more effective regulations that will examine the effectiveness of current regulations to address emerging challenges in algorithmic bias and data privacy.

To safeguard AI data privacy, institutions and organizations must adopt ethical codes in the methods used in collecting data; and it is crucial to thoroughly review how data is being collected. In order to maintain privacy and transparency, Santos (2023) asserts that organizations must adhere to the Disclosure Code by American Public Relations Association (PRSA) for the use of AI. This code emphasizes the importance of conscious decision-making in a democratic society.

Similarly, it is important to establish and publish ethical codes for the use of AI in combating election misinformation, while electoral institutions and organizations should employ experts to monitor the ethical use of AI in the electioneering process. Ethics committees should be established to oversee the use of AI in the democratic process. The committee should also address issues that are related to the potential impact of emerging technologies on the democratic processes of countries with strained democracies and ensure ethical adaptation of AI.

Data scalability issues

Data scalability refers to the ability of data mining algorithm to handle large amounts of data efficiently and effectively, and the capacity of algorithm to process data in a timely manner without sacrificing the quality of the results (Tai, 2020). It can also refer to the challenges that may arise when AI systems are applied to large, complex, and rapidly growing datasets. Many AI algorithms are not designed to handle large-scale datasets. This can lead to performance degradation, increased computational costs and errors, and slower processing time. Given the large size of the data required to be inputted into the AI system to analyze and detect false or misleading information, scalability obviously becomes a major setback in this direction.

A major challenge in data scalability according to Poole and Mackworth (2017) is complexity. The complexity as a challenge arises from the data being stored in multiple locations and in different formats, which makes it difficult to access all the information through one platform. Effective scalability helps systems to remain responsive and available even when carrying heavy loads. By scaling up or down, organizations can distribute the workload across multiple resources and prevent bottlenecks or downtime (Kehinde et al., 2024).

Data quality

Data quality is an issue of concern in the fight against election misinformation. To address misinformation using AI strategies, data must be reliable and accurate to achieve the goal of dispelling disinformation and misinformation. But if data are inaccurate, it can exacerbate the pervasive spread of misinformation and disinformation. Poor quality data can result from individuals collecting large data from individuals through their social media profiles without the user consent and then use for purposes of election information.

For example, in 2018, the *Cambridge Analytica* shocked the world by revealing that the data of up to 87 million *Facebook* profiles were collected without user consent and used for targeting purposes in the American Presidential campaign of Ted Cruz and Donald Trump (Stevenson, 2024). This development highlights the possibility that unchecked collection, and use of data can undermine AI's approach to combating election misinformation.

Also, there is a possibility that digital platforms can be used to generate massive data collection by bad actors for the purposes of generating and spreading disinformation and misinformation at a potentially massive scale. This can disproportionately hurt marginalized communities. Furthermore, the information overload on social media, which can create an overwhelming chaotic environment, can make it difficult for AI systems to determine facts from falsity since AI algorithms are not yet designed to handle large and complicated data (Singh, 2018). Thus, it may be a herculean task for AI to forestall misinformation on voting dates, polling locations, election results, and messages on the efficacy of election processes. As datasets grow, it becomes a herculean task to ensure the quality and consistency of the data. This, obviously, can impact AI model performance negatively. Without the needed consistency, it becomes difficult to use the output as basis to dispel perceived false information. Consequently, people could be exposed to inaccurate or imprecise information. This development certainly constitutes an anticlimax to a fight against election misinformation.

AI-driven electoral solutions require significant data storage and management capabilities. Inadequate data infrastructure can compromise the integrity and security of electoral data. As a strategy to address the challenge, Poole and Mackworth (2017) suggest a migration of electoral data and applications to cloud-based infrastructure to provide scalable, on-demand computing resources and secure data storage. This will enable AI-driven electoral solutions to handle large volumes of data, perform complex analytics, and ensure data integrity.

IMPACT OF INFRASTRUCTURE CHALLENGES ON AI-DRIVEN ELECTORAL SOLUTIONS

While the integration of AI in electoral processes can ensure integrity of elections and thus strengthen democracy, its effectiveness, however, may rely heavily on infrastructure. Several infrastructure challenges may impact the efficacy of AI-driven electoral solution. Salient among the infrastructure challenges that, if not addressed, could weaken the effectiveness of AI-driven electoral solutions are the ones presented in the ensuing discussion.

Network connectivity challenge is a crucial factor that can undermine the integration of AI in electoral processes. Reliable and high-speed internet connectivity is crucial for AI-driven electoral solutions. Corroborating this view, Cave et al. (2020) assert that poor network connectivity can lead to delays, errors, and inconsistencies in electoral processes. To address this challenge, it is important for governments and electoral authorities to invest in developing robust digital infrastructure, including high-speed internet connectivity, data storage, and computational power (Moller, 2018). This, according to them, will also enable faster data transmission, real-time analytics, and more efficient voter registration and verification.

Also, data storage and management represent another infrastructure challenge. This is because AI-driven electoral solutions require significant data storage and management capabilities. Thus, inadequate data infrastructure can compromise the integrity and security of electoral data. As a strategy to address the challenge, Shin et al. (2022) suggest a migration of electoral data and applications to cloud-based infrastructure to provide scalable, on-demand computing resources, and secure data storage. This will enable AI-driven electoral solutions to handle large volumes of data, perform complex analytics, and ensure data integrity.

Again, insufficient computational power can be a major hurdle in AI-driven electoral solutions. It is capable of undermining AI-driven electoral solutions. However, insufficient computational resources can impede the performance and accuracy of AI-driven solutions. As a countermeasure, electoral authorities can leverage cloud computing services that offer flexible, scalable, and cost-effective solutions to this infrastructure need. Besides, governments and electoral authorities can invest in high-performance computing systems designed to handle and process vast amounts of data quickly and efficiently. This can significantly reduce the time it would take to train AI models, thereby accelerating the process.

Cyber threats also constitute infrastructure challenges. Poor infrastructure can give rise to increased security risks, making AI-driven electoral solutions vulnerable to cyber threats and data breaches. As a mitigation strategy, it is essential to implement robust cyber security measures such as encryption, firewalls, and intrusion detection systems. This is crucial to protect electoral data and prevent cyber threats and ensure the integrity and confidentiality of electoral data, maintaining trust in AI-driven solutions. Addressing these infrastructure challenges will enhance effective development of AI-driven electoral solutions, promote transparent, efficient, and secure electoral processes.

TOWARD ADDRESSING DIGITAL LITERACY GAPS AND INFRASTRUCTURE LIMITATIONS IN DEVELOPING DEMOCRACIES AND DEVELOPING NATIONS

Regarding the pervasive digital literacy gaps withing the developing democracies in the world, it is crucial to arrest the situation to enhance the positive impact of AI-driven electoral solutions. This is because digital literacy gaps and infrastructure limitations are significant barriers to the adoption and effective use of AI in the democratic processes and structures of developing democracies, and countries, particularly those in the global south. Against this background, practical solutions are required to address these challenges, to develop and promote digital literacy, improve infrastructure, counter election misinformation, and enhance democratic governance in those countries through widespread citizen participation.

To this end, there is an urgent need to promote the development and distribution of affordable, and accessible digital devices such as low-cost laptops, smartphones, and tablets.

In addition, governments and private organizations must collaborate to invest in digital infrastructure, including high-speed internet, data centers, and cloud computing services. This can also be facilitated by developing public-private partnerships to support the development of digital infrastructure.

Furthermore, it is important to foster collaboration among stakeholders, including governments, private sector companies, educational institutions, and community organizations to establish a collective impact framework to ensure coordinated efforts toward bridging digital literacy gaps, and creating favorable conditions that could be effectively leveraged by strategic democratic actors key stakeholders for combating election misinformation.

By implementing the listed practical solutions, the issue of digital literacy gaps and infrastructure limitations could be effectively addressed, ensuring that AI benefits democratic processes, combats electoral misinformation, and promotes a more equitable and inclusive digital future.

REGULATORY GUIDELINES ON RESPONSIBLE AI USE IN ELECTIONS

To leverage AI-driven electoral solutions and strengthen democratic integrity in the developing nations, it is imperative to evolve specific regulatory guidelines for responsible AI use. These regulatory guidelines should focus on transparency, accountability, and fairness. Toward this end, the specific guidelines should focus on mandating clear labeling of AI-generated content, including social media posts, deep fakes, campaign advertisements, and election-related materials. The guidelines, too, should prohibit the use of AI for deceptive purposes in elections or require disclosure of the use of AI in campaign speeches. It will also be important to establish a registry used in elections, providing details on their purpose, functionality, and potential biases.

Similarly, it will also be important to evolve and implement mechanisms for correcting errors or biases in AI systems, including procedures for reporting and addressing issues regarding fairness and guidelines. In addition, implementing robust monitoring systems that can detect and deactivate faulty bots can help prevent the spread of electoral misinformation. This suggests that there is growing need for transparency.

Within the context of developing democracies, there is a need to foster international cooperation to share best practices, expertise, and resources for responsible AI use in elections. This calls for capacity building by providing training and capacity development programs for elections officials, policy-makers, and civil society organizations on AI-related issues.

This will promote responsible use of AI in elections. Ensure transparency, accountability, and fairness, and support the development of robust democratic institutions in the developing nations.

FUTURE DIRECTIONS OF AI INTEGRATION IN THE DEMOCRATIC PROCESS AND THE EMERGING RESEARCH NEEDS

AI in politics and by extension, in democracy, has certainly come to stay. It is poised to bring transformation to all facets of political activities with great revolutionary impact. The ultimate goal will be how AI can engender sustainable democracy in the strained democratic societies. As AI technology becomes a defining process in the modern world, wielding dominant influence on virtually every sphere of human pursuit, its role in politics and democracy will be inexorable, highlighting the imperative for nations of the world particularly the illiberal democratic nations to put greater premium on investing in AI technologies. Going forward, AI technologies will inevitably sway influence on campaigns, enhance voter engagement by offering personalized information to voters—how voters access information, and how electoral processes are managed. Furthermore, campaigns are likely to become increasingly data-driven and AI-powered. This will optimize managing, targeting, and resource allocation for campaigns. Unarguably, AI will certainly play an increasingly central role in shaping the democratic landscape (Salih, 2021).

The impact of AI on elections is a wake-up call for developing nations experiencing democratic decay to take a proactive measure by developing guidelines for AI development, deployment, and use in democratic processes. As a pragmatic step, democratically moribund nations can invest in digital infrastructure to ensure reliable internet access, digital literacy, and cyber security. This will help them derive the benefit of AI to its optimality (Bahri et al., 2024). There must be concerted efforts by those nations to foster collaboration between governments, tech companies, and civil society organizations, as shown in the cases of Kenya and Philippines discussed earlier in the chapter. Finally, the need to evolve common ethical and regulatory frameworks to ensure that AI is used responsibly and fairly in the electoral process is an urgent necessity.

AVENUES FOR FUTURE RESEARCH NEEDS

The importance of future research needs in AI-driven electoral solutions cannot be overstressed. As technologies continue to evolve and play an important role in shaping democratic processes, it is crucial to develop effective countermeasures to mitigate unintended effects of the technologies toward protecting the integrity of democracies in the developing nations of the world. To this end, further research should be carried out to develop more advanced AI-powered fact-checking systems that can quickly identify and debunk false information.

In this context, longitudinal research is a powerful research approach that will help in understanding the value and impact of AI-driven electoral solutions. By studying these solutions overtime, it will help foster a deeper understanding of their complexities and nuances that can help guide in developing more accurate models and predictions, which is particularly critical in electoral contexts where small margins can have significant consequences (Tai, 2020).This research approach can help identify patterns, trends, and potential biases, and also provide a comprehensive understanding of the effectiveness, limitations, and potential biases of AI solutions in electoral issues. This can ultimately inform the development of more robust, inclusive, and democratic AI-driven solutions for electoral processes worldwide.

Moreover, longitudinal research will enhance proper understanding of voter behavior. By studying voter behavior over time, it will help to provide a deeper understanding of how AI-driven electoral solutions influence voter decisions and behavior just as it will enable researchers to track challenges, development, and trends, and thus offer invaluable insights into how these solutions impact electoral processes and outcomes. The methodological approaches available for this kind of research can be either qualitative or quantitative or mixed methods.

In addition, cross-national research approach is another important avenue for a more encompassing understanding of AI-driven electoral solutions. The value of cross-national research approach lies in its ability to provide a comprehensive understanding of the complex interaction between technology, politics, and society (Anderson, 2019). By studying AI-driven electoral solutions across different countries and different cultural, social, and political contexts, researchers can identify the best practices, challenges, and areas of improvement. This is because the research approach will enable researchers to carry out a comparative study of data across different countries, identifying similarities, differences, and patterns that might not be apparent within a single country.

Furthermore, by examining the social, political, and cultural contexts in which AI-driven electoral solutions are deployed, researchers can gain a deeper understanding of how these solutions are shaped by, and how they shape the local context. Thus, Salih (2021) states that cross-national research can help identify generalizable principles and transferable strategies that can be applied to different contexts, enhancing the effectiveness and efficiency of AI-driven electoral solutions.

CONCLUSION

Having navigated the complex landscape of election misinformation, it is no doubt that AI-driven solutions are crucial in combating or mitigating the treat. Leveraging AI-powered fact-checking, machine learning algorithms, and other strategies discussed in this chapter, can foster a robust mechanism that can mitigate the spread of false information in democratically strained societies. This suggests that AI approaches offer a far-reaching panacea to the pervasive electoral misinformation that has defined democracies in most underdeveloped nations of the world. The sanctity and integrity of democracy rest totally on the participation of the electorate. Voters can meaningfully participate in the election when they are properly guided to enable them to reach informed decisions. This is possible when the scourge of election misinformation is addressed or minimized. Thus, integrating AI-driven strategies with the existing electoral infrastructure can unarguably mitigate election misinformation, safeguard the interest of the marginalized groups and entrench sustainable democratic governance in societies perceived to be democratically strained.

However, it is imperative to recognize some attendant pitfalls with AI-generated content, which can be used to garner false information to undermine democratic institutions. This calls for more sophisticated AI detection tools to enhance greater collaboration between policymakers and civil society organizations. AI-driven strategies have enormous potential to redeem most of the democratic challenges associated with the underdeveloped nations of the world. By being committed to developing AI-driven solutions, it can help to protect the sanctity of elections, promote fact-based information, and strengthen the foundation for democratic systems in stressed democracies.

This chapter helps to establish the understanding that AI-driven strategies can combat election misinformation, just as it will inform policy and regulatory frameworks.

REFERENCES

Akinyetun, T. S. (2022). The state of democracy in Africa: Democratic decline or autocracy? *Politcke Perspektive*, *12*(2), 89–115. Retrieved from https://www.ceeol.com/search/article-detail?id=1088987

Aleksandra, G. (2018). Coming to life: AI in Africa. *Issue Brief Atlantic Council, Africa Centre*. Retrieved from https://www.atlanticcouncil.org/wp-content/uploads/2019/09/Coming-to-Life-Artificial-Intelligence-in-Africa.pdf on November 8th, 2024.

Anderson, D. (2019). Comparative democratisation and democratic backsliding: The case for a historical institutional approach. *Comparative Politics*, *51*(4), 645–663.

Bahri, P. R., Asmara, H. G., & Risnaim, M. (2024). AI (AI)-based campaign in the implementation of General elections. *International Journal of Multidisciplinary*, *9*(2), 117–127.

Bermeo, N. (2016). One democratic backsliding. *Journal of Democracy*, *22*(1), 5–19.

Bozdag, E. (2013). Bias in algorithmic filtering and personalization. *Ethics and Information Technology*, *15*(3), 209–227.

Carrilho, S. F. (2023). AI in automated detection of disinformation: A thematic analysis. *Journal of Media*, *4*(2), 679–687.

Cave, S, & Dihal, K. (2015). Hopes and fears for intelligent machines in fiction and reality. *Nature Machine Intelligence*, *1*(2), 74–78.

Cave, S., Sihal, K., & Dillon, S. (2020). *AI Narratives: A History of Imaginative Thinking About Intelligent Machine*. Oxford University Press.

Diamond, L. (2008). The democratic rollback: The resurgence of the predatory state. *Foreign Affairs*, *87*(2), 36–48.

de Figueiredo Simao Leal, L., & de Moraes Filho, J. F. (2019). Artificial intelligence and democracy: Can algorithms influence an election? *Direitos Fundamentais & Justica*, *41*, 343.

Geissel, B. (2012). *Curing Democratic Malaise?* Routledge.

Haenlein, M., & Kaplan, A. (2019). A brief history of artificial intelligence: On the past, present, and future of artificial intelligence. *California Management Review*, *61*(4), 5–14. https://doi.org/10.1177/0008125619864925 (Original work published 2019).

Kaplan, A., & Haelein, M. (2019). Siri, Siri, in my hand: Who's the fairest in the land? On the interpretations, illustrations and implications of AI. *Business Horizons*, *62*(1), 15–25. https://doi.org/10.1016/j.bushor.2018.08.004

Kehinde, S., Simon-Ilogho, B. E., Kehinde, K., & Kehinde, T. B. (2024, July 8). *Exploring the impact of AI on voter confidence and election information in 2024*. Qeios. https://doi.org/10.32388/UT898Q

Merkel (2004). Embedded and defective democracies. *Democratization*, *11*(5), 39–58.

Moller, J. (2018). Do not blame it on the algorithms. *Information, Communication & Society*, *21*(7), 959–977.

Nsude, I., Ogbodo, J. N., & Nwamini, S. (2021). Creating and fighting fake news: Artificial Intelligence as double-edged sword. *Artificial Intelligence and the Media*, 47.

Odedinran, C. (2021). *The age of the robotic reporter*. In S. Oyeleye, & I. Ademosy (Eds). *Knowledge Societies: AI and the media*. UNESCO.

Pislaru, M., Vlad, C. S., Ivascu, L., & Mircea, I. I. (2024). Citizen-centric governance: enhancing citizen engagement through artificial intelligence tools. *Sustainability*, *16*(7), 2686. https://doi.org/10.3390/su16072686

Poole, D. L., & Mackworth A. K. (2017). *AI: Foundation of Computational Agents*. Oxford University Press.

Robinson, D. (2018 , January 14). What's the difference between data science, machine learning, and artificial intelligence? *The Way Ahead*. Society of Petroleum Engineers. Retrieved from https://jpt.spe.org/twa/whats-difference-between-data-science-machine-learning-and-artificial-intelligence

Russell, S. J., & Norvig, P. (2010) *AI: A Modern Approach* (3rd ed.). Prentice Hall

Salih, M. (2021). Africa and the decline of democracy debate. *Hungarian Journal of African Studies*, *15*(4), 5–15.

Santos, F. C. C. (2023). Artificial intelligence in automated detection of disinformation: A thematic analysis. *Journalism and Media*, *4*(2), 679–687. https://doi.org/10.3390/journalmedia4020043

Shimasaan, I. G., & Bukohwo, E. M. (2015). An artificial neural network model for Tiv character recognition. *Journal of Emerging Trends in Computing and Information Sciences*, *6*(10), 573–583.

Shin, D., Hameleers, M., Park, Y. J., Kim, J. N., Trielli, D., Diakopoulos, N., Helberger, N., Lewis, S. C., Westlund, O., & Baumann, S. (2022). Countering algorithmic bias and disinformation and effectively harnessing the power of AI in media. *Journalism & Mass Communication Quarterly*, *99*(4), 887–907. https://doi.org/10.1177/10776990221129245 (Original work published 2022).

Singh, S. (2018, December). *The impact of artificial intelligence on communication!* Medium. Retrieved August 12, 2025, from https://medium.com/@singhswati482/the-impact-of-artificial-intelligence-on-communication-d3660ce2990f

Stevenson, K. (2024). AI: A double-edged sword in elections. *Educational Administration Theory and Practice*, *30*(4), 1660–1667.

Tai, M. C. (2020). The impact of AI on human society and bio-ethics. *Tzu Chi Med*, *32*, 339–342.

Tar, U. (2010). The challenges of democracy and democratization in Africa and Middle East. *Information, Society and Justice*, *3*(2), 81–94.

Taylor & Francis (2022). Understanding democratic stress. *Journal of Representative Democracy*, *58*(1), 1–12

Ukwela, CO. (2021). AI and broadcast media presentation in Nigeria: What does the future hold? In A. Fayoyin, & I. Ademosu (Eds). *Knowledge Societies: AI and the Media* (pp. 78–95). UNESCO and the Association of Communication Scholars and Professionals of Nigeria (ACSPN).

Chapter 10

AI-driven tools as democratic equalizers for access to justice

Theodoros Falelakis

INTRODUCTION

Over the past two decades, globalization and rapid technological change has brought a significant innovation to the emersion of new technologies that have nothing to do with the traditional models of networked technologies and has profoundly brought a huge change in the court rooms and to contemporary legal profession, reshaping the justice system and the needs of people living in this era.

Given that we live in an information society largely defined by the capacity to process and disseminate information, it is no coincidence that the legal system is also profoundly influenced on a daily basis. At their core, courts are fundamentally reliant on the speed and efficiency of information processing, not to mention that law becomes increasingly complex and undergoes frequent changes. COVID-19 acted as an accelerator for the technology and the traditional legal models quickly—in a matter of weeks—restructured to become more agile.[1] It is not an overstatement to assert that even the role of judges is evolving, as courts are being restructured to align with the demands of the modern era and the acceleration of digital technologies can impact profoundly access to justice. This chapter begins by identifying barriers to access to justice, analyzing deficiencies with a literature review of global reports and scholarly perspectives while examining economic, social, and systemic obstacles to legal accessibility. Through a comparative analysis, it categorizes AI-driven legal tools, classifying them based on their use cases while highlighting their potential impact and application in judicial proceedings. The discussion then moves to how AI tools address these barriers, evaluating their effectiveness in mitigating justice accessibility issues through case studies and real-world examples. Following this, the chapter explores the risks and limitations of AI in legal systems, focusing on ethical concerns, biases, and the reliability of AI applications, as well as legal and societal challenges. Moreover, it proposes policies and guidelines for lifting barriers on AI adoption and for the incorporation of AI-tools into legal domain. Finally, it concludes by summarizing key findings.

 DOI: 10.1201/9781003594185-10

The research utilizes a qualitative methodology grounded in documentary and comparative analysis for existing AI tools and empirical examples across different jurisdictions to explore their potential to enhance access to justice. The author by reviewing academic literature, policy reports, and case studies from the European Union and the United States addresses the central research question: Can AI-driven tools function as democratic equalizers that enhance access to justice? The theme revolves around the intersection of technology, law, and governance, with a focus on how innovations like AI legal tools can either bridge or widen the justice gap.

UNDERSTANDING THE ISSUE OF ACCESS TO JUSTICE

According to the United Nations the rule of law is

> a principle of governance in which all persons, institutions and entities, public and private, including the State itself, are accountable to laws that are publicly promulgated, equally enforced and independently adjudicated, and which are consistent with international human rights norms and standards.[2]

The Sustainable Development Goal 16 of the 2030 Agenda[3] emphasizes on the paramount importance of equalizing access to justice. Access to justice directly reinforces the very concept of the rule of law. Without such access, it is impossible to implement a system that ensures the principles of the rule of law, including equality before the law; separation of powers; accountability under the law; legal certainty; and transparency.

Garth and Cappelletti in their seminal work on access to justice,[4] assert that the term encapsulates two primary objectives of a legal system as follows: first 'equal accessibility'—meaning that the legal system must be designed in such a way that everyone, regardless of any kind of factor, status, or barrier, can effectively seek legal recourse; and second 'individual and social just results'—meaning that the legal system must also ensure that the resolution of disputes and the outcomes of legal processes are addressed in a fair and just way aligned with the norms of justice. These dual pillars sustain the legal system and underscore it as the cornerstone of governance and the rule of law.

Susskind develops the concept of access to justice a step further. According to him, the concept of 'access to justice' encompasses a broader notion beyond the traditional understanding of dispute resolution through the legal system. He identifies four key elements: first, the element of 'dispute resolution', which should constitute the core of a credible justice system offering authentic mechanisms for dispute resolution with final outcomes; second, 'dispute containment', in the sense that a legal system should not encourage the escalation of disputes through litigation but rather promote their resolution; third, 'dispute avoidance', which refers to preventing legal disputes through widespread access to legal information, for citizens and society, empowering them to avoid legal issues; and fourth, 'legal health promotion', which involves promoting laws that, instead of creating problems, help individuals use legal frameworks for positive purposes, thereby enhancing their knowledge of their rights and empowering them to promote their general well-being.[5]

The discussion above helps to clarify the problem regarding the 'justice gap'. Inequality in access to justice remains, and a significant percentage of the global population faces unmet justice needs, unable to resolve legal problems or access the opportunities provided by the law. According to a 2019 report conducted by the World Justice Project (WJP), more than 5.1 billion people—two-thirds of the global population—do not receive the justice they require and face daily challenges related to access and discrimination. Furthermore, approximately 1.4 billion individuals have unresolved civil and administrative justice needs.[6]

To identify how technology can enhance access to justice, it is imperative to first examine the existing barriers to justice. According to a 2023 report[7] conducted by the WJP, these barriers can be broadly categorized into three principal domains, elaborated as follows: gender-based barriers; wealth-based barriers; and systemic-institutional barriers. Regarding the first one, it is noteworthy that women experience more family-related legal problems than men in most countries and face greater hardships due to legal problems in over 60% of countries, while they are less likely to resolve their legal issues compared to men. Regarding the second one, the report notes that people living in poverty experience more legal problems than wealthier individuals, often occurring outside formal processes, while people in poverty encounter barriers to obtaining justice either due to homelessness and debt threat, or due to high rates of lack of proof and documentation. As Schmitz notes, 'the majority of consumers remain silent because they lack the knowledge, experience, or resources to artfully and actively pursue their interests'.[8] Finally, regarding the third one, the report highlights the fact that civil justice effectiveness declined in two-thirds of countries between 2022 and 2023, while COVID-19 worsened long delays in justice proceedings. As a result, many people, due to insufficient resources, rely on informal or alternative dispute resolution.

In light of these considerations, it is imperative to scrutinize the potential impact of AI on the justice system and assess whether AI can facilitate equitable access to justice. Consequently, an enhanced discourse and deeper examination are necessary regarding the categories of AI-driven tools.

CATEGORIES OF AI LEGAL TOOLS

Before we proceed with AI legal tools, the following distinction must be drawn: rudimentary symbolic systems differ significantly from more advanced AI systems. According to Zuckerman, symbolic systems operate based on logical rules rather than advanced artificial intelligence. Specifically, they are designed to respond to pre-programmed questions by fulfilling deductive reasoning assumptions of the type 'if X, then Y' without, however, generating more complex responses. Conversely, AI systems are capable of and employed in performing more intricate legal tasks, automating sophisticated legal processes.[9]

This automated processing that augments legal tasks includes tools that involve primarily natural language processing (NLP), machine learning (ML), and knowledge-based systems (KBMS). Eliot describes the levels of automated legal reasoning as 'no automation, simple assistance, advanced assistance, semi-autonomous, domain autonomous, fully autonomous and superhuman autonomous for AI Legal Reasoning'.[10]

There is a wide array of AI tools available that can be leveraged to enhance or automate both simple and complex legal tasks as shown in Figure 10.1. Among these, certain tools focus on legal document management, enabling justice actors to organize their schedules and electronic files efficiently. Such AI-driven tools include 'iManage RAVN', which automatically organizes and summarizes documents; and 'Luminance' which is a system designed to automate routine work and ensure deadlines and compliance.

Another category is the one that pertains to legal case management, handling calendars, parties involved, case-related files, and tracking the progress of cases. Examples of such tools that incorporate AI features include 'Clio Duo', which is a Gen AI assistant for filing, serving, and delivering court documents; and 'Everlaw AI' assistant which enables users to analyze evidence, compose memos, create outlines, and generate lists. These types of tools predominantly address organizational needs and file management requirements.

On the other hand, there are tools dedicated to legal research, which grant access to legal theory, legislation, case law. These tools perform analysis and automated searches related to a specific case, notify users about legislative changes, and identify precedents. For instance, 'Westlaw Edge' can conduct legal research with intelligent analysis and AI-enabled search; 'CARA A.I.' is tailored to rank the search results based on specific legal and factual issues derived from an uploaded legal document; ROSS Intelligence is a legal

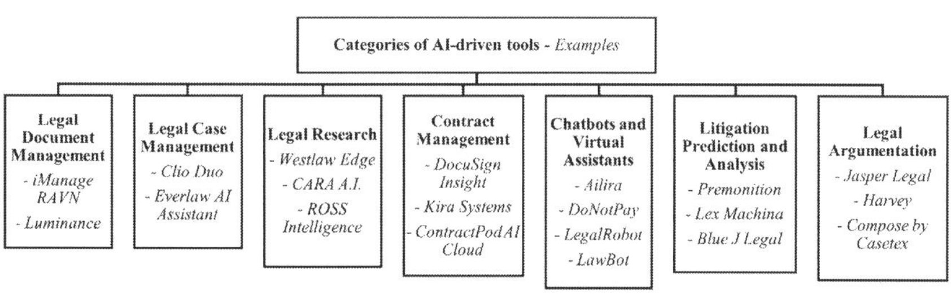

Figure 10.1 Categories of AI-drive tools. (Diagram by the author.)

research engine that uses ML, grammatical structure, word embeddings, facts, and motions to rank the best results.

Another category includes tools that assist legal experts in contract management, reviewing, and drafting. Such tools include 'DocuSign Insight' which assists in accessing, reviewing, and managing contract documents; 'Kira Systems', an application that uses ML to uncover and extract information from contracts; and 'ContractPodAi Cloud', which provides users with digital tools and capabilities to automate contract management.

Additionally, commonly used tools include chatbots and virtual legal assistants, which can respond to legal inquiries, support due diligence, and assist with legal research. Examples of AI chatbots that use NLP include 'Ailira', which automates legal research and provides legal information; 'DoNotPay', a free chatbot created to appeal parking tickets; 'LegalRobot', which is designed to simplify complex legal documents; and 'LawBot', which assists victims of crime.

Beyond these functionalities, another significant category includes litigation prediction and risk analysis tools. Examples include 'Premonition', 'Lex Machina', and 'Blue J Legal', which use machine learning and data analytics to predict case outcomes by evaluating precedents and assessing their relevance. These tools also assess the likelihood of a case failing based on the facts. Finally, there are tools designed for generating legal argumentation, which create propositions aimed at the legal analysis of laws relevant to a case. Tools such as, 'Jasper Legal', 'Harvey', and 'Compose by Casetext', are generative AI models that assist in legal drafting and argumentation.

Depending on the specific needs of laypeople and justice actors at any given time, various categories of tools may be employed. The most complex category to date remains that of legal argumentation, as an argument must inherently encompass the human factor, meaning it must incorporate elements of persuasion and holistically integrate multiple facets of legal practice.

AI-DRIVEN TOOLS LIFTING THE BARRIERS TO ACCESS JUSTICE

As stated in 1971 by Pantages, 'the archaic courts know nothing of computers. The quill is their tool, and they are run by judges, clerks and prosecutors, acting as part-time administrators'.[11] Even after nearly half a century, the situation has not changed significantly. Courts in many countries are still struggling with even the most basic computational systems, but like the rest of society, the judiciary system is gradually adapting its practices to align with the opportunities and challenges of new technologies.

The use of artificial intelligence is not a product of science fiction nor a utopia situated far in the future. On the contrary, significant advancements have been made in this field in recent years, and numerous courts worldwide are adopting policies that allow the use of artificial intelligence by lawyers and judges. Most recently, the Illinois Supreme Court issued an AI policy, which came into effect on January 1, 2025, and created a judicial reference sheet to assist judges[12] and stated that 'The integration of AI with the courts is increasingly pervasive, offering potential efficiencies and improved access to justice'.

In light of these, AI has an overarching long-term impact on justice actors. More specifically, AI-driven tools present an excellent opportunity to enhance courts and law firms, enabling them to adapt to the ever-evolving needs of justice and their clients while creating new promises for the justice system to improve access to justice for vulnerable people. Furthermore, laypeople can access legal advice without the need for an attorney.[13] In the following case studies the author looks at how such advantages of AI implementation and can be assessed regarding the obstacles to access to justice to estimate the overall value of AI-driven tools in solving the justice gap.

Diminishing bias

As previously mentioned, one of the primary barriers to access to justice arises from gender-based obstacles. This issue could be significantly mitigated through the implementation of AI. Typically, there are two types of bias. The first are the 'social biases', which refer to the impression formed by an individual about a specific person belonging to a social group. The second type is 'cognitive biases', with the most common being 'confirmation bias', where individuals seek information that confirms their beliefs while disregarding opposing information. These biases can easily infiltrate the judicial system during the administration of justice and the decision-making process. Judges, being human, often unintentionally succumb to bias. In some cases, the judges' written reasons do not assign any legal relevance to a defendant's characteristics, but on the surface, they only publicly declare or consciously adhere to the legal standards or precedent This causes a disparity between the underlying factors that truly influence the decision-making process and the apparent adherence to legal reasons. In an experiment with judges, Spamann and Klöhn concluded that a defendant's characteristics often have a stronger effect on judges than precedent.[14]

In terms of their impact on bias, there are three main strategies: first, the mitigation strategy, which works against bias; second, the insulation strategy, which removes the trigger of bias; and third, the removal strategy, which directly diminishes bias. The last two strategies are the most efficient and can be employed using tools during the decision-making process.[15]

The application of ML tools, leveraging legal data, could provide a real-time detection mechanism for such biases, thereby preventing judges from engaging in behaviors that might undermine the rule of law. The theoretical foundation for this argument is grounded in Chen's research, which posits that predictive analytics combined with ML possesses the capacity to enhance judicial processes by reducing inconsistencies and prejudices that may influence judicial decision-making.[16] Essentially, analyzing legal data through these tools, makes it possible to identify instances of bias, arbitrariness, or disproportionality.

These tools can then present their findings to judges, enabling them to apply the law more equitably. The insights derived from such evaluations empower both laypeople and justice actors to approach cases with greater transparency and consistency in legal application. Consequently, judges can make more informed choices and dispel any lingering doubts related to biases, emotional influences, or errors in judgment.[17]In 2024, a groundbreaking study on advancing legal reasoning and detecting bias was published by De'Shazer. This research is one of the most innovative studies and approaches in the analysis of judicial decisions and the mitigation of bias. By analyzing data from judicial rulings across five countries, including the United States, the United Kingdom, Rwanda, Sweden, and Hong Kong, De'Shazer developed an AI model that identifies human biases and facilitates automated, coherent argumentation aimed at ensuring the fair application of the law, irrespective of jurisdiction. The system operates as a semi-autonomous arbitration process (SAAP), which blends four AI applications to safeguard the fairness of legal decisions. According to the experiment conducted by De'Shazer, SHIRLEY—an application built on OpenAI's GPT technology—serves as the primary analyzer that detects logical inconsistencies and biases in legal documents. Its findings are then compared with SAM—a complementary AI application—which identifies deviations and patterns in different jurisdictions. To ensure an objective perspective, CRITIC is deployed to challenge SHIRLEY's findings by offering counterarguments. Finally, SARA—another AI application—acts as an AI arbitrator, synthesizing the conclusions and interpretations from the other applications.[18]

This experiment demonstrates that integrating a hybrid system of human-AI cooperation in a semi-automated arbitration process can effectively and systematically detect and quantify prejudices that may otherwise go unnoticed, paving the way for more transparent and fairer legal processes. The eradication of biases is undeniably beneficial for access to justice: it affords individuals the opportunity to seek justice and stand as equals before the law, irrespective of their personal characteristics.[19]

Decreasing wealth-based inequality

The economic turmoil induced by the COVID-19 pandemic has been a huge anomaly in this regard, as there is a growing body of evidence documenting the various ways in which the pandemic has further entrenched and expanded the disparities in access to justice.[20] Compounding the issue, another critical impediment to accessing justice is economic challenges of people and justice systems' prohibitive cost. In the United States, 92% of impoverished Americans, equating to 36 million individuals, lack the financial means to obtain legal counsel, initiate litigation in court, or defend themselves before a judicial body.[21] For this reason, individuals are compelled to engage in self-representation due to the ever-growing disparity of cost of legal services and ability to pay.[22]

A case study of a tool used to contribute to the closure of the access-to-justice gap is 'A2J Author'. This application was developed in 2005 by CALI and Chicago Kent and employs some process whereby self-represented litigants are interacting with 'Guided Interviews' to develop complex court forms. Specifically, the A2J Author application operates through logic-based framework that structures user responses into legal outputs.

Some examples of live A2J Guided Interviews are Illinois Fee Waiver, New York Support Modification and Enforcement Michigan and Answer to a Complaint on a Debt.[23] For instance, in the 'New York Support Modification and Enforcement' module, utilizing decision trees, the system queries the users for factual and legal information that upon completion provide the litigant with a court-compliant form that can be filed in person or mail. Specifically, the system first assesses jurisdictional applicability by determining whether the support order originates from a New York State court, the type of support order, the litigant's residency, and the opposing party's residency. If the support order falls under the jurisdiction of the New York State Family Court, the system further refines the inquiry by addressing the inclusion of spousal support, the number of children covered, and the litigant's relationship to the children—each factor shaping the applicable statutory framework. Each litigant's classification is carrying distinct legal consequences, ultimately ensuring that the generated court form aligns procedurally and substantively with jurisdictional mandates, enabling the unrepresented litigants access justice. To date over 3 million A2J Guided Interviews have been executed across the United States, addressing legal matters such as name changes and divorce proceedings, resulting in over 1.8 million court documents.[24]

A study published in December 2023 explored using LLMs to speed up the authoring of tools aiming to enhance access to justice for self-represented litigants. Deploying the open source 'Docassemble' platform together with a tool created at Suffolk University Law School called the 'Assembly Line Weaver' the research concludes with a human-AI approach, combining AI automated drafting with human review, to be most effective in this context.[25] Notably, a research conducted in Michigan demonstrated that self-represented litigants achieve divorce outcomes with utilizing automated forms, while similar successes have been observed in Arkansas, where over 85% of divorces without property or without child support were filled using such tools.[26] These empirical data underscore the operational capacity of such automated legal tools in facilitating access to legal services and in narrowing the justice gap.

Beyond tools explicitly designed to aid the poor, the general integration of AI-driven tools by the judiciary and legal experts fundamentally enhances efficiency while conserving resources, time, and financial expenditures. The use of algorithms facilitates the prediction of judicial outcomes based on empirical data. This enables the avoidance of unnecessary litigation and promotes recourse to alternative dispute resolution mechanisms. In 2016, a study research was published for predicting judicial decision of the European Court of Human Rights with accuracy up to 79% using 584 Court cases and an AI method developed by researchers at UCL, the University of Sheffield, and the University of Pennsylvania.[27] Similarly, in Brazil, a ML algorithm was developed by using 4,043 cases from Brazilian courts for predicting Brazilian court decision with an estimated 80.2% accuracy.[28] Another, study achieved the rate of 65% accuracy in predicting decision-making outcomes based only on the surnames of the ECHR judges.[29]

Automated analysis and statistical prediction of outcomes in judgements give litigants a great opportunity to check and formulate their arguments. On the other hand it can be used by judges to improve their decision.[30] In that sense, there is a dual benefit: AI applications like these alleviate the burden on the judicial system, expediting the delivery of justice, while simultaneously reducing superfluous litigation costs for the parties.[31] Importantly, outcome prediction does not aim to supplant judicial reasoning; rather, it seeks to identify, through statistical and probabilistic means, the trajectory of a judge's reasoning process.[32]

Overcoming systemic-institutional barriers to justice

However, the justice gap is not exclusively attributable to the obstacles encountered by individuals seeking legal assistance; it equally arises from the inherent complexities and systemic challenges confronting those endeavoring to deliver such services. AI, equipped with its diverse array of tools, could serve as an invaluable asset to justice actors in crafting layperson-friendly guidelines for legal procedures and their rights. Furthermore, it enhances the capacity of law experts to supply more efficient client services by eliminating the burden of bureaucratic and time-consuming tasks, such as document preparation, management, and archiving. This allows professionals to concentrate on more substantive legal issues and negotiation matters.

Within legal services, Massachusetts Defense for Eviction ('MADE') is a 'clinic in a box' solution designed to address inefficiencies in traditional in-person eviction clinics. [33] This AI-driven platform was developed by GBLS and enables tenants in Massachusetts facing the threat of eviction to navigate the legal process effectively. Through a thoughtfully crafted questionnaire, tenants are assisted in generating legally sound documents, while the platform provides comprehensive guidance throughout the eviction proceedings, ensuring they secure at least a two-week reprieve. Leveraging sophisticated decision trees and automated document generation, the system dynamically adapts to users' unique circumstances through tailored and highly specific questionnaires.

According to Steenhuis, consider, for instance, the defense of improper notice by the landlord. Such a failure to provide proper notice obligates the landlord to recommence the eviction process. To determine the viability of this defense the clinic developed a guided interview that asks specific information from the tenant regarding the notice, the address, the language, the nature of the tenancy arrangement and the formality of the lease agreement, the notice period stipulated within the agreement, and the date the eviction was filed. Based on the tenant's responses, the system assesses whether the notice was legally valid. Meanwhile, the same facts are employed to automatically generate discovery queries for legal preparation. Upon completion the system follows integrated guidance on the eviction process, offering an electronic legal intake option.

By the numbers, MADE increased access to legal services aiding over 4,000 tenants in 2023. A typical completion time for an answer via MADE is around 20 minutes, compared to the three- to five-hour duration observed in traditional legal services.[34] Within the judicial system, AI facilitates the comprehension of legal norms and state policies while enabling the rapid identification of legal issues and the guidance of laypersons through their available legal options and strategies. Moreover, predictive capabilities regarding potential outcomes increase consistency and predictability, streamlining the resolution of disputes through alternative mechanisms, fostering the pursuit of mutual solutions, and reducing the backlog of cases.[35] This extends to the preparation of legal documents and evidentiary materials, further optimizing the functionality and accessibility of justice. In this context, structural determinants influencing the availability of dispute resolution mechanisms will similarly affect the degree to which proportionality objectives are achievable. It can be contended that technologies capable of facilitating the creation of more transparent pathways for litigants, or potential litigants, could foster both public and private sector efficiencies, thereby advancing more proportionate outcomes.[36]

According to Susskind, technology can affect the courts in two ways: firstly, with the process of 'automation', new technology can be grafted into traditional working practices to optimize justice actors in more efficiently, but at the same time it sustains the current court system; and secondly, with the process of 'transformation', new technology can displace conventional working practices and introduce radical changes in court services.[37] EU jurisdictions have all implemented modalities of e-justice, while the UK and American jurisdictions focus more on online courts.[38] In the context of transformation, the example of the Colombian court is particularly compelling[39]. In February 2023, a court hearing was conducted within the metaverse, with each participant in the proceedings represented by an avatar. This case underscores the future proximity of a comprehensive reformation of the traditional justice delivery model.

AI-based case management systems, such as the one deployed by the Hebei High Court in China, enable more efficient handling of judicial processes by automating time-consuming and costly procedures such as digitizing documents, matching incoming documents with existing case files, and identifying relevant legislation and case law. These systems also facilitate the automatic generation of procedural documents and the distribution of cases to judges based on the subject matter.[40]

Beyond the case management system, machine learning tools can be employed to analyze Big Data. Groundbreaking research introduced 'INACIA' (Instrução Assistida com Inteligência Artificial), an LLM application designed for the Brazilian Federal Court of Accounts' (Tribunal de Contas da União—TCU).[41] According to Pereira et al. when a case is initiated through the filing of audits or complaints, INACIA processes the submitted documents including those related to financial mismanagement and supporting evidence. INACIA integrates an advanced text extraction pipeline and several applications for optimal character recognition (OCR) of text and scanned images to extract data. Using LLMs combined with Retrieval-Augmented Generation (RAG) techniques it proceeds to identify case details and interpret the plaintiff's claims and requested legal remedies. Also, by interfacing with TCU's internal jurisprudence databases, statutory provisions, and prior rulings it ensures that each case is scrutinized against predefined admissibility criteria such as legitimacy, competency, availability of evidence, public interest, and clarity of submission. Once the case passes the admissibility test, INACIA generates a preliminary document containing the synthesized legal analysis and the recommended adjudicatory stance, assisting auditors in drafting their official recommendations to the judicial panel. Overall, INACIA serves as an application that integrates LLMs into administrative judicial processes to extract data, retrieve information from documents, assess legal plausibility, and automate case analysis, ensuring audit processes are conducted efficiency and enhancing compliance with jurisprudential frameworks.

Similarly, another system in Brazil, the 'Socrates' program has been trained on more than 300,000 judicial decisions. By utilizing this program, it consolidates cases addressing similar legal issues for concurrent adjudication and automates tasks to expedite the processing of cases.[42] Moreover, in 2021, in Düsseldorf, Germany, the Ministry of Justice of North Rhine-Westphalia, the Central Cybercrime Department and Microsoft Germany developed an AI tool capable of categorizing image and automatically detecting child pornography with a 92% of accuracy.[43]

Notably, access to justice is a multifaceted social issue that has been a persistent problem across all societies, demanding substantial investment and attention from governments to be fully resolved. However, the utilization of AI tools within the field of justice, particularly in judicial settings, has the potential to augment transparency in the decision-making process, enhance the efficacy of judges, and, more broadly, optimize the delivery of justice through expedited and fairer procedures.

In that sense, the deployment of AI tools optimizes the functionality of the judicial system and reinforces access to justice across multiple dimensions, in alignment with Susskind's four-tier theory of access to justice:

1. *Dispute Resolution*: AI tools can accelerate the delivery of justice and achieve efficiency and fairness in the decision-making process.

2. *Dispute Containment*: AI tools do not encourage the escalation of disputes through litigation but rather promote alternative resolution methods to avoid litigation costs.
3. *Dispute Avoidance*: AI tools provide legal advice and information, helping laypeople understand their legal strategies.
4. *Legal Health Promotion*: AI tools enhance people's knowledge of their rights.

Tools for legal decision support provide citizens with the opportunity to be informed and offer them solutions to their legal issues enhancing overall societal well-being.

RISKS AND OBSTACLES TO THE IMPLEMENTATION OF AI-DRIVEN TOOLS

AI can, in essence, only serve as a supplementary, adjunctive, and enhancing tool within the decision-making process and the provision of legal services with constant human intervention and supervision. AI is fundamentally predicated on Big Data, drawing conclusions from the analysis of statistical data to form judgments; yet in practice, decision-making is considerably more intricate and complex than a mere probabilistic model. As Mingtsung and Shuling noted 'just as there are no two identical people in the world, the parties in each case have a unique personality, and the limitation of artificial intelligence can only realize the general and mechanized justice'.[44] Bearing this in mind, it is crucial to examine the risks and obstacles to the adoption of AI-driven tools in justice systems.

Inherent limitations in fully replicating the nuances of legal reasoning: AI fallacy

The law is characterized by complexity, and often the use of AI to resolve legal issues can introduce uncertainty. In most cases, the applicable law in a lawsuit is not straightforward. For instance, in the case of contract invalidity due to contradiction with public order, it is difficult to identify and delineate public order based on the factual circumstances and prevailing conditions in a country with certainty and automation through AI. This is because public order is a broad concept that could apply to an indeterminate number of cases and variations. Similarly, the application of AI is quite uncertain in cases where the algorithm is required to develop legal reasoning and form an argument through legal analysis. Susskind calls this 'AI fallacy'—'the view that the only way to get machines to outperform the best human lawyers will somehow be to copy the way that human lawyers work'.[45]

To solve this, Eliot suggests following the 'CARE' model, which stands for: create, assess, and refine a legal argument; and engage in legal argumentation.[46]

Other perspectives suggest that for AI to fully automate the process, it must be capable of extracting from legal texts a comprehensive representation of legal concepts and their interconnections.[47] Turing, suggested, in a seminal paper, a behavioral test in order to determine whether machines are capable of thinking like a human being.[48] Nonetheless, years after the establishment of the Turing test, there are programs that reach or surpass human-level performance, but outside of specific tasks, they cannot be human-like.[49] However, people, in contrast to machines, possess a distinct advantage: they have the ability to employ their own subjective experience as a means of assessing and understand the subjective experiences of others.[50] Analogously, AI cannot fully replicate the process of legal reasoning without the human intervention.

In this regard, artificial intelligence, precisely because it is grounded in algorithms rather than awareness and cognition, cannot replicate the process of a trial, particularly in the context of automated justice systems. In a traditional trial, the judge is the authority who renders a decision based on the trial's experiential dynamics, including the forum, often facing challenges between legal systems and possessing the discretion to interpret broad and vague legal concepts such as fairness, reasonableness and proportionality, ethical values, security, trust, equity, public health, public policy, public order norms, good morals, and commercial practices, the experience and the rationality of an individual, and so on. Algorithms cannot understand modern social attitudes and policy concerns;[51] rather they merely use data to make predictions based on their analytics to fit these factors.

Additionally, judges frequently engage in implicit corrective interpretation of the law, apply analogical reasoning, or determine the constitutionality and scope of rules. In this way, operating within a complex socioeconomic and political environment, the judge makes decisions based on rationality and equitable judgment, determining which legal provisions are applicable or not to specific cases. Conversely, artificial intelligence cannot supplant the discretion of judges in instances where no explicit provision exists, functioning as a complementary aspect of the law. These are intricate issues that often cannot be resolved using a logic of 'if X then Y'; plus, it must be emphasized that many arguments do not derive from logic and do not conform to ontological rules, but instead rely on empirical or emotional data.

Lack of transparency and accuracy

In 1998, in the United States, the company Equivant developed an algorithm known as COMPAS, designed to classify offenders based on the likelihood of recidivism in criminal behavior. This likelihood was utilized to determine the severity of sentencing or the potential for early release. The deployment of this risk assessment tool in sentencing revealed inherent biases against individuals with darker skin tones, consistently attributing a higher risk of recidivism compared to individuals with lighter skin tones.[52] This led to the Supreme Court of Wisconsin, in the State v. Loomis case,[53] where the Court rejected Loomis' claim regarding the inherited bias in COMPAS, receiving heavy criticism.[54]

A similar case involving risk assessment tools, was adjudicated by the Supreme Court in Ewert v Canada.[55] The Court held that the impugned tools concerning a specific minority are susceptible to bias, as they were developed based on studies conducted predominantly on individuals from the majority, and are, therefore, more likely to exhibit some degree of variance when applied to the minority group. Analogously, because of the risks, such automated tools with significant legal consequences should not be applied to determine the outcome of a decision. Nonetheless, as Zuckerman argues, 'it should be easier to deal with algorithm bias than with human unconscious bias'.[56]

Furthermore, it is quite easy for a user of such tools to fall victim to deception, deepfakes, or even false data or news if they do not verify the results of the processing. For instance, several instances have already been identified where Generative AI tools have created fake jurisprudence.[57] Specifically, the case Mata v. Avianca[58] emerged, where the judge discovered a document full of references to non-existent cases, as they had been fabricated using AI.[59] Similarly, in Missouri, in Kruse v. Karlen,[60] the litigant submitted an appeal in which 22 out of 24 case laws were fictitious, bearing generic titles such as 'Jones v. XYZ Corporation'. Moreover, in Massachusetts, in Smith v. Farwell,[61] three legal briefs were submitted, which were also based on fake and fabricated jurisprudence.[62] Court users may feel safer if the AI systems protect their right to a fair trial. But efficiency is not the only achieving goal; such systems should always be in accordance with the rule of law and established standards of protection.[63]

Technological and economic barriers

The success or failure of AI adoption across jurisdictions is contingent upon an intricate interplay of legal, technological, and socio-cultural factors. The European Union, the United States, and China for instance are having totally different approaches shaped by their respective legal cultures, regulatory frameworks, and infrastructural capabilities. On the one hand the EU regulatory environment, following the GDPR, prioritizes data protection and the AI Act is linked to AI deployment and risk assessment, fostering public trust. Conversely, the United States embraces a market-driven approach, characterized by regulatory fragmentation while, China, by contrast, leverages a state-led strategy, integrating AI development with state-backed investments. Compared to the laissez-faire approach in the United States and the state-driven model in China, the EU's heavily regulated approach may seem to slow AI commercialization. However, the lack of funding compared to its Chinese and American counterparts, is the crucial barrier to development and adoption, followed by the limited talent pool of AI academics transitioning into practical AI.[64]

Other than that, the integration of AI into institutional frameworks, particularly within the judicial system, is encumbered by both technical complexities and deep-seated skepticism.[65] From a technical standpoint AI demands substantial modification to existing infrastructures, which in many cases are built on outdated, monolithic legacy systems, while it also necessitates the appropriate technical and educational support that many courts lack. The transition demands not only significant financial investment but also expertize in machine learning, data science, and cybersecurity resources—that are often limited. Beyond technical impediments, judicial systems worldwide exhibit an entrenched reluctance to embrace technology within their systems.

An example that reveals the skepticism and delay of the judicial system in adopting new technologies is Greece where the practical relevance of AI applications for Greek justice has been limited and the AI applications have not yet been harnessed in a consistent manner, since within the Greek legal order AI is seldom addressed directly,[66] while even the existing electronic filing system[67] is questioned by the Greek Supreme Court. This is reflected in two decisions: Supreme Court Decision 1014/2024,[68] where electronic filings made after judicial services' working hours are rejected as late—despite the specific regulation regarding the filing of documents through electronic means—while in Decision 1765/2023,[69] such a filing is accepted. This inconsistency in case law, even for simple issues related to e-justice systems, underscores the difficulties judicial actors face in keeping pace with technology and incorporating technological changes in a manner that facilitates access to justice.

RECOMMENDATIONS REGARDING INCORPORATING AI-DRIVEN TOOLS IN JUSTICE SYSTEMS: OVERCOMING THE RISKS AND BARRIERS

Lifting barriers to AI adoption by EU requires targeted strategies to address economic, infrastructural, and socioeconomic challenges. Meyers and Springford propose four areas of focus: fostering robust competition among AI foundation models to guarantee European enterprises equitable pricing and unobstructed access to the technology; incentivizing AI adoption within European businesses; ensuring the just and equitable distribution of AI-derived benefits to mitigate opposition and facilitate societal acceptance; and upholding strict compliance with European values and regulatory frameworks, irrespective of whether AI providers originate within or beyond the Union's jurisdiction.[70]

The incorporation of AI in the legal domain also requires careful consideration, especially with laypeople, who often encounter significant barriers in navigating legal procedures. The key approach is to enhance AI acceptance and to build trust through clear and understandable explanations about AI processes.[71]To address the risks of incorporating AI into judicial field guidelines regarding three key subcategories are recommended for the design of AI tools, the transparency risks and the trustworthiness.

Regarding the design of AI systems, they must translate factual information into legal contexts but simplifying the legal terminology and providing accessible and transparent explanations for everyone. To accommodate their needs and to maintain the reliability of AI-generated outputs, safeguards must be implemented, such as disclaimers on AI limitations and citations of legal references. Regarding the practical implementation and design considerations of AI-based legal tools, the system should primarily be able to address high-volume, low-intensity legal matters, such as consumer rights, rental disputes, and employment claims. Through procedure steps the systems should integrate automated case triage, template-based guidance, and do-it-yourself features in order to provide personalized legal recommendations while maintaining compliance with judicial frameworks. The systems should also ensure real-world applicability which presupposes continuous updates and integration of data regarding legislative changes, case law, and interpretation.[72]

Despite the advantages of fostering AI innovation, critical concerns maintain regarding the legitimacy of algorithmic decision-making tools that inherently risk reinforcing bias and undermining public trust. To address these concerns a framework of 'guaranteed transparency' has been developed by Gans-Combe[73] that is grounded in four core principles: (i) Transparency of AI stakeholders, to ensure accountability; (ii) algorithmic transparency of the core learning methodologies and bias-mitigation mechanisms; (iii) data transparency, regarding the sources, structure and preprocessing methods of data used to train the AI models; and (iv) use transparency and oversight, meaning that AI applications in justice should be tracked through a supranational registry to ensure responsible use and monitoring.

Notwithstanding, AI systems integrated into the legal domain necessitate a structured and legally sound approach to ensure both procedural and substantive access to justice. While AI presents transformative opportunities for laypeople, legal services and judicial actors, the aforementioned risks should be mitigated in alignment with fundamental rights, due process, and the rule of law. Critical normative and operational criteria of AI-driven legal decision-support systems are articulated in the 'Ethics Guidelines for Trustworthy Artificial Intelligence', presented by the High-Level Expert Group on AI (AI HLEG) on April 8, 2019.[74] These guidelines suggest that AI deployed must satisfy three essential conditions: (1) lawfulness, requiring compliance with all applicable statutory and regulatory provisions; (2) ethical integrity, mandating adherence to fundamental rights and moral imperatives; and (3) technical robustness, ensuring operational security, reliability, and resilience in varied socio-legal contexts. The following seven requirements, while non-exhaustive, encompass systemic, individual, and societal aspects all of which are of equal importance, are utilized with interdependence and should continuously be implemented and evaluated (Table 10.1):

Table 10.1 Requirements for trust-worthy AI

The seven requirements entail						
Human agency and oversight	*Technical robustness and safety*	*Privacy and data governance*	*Transparency*	*Diversity, non-discrimination, and fairness*	*Societal and environmental well-being*	*Accountability*
The safeguarding of fundamental rights; the empowerment of human agency; and the institutionalization of human oversight mechanisms.	The resilience of AI systems against adversarial threats, ensuring robust security protocols; the establishment of contingency mechanisms; and the overarching guarantees of accuracy, reliability, and reproducibility.	The rigorous respect for privacy, the maintenance of high standards of data quality and integrity; and the establishment of stringent governance mechanisms regarding data access.	The implementation of traceability, the provision of clear explanations regarding system operations; and the communication of relevant information to stakeholders.	The prevention of unfair bias; the fostering of accessibility and universal design principles, and the active participation of relevant stakeholders throughout the life cycle of the AI system.	The promotion of sustainability, environmental responsibility, and the social impact of AI systems, ensuring that their design and deployment serve the broader interests of society and democratic principles.	Mechanisms for auditability; the minimization and transparent reporting of negative impacts, the management of trade-offs, and the provision of accessible redress mechanisms.

Source: AI HLEG.

By implementing these strategies and principles, aligning AI deployment into legal domain with ethical and legal standards, the AI-driven tools can offer significant potential to enhance accessibility, efficiency, and fairness in legal procedures.

CONCLUSION

AI constitutes a powerful tool and creates immense prospects for equalizing access to justice, but at the same time, it entails risks of exacerbating inequalities. Its use is promising; however, it should be noted that legal and judicial actors do not always align with technology and are notoriously skeptical of it.

For this reason, lawmakers must act promptly to mitigate any negative impacts that technology may have on the legal system, while simultaneously ensuring that, through appropriate reinforcement measures, it can narrow the justice gap and ensure access to justice. Lifting barriers to AI adoption by states requires targeted strategies to address economic, infrastructural, and socioeconomic challenges. The use of AI should be employed prudently, with oversight and without extremes, aligning with statutory and ethical requirements. After all, as Russell and Norvig highlight, 'Let technology integrate into our system or ethical framework, or our system or ethical framework is improved because of the system'.[75]

NOTES

1. Cohen, M. A. (2020, September 15). Covid-19 is transforming the legal industry: Macro and micro evidence. *Forbes*. https://www.forbes.com/sites/markcohen1/2020/09/15/covid-19-is-transforming-the-legal-industry-macro-and-micro-evidence/
2. United Nations, Security Council. (2004). *The Rule of Law and Transitional Justice in Conflict and Post-Conflict Societies (S/2004/616)* (p. 4). https://documents.un.org/doc/undoc/gen/n04/395/29/pdf/n0439529.pdf
3. United Nations. (2015). *Resolution Adopted by the General Assembly on 25 September 2015. (A/RES/70/1). Transforming our world: the 2030 Agenda for Sustainable Development*. https://www.un.org/en/development/desa/population/migration/generalassembly/docs/globalcompact/A_RES_70_1_E.pdf
4. Garth, B., & Cappelletti, M. (1978). Access to justice: The newest wave in the worldwide movement to make rights effective. *Buffalo Law Review*, *27*, 181. https://www.repository.law.indiana.edu/facpub/1142/
5. Susskind, R. E. (2019). *Online Courts and the Future of Justice* (1st ed., p. 66). Oxford University Press.
6. World Justice Project. (2019). *Measuring the Justice Gap: A People-Centered Assessment of Unmet Justice Needs Around the World*. https://worldjusticeproject.org/our-work/research-and-data/access-justice/measuring-justice-gap
7. World Justice Project. (2023). *Disparities, Vulnerability, and Harnessing Data for People-Centered Justice: WJP Justice Data Graphical Report II*. https://worldjusticeproject.org/our-work/research-and-data/wjp-justice-data-graphical-report-ii

8. Schmitz, A. J. (2020). Measuring "Access to Justice" in the rush to digitize. *Fordham Law Review*, *88*(6), 2382. https://ir.lawnet.fordham.edu/flr/vol88/iss6/11
9. Zuckerman, A. (2020). Artificial intelligence-implications for the legal profession, adversarial process, and rule of law. *Law Quarterly Review*, *136*, 427.
10. Eliot, L. (2020). *AI and Legal Argumentation: Aligning the Autonomous Levels of AI Legal Reasoning*. ArXiv (Cornell University). https://doi.org/10.48550/arxiv.2009.11180
11. Pantages, A. (1971–1972). No glory in chaos. *Jurimetrics Journal*, *12*, 193–194.
12. Illinois Supreme Court. (2024). *Illinois Supreme Court Policy on Artificial Intelligence*. Administrative Office of the Illinois Courts. https://www.illinoiscourts.gov/News/1485/Illinois-Supreme-Court-Announces-Policy-on-Artificial-Intelligence/news-detail/
13. Kahale, Ö. (2021). How can law firms contribute to access to justice in an age of technology and digitalisation? Pro bono, law firm innovation and ideas for the legal community. In S. Peter De Souza, & M. Spohr (Eds). *Technology, Innovation and Access to Justice: Dialogues on the Future of Law* (pp. 19–31). Edinburgh University Press EBooks. https://doi.org/10.1515/9781474473880-008
14. Spamann, H., & Klöhn, L. (2016). Justice is less blind, and less legalistic, than we thought: Evidence from an experiment with real judges. *The Journal of Legal Studies*, *45*(2), 255–280. https://doi.org/10.1086/688861
15. Stafford, T. (2017). *Biases in Decision Making Anti-Bias Strategies*. https://www.judiciary.uk/wp-content/uploads/2018/02/stafford-biases-in-decision-making-winter-2017.pdf
16. Chen, D. L. (2019). Machine learning and the rule of law. In M. A. Livermore, & D. N. Rockmore (Eds), *Law as Data: Computation, Text, and the Future of Legal Analysis*. Santa Fe Institute Press.
17. Pavón, J., & González-Espejo, M. J. (2020). *An Introductory Guide to Artificial Intelligence for Legal Professionals*. Kluwer Law International B.V. 11.01.
18. De'Shazer, M. (2024). *Advancing Legal Reasoning: The Integration of AI to Navigate Complexities and Biases in Global Jurisprudence with Semi-Automated Arbitration Processes (SAAPs)*. ArXiv (Cornell University). arxiv:2402.04140v3.
19. Kyriakides, N., Plevri, A., & Zentani, Y. (2022). AI and access to justice: An expansion of Adrian Zuckermans findings. In *Frontiers in Civil Justice* (pp. 121–141). Edward Elgar Publishing. https://doi.org/10.4337/9781802203820.00014
20. Simshaw, D. (2022). Access to A.I. justice: Avoiding an inequitable two-tiered system of legal services. *Yale J.L. & Tech*, *24*, 150. Gonzaga University School of Law Research Paper. https://ssrn.com/abstract=4090984
21. Telang, A. (2023). The promise and peril of AI legal services to equalize justice. *Harvard Journal of Law & Technology*. https://jolt.law.harvard.edu/digest/the-promise-and-peril-of-ai-legal-services-to-equalize-justice
22. Lowenberger, B., Selensky, E., & McCutcheon, J. (2024). Reducing the 'Justice Gap' through access to unbundled legal services: Utilizing an A2J measurement framework to measure unbundling effectiveness. *Windsor Yearbook of Access to Justice*, *40*, 103. https://doi.org/10.22329/wyaj.v40.9182
23. What does an A2J Guided Interview look like? | A2J Author. (2020). A2jauthor.org.
24. Frank, J. (2017). A2J Author, Legal Aid Organizations, and Courts: Bridging the civil justice gap using document assembly. https://digitalcommons.law.wne.edu/lawreview/vol39/iss2/3

25. Steenhuis, Q., Colarusso, D., & Willey, B. (2023). *Weaving Pathways for Justice with GPT: LLM-Driven Automated Drafting of Interactive Legal Applications.* ArXiv (Cornell University). https://doi.org/10.48550/arxiv.2312.09198
26. Frank, J. (2017). A2J Author, Legal Aid Organizations, and Courts: Bridging the civil justice gap using document assembly. https://digitalcommons.law.wne.edu/lawreview/vol39/iss2/3
27. Aletras, N., Tsarapatsanis, D., Preoţiuc-Pietro, D., & Lampos, V. (2016). Predicting judicial decisions of the European Court of Human Rights: a Natural Language Processing perspective. *PeerJ Computer Science*, *2*(1), e93. https://doi.org/10.7717/peerj-cs.93
28. Lage-Freitas, A., Allende-Cid, H., Santana, O., & de Oliveira-Lage, L. (2022). Predicting Brazilian court decisions. PeerJ Computer Science, *8*, e904–e904. https://doi.org/10.7717/peerj-cs.904
29. Medvedeva, M., Vols, M., & Wieling, M. (2020). Using machine learning to predict decisions of the European Court of Human Rights. *Artificial Intelligence and Law*, *28*, 237–266. https://doi.org/10.1007/s10506-019-09255-y
30. Bernhardt, W. (2021). *The Use of Artificial Intelligence in the Field of Justice* (pp. 173–196). Nomos Verlagsgesellschaft MbH & Co. KG EBooks. https://doi.org/10.5771/9783748926979-173
31. Ferrari, F., & Mustari, D. (2023). The new technologies and the civil justice commons. *Revista Ítalo-Española de Derecho Procesal*, *1*, 124–142. https://doi.org/10.37417/rivitsproc/1443
32. Castelli, C., & Piana, D. (2018). *Giustizia predittiva. La qualità della giustizia in due tempi.* Questionegiustizia.it. https://www.questionegiustizia.it/articolo/giustizia-predittiva-la-qualita-della-giustizia-in-due-tempi_15-05-2018.php
33. Steenhuis, Q. (2024). *AI and Tools for Expanding Access to Justice* (forth coming). https://doi.org/10.2139/ssrn.4876633
34. Steenhuis, Q. (2024). *AI and Tools for Expanding Access to Justice* (forth coming). https://doi.org/10.2139/ssrn.4876633
35. Kyriakides, N., Plevri, A., Zentani, Y. (2022). AI and access to justice: An expansion of Adrian Zuckermans findings. In *Frontiers in Civil Justice* (pp. 121–141). Edward Elgar Publishing. https://doi.org/10.4337/9781802203820.00014
36. Sourdin, T. (2021). *Judges, Technology and Artificial Intelligence: The Artificial Judge* (pp. 168–169). Edward Elgar Publishing.
37. Susskind, R. E. (2019). *Online Courts and the Future of Justice* (1st ed., p. 33). Oxford University Press.
38. Sourdin, T. (2021). *Judges, Technology and Artificial Intelligence: The Artificial Judge* (pp. 173–175). Edward Elgar Publishing.
39. Bertovskiy, L. V., Devyatkin, G. S., & Fedorov, A. R. (2024). Interdisciplinary aspects of the introduction of virtual reality technologies in court proceedings. *Kutafin Law Review*, *11*(1), 124–141. https://doi.org/10.17803/2713-0533.2024.1.27.124-141
40. Wu, J. (2019). *AI Goes to Court: The Growing Landscape of AI for Access to Justice.* Medium. https://medium.com/legal-design-and-innovation/ai-goes-to-court-the-growing-landscape-of-ai-for-access-to-justice-3f58aca4306f
41. Pereira, J., Assumpcao, A., Trecenti, J., Airosa, L., Lente, C., Cléto, J., Dobins, G., Nogueira, R., Mitchell, L., & Lotufo, R. (2024). *INACIA: Integrating Large Language Models in Brazilian Audit Courts: Opportunities and Challenges.* ArXiv (Cornell University). https://doi.org/10.48550/arxiv.2401.05273
42. Folha de S.Paulo. (2020, March 10). *Artificial Intelligence Makes its Mark in the Brazilian Judicial System.* Folha de S.Paulo. https://www1.folha.uol.com.br/internacional/en/brazil/2020/03/artificial-intelligence-makes-its-mark-in-the-brazilian-judicial-system.shtml

43. Süddeutsche Zeitung. (2021). *Ergebnis: Künstliche Intelligenz erkennt Kinderpornografie*. Süddeutsche.de; Süddeutsche Zeitung. https://www.sueddeutsche.de/panorama/duesseldorf-ergebnis-kuenstliche-intelligenz-erkennt-kinderpornografie-dpa.urn-newsml-dpa-com-20090101-210524-99-725248
44. Mingtsung, C., & Shuling, L. (2020). Research on the application of artificial intelligence technology in the field of justice. *Journal of Physics: Conference Series*, *1570*(1), 012047. https://doi.org/10.1088/1742-6596/1570/1/012047
45. Susskind, R. E. (2019). *Online Courts and the Future of Justice* (1st ed., p. 272). Oxford University Press.
46. Eliot, L. (2020). *AI and Legal Argumentation: Aligning the Autonomous Levels of AI Legal Reasoning* (p. 11). ArXiv (Cornell University). https://doi.org/10.48550/arxiv.2009.11180
47. Frankenreiter, J., & Nyarko, J. (2023). Natural language processing in legal tech. In D. F. Engstrom (Ed.), *Legal Tech and the Future of Civil Justice* (p. 82). Cambridge University Press.
48. Turing, A. M. (1950). Computing machinery and intelligence. *Mind*, *59*(236), 433–460. http://www.jstor.org/stable/2251299?origin=JSTOR-pdf
49. Russell, S., & Norvig, P. (2020). *Artificial Intelligence: A Modern approach* (4th ed., p. 1035). Prentice Hall.
50. Mingtsung, C., & Shuling, L. (2020). Research on the application of artificial intelligence technology in the field of justice. *Journal of Physics: Conference Series*, *1570*(1), 012047. https://doi.org/10.1088/1742-6596/1570/1/012047
51. Kyriakides, N., Plevri, A., Zentani, Y. (2022). AI and access to justice: An expansion of Adrian Zuckermans findings. In *Frontiers in Civil Justice* (pp. 121–141). Edward Elgar Publishing. https://doi.org/10.4337/9781802203820.00014
52. Larson, J., Mattu, S., Kirchner, L., & Angwin, J. (2016). *How We Analyzed the COMPAS Recidivism Algorithm*. ProPublica. https://www.propublica.org/article/how-we-analyzed-the-compas-recidivism-algorithm
53. *State v. Loomis*, 881 N.W.2d 749 (Wis. 2016).
54. Freeman, K. (2016). Algorithmic injustice: How the Wisconsin Supreme Court failed to protect due process rights in State v. Loomis. *North Carolina Journal of Law & Technology*, *18*(5), 75. https://scholarship.law.unc.edu/ncjolt/vol18/iss5/3
55. *Ewert v. Canada*, 2018 SCC 30, [2018] 2 S.C.R. 165.
56. Zuckerman, A. (2020). Artificial intelligence-implications for the legal profession, adversarial process, and rule of law. *Law Quarterly Review*, *136*, 427.
57. Boahenaa, F. J. (2019). The Impact of Artificial Intelligence on Justice Systems. Paper N. 25. Trento BioLaw Selected Student Papers.
58. Mata v. Avianca, Inc., 1:22-cv-01461 (S.D.N.Y. Feb. 22, 2022).
59. *Why the Avianca "Bogus Cases" News Is Not About Either Generative AI or Lawyers' Tech Competence*. (2023). LawSites. https://www.lawnext.com/2023/05/why-the-avianca-bogus-cases-news-is-not-about-either-generative-ai-or-lawyers-tech-competence.html
60. Kruse v. Karlen, No. ED111172 (Mo. Ct. App. Feb. 13, 2024).
61. Ewert v. Canada, 2018 SCC 30, [2018] 2 S.C.R. 165, 37233.
62. *Not Again! Two More Cases, Just this Week, of Hallucinated Citations in Court Filings Leading to Sanctions*. (2024). *LawSites*. https://www.lawnext.com/2024/02/not-again-two-more-cases-just-this-week-of-hallucinated-citations-in-court-filings-leading-to-sanctions.html
63. Terzidou, K. (2022). The Use of Artificial Intelligence in the Judiciary and Its Compliance with the Right to a Fair Trial. 31. JJA. 154.
64. Hoffmann, M., & Nurski, L. (2021). What Is Holding Back Artificial Intelligence Adoption in Europe? Policy Contribution Issue n°24/21. https://www.bruegel.org/sites/default/files/private/wp_attachments/PC-24-261121.pdf

65. Rane, N., Choudhary, S., & Rane, J. (2024). Acceptance of artificial intelligence: Key factors, challenges, and implementation strategies. *Journal of Applied Artificial Intelligence, 5*(2), 50–70. https://doi.org/10.48185/jaai.v5i2.1053
66. Gbandi, M., Sachoulidou, A., & Lima, D. (2023). *Greek Report on AI and Administration of Justice.* e-Revue Internationale de Droit Pénal. https://penal.org/sites/default/files/files/A-06-23.pdf
67. Plevri, A. (2024). Presentation: Applications of artificial intelligence and technology in political civil litigationproceedings: New tools or new risks? 8th Conference of Young Lawyers: Legal Issues in the Contemporary Economic World. ELSA Thessaloniki.
68. Areios Pagos 1014/2024. dsanet.gr.
69. Areios Pagos 1765/2023. areiospagos.gr
70. Meyers, Z., & Springford, J. (2023). How Europe can make the most of AI (Policy brief). Centre for European Reform. https://www.cer.eu/publications/archive/policy-brief/2023/how-europe-can-make-most-ai
71. Rane, N., Choudhary, S., & Rane, J. (2024). Acceptance of artificial intelligence: Key factors, challenges, and implementation strategies. *Journal of Applied Artificial Intelligence, 5*(2), 50–70. https://doi.org/10.48185/jaai.v5i2.1053
72. Westermann, H. (2023). Using artificial intelligence to increase access to justice (Doctoral dissertation, Université de Montréal). Université de Montréal, 241–245.
73. Gans-Combe, C. (2022). Automated justice: Issues, benefits and risks in the use of artificial intelligence and its algorithms in access to justice and law enforcement. In D. O'Mathúna, & R.Iphofen, (Eds). *Ethics, Integrity and Policymaking. Research Ethics Forum* (vol. 9). Springer. https://doi.org/10.1007/978-3-031-15746-2_14
74. High-Level Expert Group on AI (AI HLEG). (2019). Ethics guidelines for trustworthy AI | Shaping Europe's digital future. https://digital-strategy.ec.europa.eu/en/library/ethics-guidelines-trustworthy-ai
75. Russell, S., Norvig, P. (2020). *Artificial Intelligence: A Modern approach* (4th ed., p. 1037). Prentice Hall.

Chapter 11

AI algorithms for democratic processes

Rajasekhara Mouly Potluri, Assel Kenesovna Jumasseitova, Yerzhan B. Mukashev, and Lohith Sekhar Potluri

INTRODUCTION

Democracy, as a system of governance, is established on the philosophy of political equality, civilian involvement, free and fair elections, accountability, and the rule of law. Democratic progressions comprehend a broad array of organized institutional mechanisms and civic procedures that facilitate citizens to express their political will, guide policymaking, and hold elected and designated representatives responsible. These procedures comprise electoral involvement, public discussion, policy preparation, civic engagement, and institutional precision. In the current millennium, democratic systems are being shaped and reshaped by rapid technological advancements, especially in digital communication and data-driven governance. While these advancements offer enormous potential for increasing democratic engagement, they also present substantial challenges. Van den Hoven et al. (2024) stated that democracy has been severely affected by the current digital technologies, and these sways will only enhance as technologies continue to progress at a radical pace. The digital era has renovated the panorama of democratic structures, depicting both prospects and perils or challenges for the preservation and evolution of democratic principles. The digital age has pointed to an era of hyperconnectivity, where social media platforms and digital communication tools can both facilitate citizens and differentiate public discourse. Promptly, hesitations over data privacy, algorithmic bias, electoral interference, cyber threats, and the proliferation of misinformation have evolved gradually, projecting floating critical questions about the resilience and integrity of democratic institutions.

AI is omnipresent, as a promise or dreadful, and extensively pervasive from one field to another. It is associated with the prospects of solving tedious problems, making better use of material resources, and saving time. This sensational and game-changing technology transforms the world of democracy into artificial democracy. The underlying principle for integrating AI into democratic frameworks is multifaceted. First, AI extends the capacity to process vast amounts of data in real time, authorizing policymakers and election administrators to make informed decisions quickly. Second, AI-driven

DOI: 10.1201/9781003594185-11

systems can help recognize patterns of irregularities or menaces that may not be easily detected through conservative methods. Third, by distinguishing citizen engagement and optimizing communication strategies, AI can advance more comprehensive and approachable governance. Likewise, AI can help bridge gaps in democratic participation by facilitating access to information and presenting digital platforms for marginalized communities to voice their concerns. However, the application of AI in democratic contexts must be considered cautiously. The same technologies that undertake heightened efficiency and involvement also establish substantial risks, including the potential for surveillance, manipulation, and the erosion of public trust. Authoritarian regimes may exploit AI tools to suppress dissent and engineer consent, thereby challenging democratic values. As such, the implementation of AI in democratic systems must be guided by robust ethical frameworks, legal safeguards, and participatory oversight mechanisms. This chapter essentially explores the intersection of sophisticated AI algorithms and democratic processes. It starts by contextualizing the challenges encountered by democracies in the digital age and articulates the need for AI-enabled solutions. It then investigates the realistic relevance of AI in electoral management, voter analytics, policy development, and civic engagement, supported by case studies from diverse geopolitical contexts such as India and the United States. The chapter concludes by outlining the ethical, legal, and governance considerations necessary to ensure that the integration of AI strengthens rather than compromises democratic ideals.

AI FOR ELECTORAL SYSTEMS

AI has become a powerful tech tool thanks to technological advances, access to substantial amounts of data, machine learning, and increased computing power. The introduction of ChatGPT at the end of 2022 was a sensational breakthrough in AI. It revealed the vast range of prospects involved in adapting general-purpose AI to a wide array of tasks and in getting generative AI to generate synthetic content based on prompts entered by the user (Michael, 2023). Michael stated that these technologies can help citizens of the world to get a comprehensive view and better cohesion of politics and engage more easily in democratic debate, and reiterated that by 2026, 90% of online content may be synthetically generated, and AI is an opportunity to improve the democratic process in our societies. Similarly, many politicians from different parts of the globe can move closer to their voters and get involved in more lifelike political campaigns. Such a kind of synchronization between public and political parties could change the face of the election process and campaigns and considerably enhance the electioneering process, which is more accurate and efficient. The evolution of AI and its application in the political process has been present for the past 15 years. During the quinquennium, the usage of AI in democracies and the election process in particular has grown abnormally.

This emerging technology poses multiple risks to democracies as a potential tech tool for disinformation and misinformation, which can lead to tensions, resulting in electoral-related conflicts and even violence. Many political parties, specifically from the world's largest democratic country, India, tend to extensively use AI and its supportive technological tools to create fake or false propaganda to create impressions against their opposition parties and have succeeded since 2015. This tendency is significantly and severely used by political parties to develop character assassination comparisons with photos, generate false information, or spread biased opinions that do not represent societal sentiments. Even though numerous benefits have been exposed by AI, irrespective of the field of operation, it has the potential to affect the democratic process negatively. The challenges briefly discussed above also identified a meaningful solution from the same technology, which can prove helpful to democratic countries as well as their electioneering process to safeguard their political set-up. For instance, specific tools can be employed to detect the use of AI-generated content, and techniques such as watermarking can clearly indicate that AI has generated content. The EU is currently adopting its legal framework to address the dangers of AI and to promote the use of trustworthy, transparent, and accountable AI systems (Michael, 2023).

In many countries, the lower and upper houses elect their representatives based on their durations, either with direct or indirect elections, with the responsibilities to lead the people, represent them in different capacities, and, most significantly, manage their limited resources of people for their well-being (Esiefarienrhe & Maine, 2024). Keep in mind the general prevailing factors, specifically in Africa and other Southeast Asian countries, like illiteracy, poverty, corruption, and red-tapes; AI, which is the sensational technology of making computers think, act, and behave like humans, transformed as a viable tool at the discarding of electoral authorities to enable a smooth, free, and fair election process. The AI-driven election process ensures that the outcomes are delivered immediately after voting concludes while confidently upholding the core principles of democracy with transparency, accuracy, and efficiency. Academicians like Esiefarienrhe and Maine (2024) conducted an extensive systematic review methodology using expert judgment. They analyzed the use of AI in elections in different parts of the world and their performances and challenges. Ingbae (2025) stated that AI and predictive analytics are reshaping the landscape of political campaigns by offering new insights into voter behavior, election outcomes, and campaign strategies. The Chairman of the Board of Management of MBANK, Mr. Ingbae, emphasized that the following areas greatly influence politics and campaigning. These areas are data-driven voter insights, targeted campaign strategies, optimizing ad spending and media buying, enhancing get-out-the-vote (GOTV) efforts, identifying swing voters and battleground states, analyzing opponent strategies, forecasting election outcomes, and strengthening political communication.

The predictive behavior of voters and fraud detection in voting are also notable, debatable topics in this chapter. The security and accessibility of voting procedures in the United States have caused the matter of electoral integrity to become a point of contention. Public confusion regarding the federal government's response to allegations of voter fraud has contributed to a decline in trust in governmental institutions and a rise in voter apathy. This study contextualizes its empirical methodology by examining the historical evolution of electronic voting, concerns over voter security, and the sensationalism often surrounding claims of voter fraud. The research employs a custom-developed software application to analyze the geographic proximity of voters to polling stations, aiming to understand voting behaviors better and identify potential vulnerabilities to fraud. The chapter details the software's development cycle, design architecture, and key use cases, offering a foundation for further innovation (Granger, 2022). Bach et al. (2021) emphasized that a significant concern arising from the ubiquitous tracking of individuals' online activity is that algorithms may be trained to predict sensitive personal information, even for users who do not wish to reveal such information. These scholars investigated in this research the possibility of predicting voting behavior, which is considered personally sensitive information in Germany and is subject to strict privacy regulations. By analyzing web browsing records and mobile device usage data from approximately 2,000 online users eligible to vote in the 2017 German federal election, supplemented with corresponding survey responses, we find that online activity is a poor predictor of self-reported voting behavior within this population. These findings contribute to the broader discourse on the limitations of user control over the flow and accuracy of personal information. Electoral data sets typically consist of spreadsheets containing information about the number of votes received by each party or candidate, the number of invalid and blank votes, and the number of eligible ballots for each electoral unit (Levin et al., 2016; Rozenas (2017) developed a novel method to detect election fraud from irregular patterns in the distribution of vote shares and built on a widely deliberated observation that in some elections where fraud allegations abound, suspiciously, many polling stations return coarse vote shares for the ruling party, which seems highly implausible in large electorates.

An electronic voting machine (EVM) is an innovative electronic apparatus that registers votes and maintains the electoral system's transparency. It considerably reduces certain types of fraud, provides accurate counts by eliminating spoiled ballots, improves voter turnout, reduces electoral operating costs, and allows marginalized communities to vote. It has been used by many countries around the world, like the United Kingdom, the United States, Brazil, Belgium, and Switzerland. India is one of those states that utilized this machine for the first time in their electoral system in 1982 in the Paravur assembly during a biennial election in the state of Kerala. After its immediate accomplishment, the Election Commission of India (ECI) purchased 150,000 machines in 1990 to use in the entire country. Though many political parties raised questions and criticized the genuineness of the machines for security concerns at the time, they were used in 16 selected constituencies in the state elections following the amendment to the Constitution in December 1998. Previously, India used a manual voting system (paper ballot) in their electoral system, due to which electoral fraud, inefficiency, rigging, and other evil practices were at their peak. Hence, to address these issues, India has implemented EVMs to bring transparency to their electoral system. Kumar and Begum's (2012) study revealed that it aims to evaluate the performance of EVMs in terms of improving transparency and efficiency in the electoral process in India and analyze the perspectives of various stakeholders such as voters, political parties, media, intelligentsia, and the judiciary regarding the introduction of EVMs in India. This chapter employs transparency and efficiency theory and system theory to emphasize the significance of free and fair elections.

AI AND PUBLIC POLICY MAKING AND POLITICAL CAMPAIGNS

Ngai et al. (2025) emphasized the use of natural language processing (NLP) in government applications and analyzed the findings from diverse perspectives, including elections at all levels of government. They found that the key techniques supporting these applications, while the NLP societal value grid provides an overview of NLP's societal benefits in the government sector. Around the globe, many research studies have used social media data to estimate electoral outcomes and public opinion. The paper highlighted a meta-analysis examining the predictive power of social media data by focusing on various sources of data and different methods of prediction, i.e., (1) sentiment analysis and (2) analysis of structural features. The study depicted that machine learning-based guesses are superior primarily to those descended from pre-existing lexica and that a combination of structural features and sentiment analyses specifies the most precise projections. Moreover, the same study shows some differences in the predictive power of social media data across different levels of political democracy and various electoral systems. The academicians noted that since the accuracy of elections and public opinion estimates varies depending on which statistical estimates are used, the scientific community should aim to adopt a more standardized approach to analyzing and reporting social media data-derived predictions in the future. Data-driven decision support systems have been used to manage and administer elections in different countries. This digital revolution has tremendously enhanced the efficacy and efficiency of policymaking across all departments of government, including the electoral systems. The integration of AI and its allied technologies has enormously improved the productivity of governance systems. Many countries' governments essentially needed a substantial amount of data and AI algorithms, which are used to analyze and extract insightful data that enables decision-making based on facts. Decision support systems can analyze and understand complicated information by utilizing cutting-edge machine learning and data analytics approaches, revealing trends, patterns, and correlations that would be challenging for human analysts to find manually. Because of this kind of situation, government officials who are specifically and actively involved in decision-making can make accurate decisions based on well-informed choices based on impartial and precise data. Arora et al. (2024), with their comprehensive research, examine the difficulties and factors to be considered when implementing AI in decision support systems for e-governance. With an emphasis on the significance of responsible AI governance frameworks, ethical issues, including algorithmic bias, transparency, and accountability, are addressed. The article also explores the effects of incorporating AI into decision-making processes, including potential sociopolitical effects and the requirement for stakeholder participation and public confidence. The results of this study show how data-driven decision support systems may revolutionize e-governance policies when equipped with AI technology.

There is a widespread belief that elections can be won and lost based on the candidate and that a political party has better data on the preferences and behavior of the electorate. However, there are myths and realism about data-driven elections in many parts of the globe. It is time to evaluate the actual implications of data-driven polls considering the Facebook/Cambridge Analytical scandal and to reconsider the broader terms of the international debate. Political micro-targeting and voter analytics are essentially forms of surveillance. We know a lot about how surveillance harms democratic values. TheThe balance between the rights to privacy and the rights of political actors to communicate with the electorate is struck in different ways in different jurisdictions depending on a complex interplay of various legal, political, and cultural factors (Bennett & Lyon, 2019).

The current digital era greatly influenced electioneering in many countries, as well as governance, including all kinds of services. The application of AI-powered tools and techniques has become indispensable in the world's political circles while communicating the philosophies of political parties with their public, who decides their fate. The integration of AI-powered solutions into political marketing has revolutionized the way political campaigns engage with voters. By leveraging sophisticated algorithms and data analytics, political marketers are now able to deliver highly personalized advertisements tailored to specific demographic segments. This capability facilitates the precise targeting of content and enables the crafting of messages that resonate directly with the intended audience. Such technological advancements significantly enhance the accuracy and efficiency of identifying, reaching, and persuading voters. However, alongside these strategic benefits, the use of AI in political advertising raises critical ethical considerations. This chapter explores the moral dimensions associated with AI-driven campaign strategies, with particular emphasis on issues related to privacy, data security, and the potential manipulation or exploitation of voters. The growing reliance on personal data and predictive analytics not only challenges traditional notions of informed consent but also raises concerns about transparency and accountability in democratic processes. As such, the discussion seeks to balance the promise of AI-enhanced political communication with the imperative to uphold ethical standards and protect individual rights in the digital age (Kamal & Kaur, 2025).

The application of AI in India's general elections, along with specific state elections, has completely changed the political landscape since 2019. The several ways that AI might improve campaign tactics, voter turnout, and election administration are examined in this review study. This chapter discusses the potential of key AI technologies—such as chatbots, sentiment analysis, microtargeting, and voter profiling—to enhance political communication and outreach strategies. By examining case studies from recent Indian elections, this analysis demonstrates how AI-powered digital campaign tools—such as microtargeting, sentiment analysis, and automated content delivery—have played a pivotal role in shaping voter perceptions, customizing political messaging, and ultimately influencing electoral outcomes. These technologies have not only enhanced the precision of political outreach but have also transformed the dynamics of voter engagement in the digital age. In addition to evaluating these innovations, the discussion also addresses the ethical and privacy concerns associated with the deployment of AI in political contexts. It proposes regulatory frameworks aimed at mitigating potential risks and ensuring the responsible use of these technologies (Kumar & Kumar, 2024). Since 2016, the widespread availability of affordable smartphones and internet access has significantly increased the influence of social media on political campaigning, particularly evident in the 2019 elections across several Indian states. This volume presents empirical insights through two thematic case studies one examining how political parties leverage large-scale campaign rallies to shape prime-time news coverage and the other exploring the spread of misinformation on social media platforms.

Additionally, it includes five in-depth case studies that highlight distinctive political campaigning strategies within the diverse regional contexts of West Bengal, Assam, Karnataka, Kerala, and Andhra Pradesh (Varughese & Semetko, 2022). Tomar et al. (2023) stated that India's political landscape has undergone a profound transformation with the advent of the digital revolution, marked by the rapid expansion of social media and the integration of AI technologies. This chapter draws upon secondary data to critically assess the impact of AI-powered tools on political campaigning, voter behavior, and electoral outcomes within the Indian democratic framework. AI technologies have empowered political actors to conduct advanced voter profiling, deliver precision-targeted advertisements, and perform real-time sentiment analysis. However, these innovations also present significant challenges, including the proliferation of misinformation, fake news, and deepfake content. Such AI-enabled manipulative tactics pose a threat to public discourse, potentially distorting voter perceptions and compromising the credibility of democratic processes. Through an examination of case studies from recent

Indian elections, alongside comparisons with global experiences, this analysis highlights the urgent need for comprehensive regulatory mechanisms and widespread digital literacy programs to preserve democratic values in the era of AI-driven politics.

TOOLS AND FRAMEWORKS FOR FAIR AI IN DEMOCRACY

The rapid advancement and widespread application of AI across social, economic, and political domains have prompted growing concern over its implications for democracy. While democracy is a complex and contested concept, often debated in terms of its normative, procedural, and structural dimensions (Landemore, 2022; Przeworski, 2018), this analysis focuses on key features where AI is likely to have the most significant impact. These include individual autonomy and self-governance, group-level equality of rights, institutional trust in fair electoral processes, and systemic competition between democratic and authoritarian regimes (Jungherr, 2023). Although this simplification may forgo some theoretical depth, it enables a practical framework for evaluating AI's influence on democratic systems. The rapid advancement and widespread adoption of AI have brought increasing attention to its broader economic, social, and political implications. With each significant development in AI technologies, especially in the realm of large language models (LLMs), public discourse often includes speculative narratives about the emergence of artificial general intelligence (AGI) possessing human-like or even superhuman capabilities. These debates have intensified in the wake of tools like ChatGPT, reflecting both genuine interest and exaggerated expectations surrounding AI's potential (Jungherr, 2023). Contemporary AI models, profound neural networks (DNNs), face two critical limitations: their reliance on expert-driven manual design and their lack of interpretability. These challenges hinder broader accessibility and trust in AI systems, obstructing efforts to democratize technology. Enhancing interpretability and automating model development without expert intervention could address key concerns around transparency, accountability, and integration of human knowledge. Halgamuge (2021) proposes innovative approaches to overcome these barriers, aiming to make AI more accessible, reliable, and impactful across disciplines.

RECOMMENDATIONS FOR ETHICAL AI GOVERNANCE IN DEMOCRACIES

In recent years, the deployment of AI technologies has expanded rapidly, offering a wide range of benefits and efficiencies across various sectors, including electioneering in many countries in different parts of the world. However, this rapid growth has also raised pressing ethical concerns, including threats to privacy, algorithmic bias, issues of security and reliability, lack of transparency, and other unintended societal consequences. This chapter identifies areas of alignment that can serve as foundational elements for international AI governance efforts (Corrêa et al., 2023). The integration of AI and Big Data into digital media has raised significant ethical concerns, particularly regarding their alignment with democratic values. Amid rising populism, digital surveillance, and data manipulation, AI and big data practices often undermine transparency, individual autonomy, and informed citizen participation—fundamental principles of democracy. This study highlights the ethical dilemmas stakeholders face in addressing these challenges, drawing on insights from six European focus groups. The findings underscore the urgent need for responsible innovation and policy frameworks that safeguard democratic integrity while promoting digital well-being (Christodoulou & Iordanou, 2021). As AI becomes increasingly embedded in society, its benefits—such as enhanced speed, accuracy, and innovation—are accompanied by serious ethical and political concerns. While numerous national strategies and ethical guidelines have emerged to guide AI development, they often fall short of ensuring democratic oversight and public involvement. A key ethical gap lies in the limited inclusion of civil society in shaping AI objectives and governance frameworks. To address these shortcomings, Gianni et al. (2022) propose a model of democratic experimentation rooted in social inquiry, emphasizing participatory governance to align AI implementation with ethical principles and democratic values.

CONCLUSION

The assimilation of advanced AI algorithms into democratic processes marks a pivotal moment in the evolution of governance, citizen engagement, and political communication. As this chapter has explored, modern technologies—specifically AI—are redefining the foundational mechanisms of democracies around the world. From electoral systems and public policy formulation to political campaigns and governance frameworks, AI has the potential to both strengthen and challenge the democratic ideal. AI's role in electoral systems has become increasingly prominent, offering innovative tools for voter profiling, real-time sentiment analysis, predictive modelling, and digital outreach. These technologies enhance campaign precision and efficiency, allowing political actors to connect with citizens in more personalized and data-informed ways. However, they also pose risks—such as misinformation, manipulation, and voter polarization—that must be addressed through transparent and accountable implementation. In the domain of public policy, AI enables data-driven decision-making, improves administrative efficiency, and fosters responsiveness in governance. By analyzing vast datasets, AI can uncover patterns and insights that inform more inclusive and evidence-based policies. Yet, the deployment of these tools must be carefully regulated to prevent algorithmic bias, ensure data protection, and preserve the autonomy of human decision-makers. Political campaigning has also undergone a digital transformation, with AI reshaping the landscape of communication and engagement. Campaigns now leverage AI for content optimization, message targeting, and even predicting voter turnout. While these advancements offer strategic advantages, they raise serious ethical considerations about transparency, digital consent, and the influence of automated systems on democratic discourse. There is an urgent need to develop and implement tools and frameworks that prioritize fairness, accountability, and inclusiveness to ensure that AI contributes positively to democracy. The creation of explainable AI systems, independent oversight bodies, and participatory design processes are essential steps toward safeguarding democratic values in the age of intelligent technologies.

This chapter recommends essential ethical principles for AI governance in democratic societies: transparency and explainability in AI systems used in governance and elections to enable public understanding and scrutiny; data protection and privacy standards that ensure citizens' information is handled with informed consent, confidentiality, and protection against misuse; inclusivity and equity to serve all citizens without discrimination while promoting marginalized voices; meaningful public participation in the development and evaluation of AI systems affecting democratic processes; and robust regulatory oversight with international collaboration to monitor and enforce responsible AI use. As democracies continue to evolve in the digital age, the challenge lies not in resisting technological progress but in steering it toward outcomes that reinforce democratic resilience, protect individual rights, and promote societal well-being. While AI introduces complex challenges to democratic governance, it simultaneously opens new pathways for innovation, engagement, and accountability. The future of democracy in an era increasingly shaped by intelligent technologies will depend on our collective commitment to governing AI systems with integrity, foresight, and steadfast dedication to democratic ideals, embedding ethics at the core of implementation to harness AI's full potential while enhancing participation, transparency, and trust in public institutions.

REFERENCES

Arora, A. *et al.* (2024). Data-Driven Decision Support Systems in E-Governance: Leveraging AI for Policymaking. In: Sharma, H., Chakravorty, A., Hussain, S., Kumari, R. (eds) Artificial Intelligence: Theory and Applications. AITA 2023. *Lecture Notes in Networks and Systems*, *844*. Springer, Singapore. https://doi.org/10.1007/978-981-99-8479-4_17

Arora, A., Vats, P., Tomer, N., Kaur, R., Saini, A. K., Shekhawat, S. S., & Roopak, M. (2024). Data-driven decision support systems in e-governance: Leveraging

AI for policy-making. In *International Conference on Artificial Intelligence on Textile and Apparel* (pp. 229–243). Springer Nature Singapore.

Bach, R. L., Kern, C., Amaya, A., Keusch, F., Kreuter, F., Hecht, J., & Heinemann, J. (2021). Predicting voting behavior using digital trace data. *Social Science Computer Review*, *39*(5), 862–883.

Bennett, C. J., & Lyon, D. (2019). Data-driven elections: Implications and challenges for democratic societies. *Internet Policy Review*, *8*(4), 13–19.

Christodoulou, E., & Iordanou, K. (2021). Democracy under attack: Challenges of addressing ethical issues of AI and big data for more democratic digital media and societies. *Frontiers in Political Science*, *3*, 682945.

Corrêa, N. K., Galvão, C., Santos, J. W., Del Pino, C., Pinto, E. P., Barbosa, C., & de Oliveira, N. (2023). Worldwide AI ethics: A review of 200 guidelines and recommendations for AI governance. *Patterns*, *4*(10), 1–14.

Esiefarienrhe, B. M., & Maine, I. M. (2024). Artificial intelligence and the electoral process: The benefits and the challenges. *African Journal of Development Studies (Formerly AFFRIKA Journal of Politics, Economics and Society)*, *2024*(No. si1), 213–226.

Gianni, R., Lehtinen, S., & Nieminen, M. (2022). Governance of responsible AI: From ethical guidelines to cooperative policies. *Frontiers in Computer Science*, *4*, 873437.

Granger, H. (2022). An Analysis of Voter Fraud and Proposed Methodology for Recording Numerical Anomalies in Polling Data. https://digitalcommons.liberty.edu/honors/1210/

Halgamuge, S. (2021). Fair AI: A conceptual framework for democratization of 21st century AI. In *2021 International Conference on Instrumentation, Control, and Automation (ICA)* (pp. 1–3). IEEE.

Ingbae, T. I. (2025). Predictive analytics in politics: How AI influences campaigns. AI and Politics. https://www.linkedin.com/pulse/predictive-analytics-politics-how-ai-influences-inamdar–wtzjf/

Jungherr, A. (2023). Artificial intelligence and democracy: A conceptual framework. *Social Media + Society*, *9*(3), 1–14. https://doi.org/10.1177/20563051231186353

Kamal, R., & Kaur, J. (2025). Artificial intelligence and electoral decision-making: Analyzing voter perceptions of AI-driven political Ads. In *Recent Advances in Sciences, Engineering, Information Technology & Management* (Eds) Dinesh Goyal, Bhanu Pratap, Sandeep Gupta, Saurabh Raj, Rekha Rani Agrawal, Indra Kishor (pp. 890–896). CRC Press.

Kumar, D. A., & Begum, T. U. S. (2012, March). Electronic voting machine—A review. In *International Conference on Pattern Recognition, Informatics and Medical Engineering (PRIME-2012)* (pp. 41–48). IEEE.doi: 10.1109/ICPRIME.2012.6208285.

Kumar, N., & Kumar, R. (2024). Review of implementation of AI in Parliamentary Election Campaign in India. In *2024 1st International Conference on Sustainable Computing and Integrated Communication in Changing Landscape of AI (ICSCAI)* (pp. 1–16). IEEE.

Landemore, H. (2022, October). Can AI bring deliberative democracy to the masses. In *Human Centered Artificial Intelligence Seminar*, 166–191. Stanford University.

Levin, I., Pomares, J., & Alvarez, R. M. (2016). Using Machine Learning Algorithms to Detect Election Fraud. https://books.google.kz/books

Michael, A. (2023). Artificial Intelligence, Democracy, and Elections. https://policycommons.net/artifacts/4851173/artificial-intelligence-democracy-and-elections/5688039/

Ngai, E. W., Lui, A. K., & Kei, B. C. (2025). Natural language processing in government applications: A literature review and a case analysis. *Industrial Management & Data Systems*. 27 May 2025; 125 (6): 2067–2104. https://doi.org/10.1108/IMDS-07-2024-0711

Przeworski, A. (2018). *Why Bother with Elections?* John Wiley & Sons.

Rozenas, A. (2017). Detecting election fraud from irregularities in vote-share distributions. *Political Analysis*, *25*(1), 41–56.

Tomar, M., Raj, N., Singh, S., Marwaha, S., & Tiwari, M. (2023). The role of AI-driven tools in shaping the democratic process: A study of Indian elections and social media dynamics. *Industrial Engineering Journal*, *52*(11), 143–153.

Van den Hoven, J., Stauch, M., Musiani, F., Domingo-Ferrer, J., Ruggieri, S., Pratesi, F., & Comandé, G. (2024). Democracy in the Digital Age. Halshs-04844505, version 1 (17-24-2024), https://doi.org/10.15488/18259

Varughese, A. M., & Semetko, H. A. (2022). Political campaigning in India: Changing contexts of political communication. *South Asian History and Culture*, *13*(3), 267–284.

Index

D

M

N

O

P

Made in the USA
Las Vegas, NV
19 September 2026

28ba47b6-6c5b-477b-a28a-e72f5fffc014R02